THE QUEER CHILD,

OR
GROWING
SIDEWAYS
IN THE
TWENTIETH
CENTURY

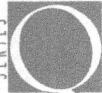

SERIES Q

EDITED BY

MICHÈLE AINA BARALE,

JONATHAN GOLDBERG,

MICHAEL MOON, AND

EVE KOSOFSKY SEDGWICK

THE QUEER CHILD,

OR

GROWING

SIDEWAYS

IN THE

TWENTIETH

CENTURY

Kathryn Bond Stockton

DUKE UNIVERSITY PRESS

Durham and London 2009

Designed by Amy Ruth Buchanan
Typeset in Dante by Tseng
Information Systems, Inc.
Library of Congress Cataloging-in-
Publication Data appear on the last
printed page of this book.

*Frontispiece: detail of a photograph
by Sean Graff, © Sean Graff Photography.*

For Marilyn, Ed, and Dave

CONTENTS

ACKNOWLEDGMENTS

Gratitude grows as I think of people who have schooled me on these topics: Henry Abelove, Stephen Barber, Lauren Berlant, Scott Black, Steven Bruhm, Debra Burrington, Melanee Cherry, Beth Clement, William Cohen, Peter Coviello, Stuart Culver, Ann Cvetkovich, Chris Decaria, Nadja Durbach, Lee Edelman, Angie Elegante and Natalie Avery, Karen Engle, Martha Ertman, Kathryn Flannery, Beth Freeman, Jane Garrity, Jake Grace, J. Halberstam, Randall Halle, Ellis Hanson, Jonathan Gil Harris, Becky Horn, Natasha Hurley, Karen Jacobs, Annamarie Jagose, Ratna Kapur, David Kennedy, Marilee Lindemann, Joe Litvak, Dana Luciano, Heather Lukes, Stacey Margolis, Ellen McCallum, Molly McGarry, Tom McWhorter, Madhavi Menon, José Muñoz, Mary Ann O'Farrell, Stephanie Pace, Ann Pellegrini, Ellen Pollak, Masha Raskolnikov, Todd Reeser, Jocelyn Romano, Stella Rozanski, Martha Nell Smith, and especially Barry Weller, who gave such kind and careful help in this book's final stages. And a shout goes out to my intellectual comrades in the canyons—Laura Briggs and Lisa Duggan—for their love of ledges and talking while walking.

I have felt tremendously supported in Utah: by my department and its chairs, Stuart Culver and Vincent Pecora; by my dean, Robert Newman; by Associate Vice-President for Diversity Karen Dace, and now her successor, Octavio Villalpando; and especially by my students, both graduate and undergraduate, in a range of literature and theory courses, particularly those in "Queer Theory," "Canonical Perversions," and "The Semiotics of Race." The Gender Studies Program has been my second home, both intellectual and political, and warmest, deepest thanks are owed to my associate director Gerda Saunders, whose intellect, modesty, and kindness humble me, and my inspiring colleagues Matt Basso, Gunseli Berik, Kandi Brinkman, Lisa Diamond, Kirsten Jorgenson, Jo Tiffany Merrill, Ella Myers, Susie Porter, Nick Russell, Angela Smith, Chris Talbot, Jodee Taylor, and Claudia Wright. Once again, in bringing a book to completion, I have been graced to work with kt farley, whose sheer cleverness endlessly charms me, and Erin Menut, whose exquisite astuteness anchors me.

And, again, I have been lucky to be in the hands of the people at Duke University Press: my incomparable editor, Ken Wissoker, who has singularly nurtured this project; his assistant, Mandy Earley, who has been enormously helpful, responsive, and fun to work with; and Molly Balikov, who has gracefully led me to the finish (where the magic of Amy Ruth Buchanan has me covered). Michael Cobb and a second, anonymous reader for the press made incisive, wonderfully smart, and persuasive suggestions for revision, alongside their evident intellectual generosity.

Three previously published essays of mine have lent materials to this book, ideas appearing here with kind permission from the publishers: my essay "Growing Sideways, or Versions of the Queer Child: The Ghost, the Homosexual, the Freudian, the Innocent, and the Interval of Animal," in the collection *Curiouser*, ed. Steven Bruhm and Natasha Hurley (Minneapolis: University of Minnesota Press, 2004): 277–315; "Eve's Queer Child," from *Regarding Sedgwick: Essays on Queer Culture and Critical Theory*, ed. Stephen M. Barber and David L. Clark (New York: Routledge, 2002): 181–99; and "Feeling Like Killing? Queer Temporalities of Murderous Motives among Queer Children," in GLQ: *A Journal of Lesbian and Gay Studies* 13: 2–3 (2007): 301–25.

In many respects, this book owes its life and support to several of my favorite playmates: Dave, Judy, Adam, Jonathan, Julie, and Harriett, who have emboldened my thinking and living; my parents, Ed and Marilyn, who, not knowing who or what they had before them, loved what they found, which I will not forget; and Shelley White, my household saint, who has birthed me forward and backward simultaneously, as only she could.

Growing Sideways, or Why
Children Appear to Get Queerer
in the Twentieth Century

If you scratch a child, you will find a queer, in the sense of
someone "gay" or just plain strange.[1] One boy says that he
called himself a "filly"—the word, he thought, for a "homosexual seagull."[2] A girl of nine thought herself a vampire, a
shadowy figure with shadowy secrets surrounding women.
Someone else tells how, "idiotic as it may seem, watching *The
Bible* on a lousy TV during an acid trip [in college] with my best
friend" brought up childhood sexual memories surrounding
this film and thus enabled him to "half-acknowledge" himself
"sexually" for the first time.[3] Certain queer comedians, who
grew up in the sixties before there were any gays on TV, wryly
explain that they "found themselves" as children in TV personas
(some of these almost forgotten today): Ernie, the odd boy on
My Three Sons; Robin of *Batman*; *The Beverly Hillbillies'* Miss
Jane Hathaway; or Josephine the Plumber (in ads for bathroom
cleaners).[4]

Aside from these confessions, there are dark and beautiful
renderings, emerging, extending, from novels and films, such
as I privilege throughout this book, beyond the puzzles they
tease us with here: children who hang, suicide-like, in spectral
forms from flowering trees; lying children spying in a Hitchcock fashion (an isolated eye peering out from a stairwell,
making a diagonal visual plane), spying on their teachers who

DREAMING
IS NURSED IN
DARKNESS.
—JEAN GENET

they claim are lovers; the portrait of a twelve-year-old acting like a child and a wife to a man, to whom she prefers both dogs and souvenirs; a black hustler who births a white mother to love him and mourn him; even a highly complicated image of a ghostly woman-child — she with the charming "look of cherubs in Renaissance theatres," who, "strangely aware of some lost land in herself . . . took to going out" — wandering and looking for her motherly lover, while speaking to animals, "straining their fur back until their eyes were narrowed and . . . teeth bare, her own teeth showing as if her hand were upon her own neck."[5]

Have such children largely eluded us?

Even if we meet them in our lives and reading (inside an Anglo-American frame), they are not in History, as we are going to see.[6] They are not a matter of historians' writings or of the general public's belief. The silences surrounding the queerness of children happen to be broken — loquaciously broken and broken almost only — by fictional forms. Fictions literally offer the forms that certain broodings on children might take. And certain broodings on children are facilitated, generally, dramatically, by our encountering a still ghostly child.

A Ghost and Its Peers: What the "Gay" Child Says about Children

What a child "is" is a darkening question. The question of the child makes us climb inside a cloud — "a shadowy spot on a field of light" — leading us, in moments, to cloudiness and ghostliness surrounding children as figures in time.[7]

One kind of child brings these matters into view. And, to my mind, it is the means, the fine-grained lens, by which to see any and *every* child as queer, even though the troubles of this specific child seem to be unique. This strange child particularly leads us to perceive ghosts and the darkening of children. The questions, in fact, "When did you know?" "Did you know as a kid?" ask queer adults to account for this child (as if they could): a child who was knowing something of "gay" or of things turning strange on her. Is there a gay child? Is there a notion of a child lingering in the vicinity of the word *gay*, having a ghostly, terrifying, complicated, energizing, chosen, forced, or future connection to this word? Or to what it means, to its umbrageous web, *without* the word itself? Have we been thinking there are such children? What might the notion of a gay child do to conceptions of the child? What might this ghost have to say about its peers? Quite a lot, it seems. In this study of children's queerness in the broadest sense, it speaks volumes. As it emerges as an idea, it begins to outline, in shadowy form, the pain, closets, emotional labors, sexual motives, and sideways movements that attend all children, however we deny it. A gay child illuminates the darkness of the child.

For queer adults, it does something else. Something unexpected for those who would pride themselves on irony or resist "gay" (the concept and word) as too naively identity-laden.[8] For these adults, talk of a gay child may trip a tenderness. It may release, however unsought, a barely allowable, barely admitted sentimentality. One may be pricked by, pained by, feelings — about one's childhood — that, even now, are maudlin, earnest, melodramatic, but understandable pangs of despair or sharp unease. One can remember desperately feeling there was simply nowhere to grow. What would become of the child one feared oneself to be? For adults, then, who from a young age felt they were attracted to others in wrong ways, the notion of a gay child — however conceptually problematic — may be a throwback to a frightening, heightened sense of growing toward a question mark. Or growing up in haze. Or hanging in suspense — even wishing time would stop, or just twist sideways, so that one wouldn't have to advance to new or further scenes of trouble. Truly, one could feel that one more readily had a future with a word — homo, faggot, gay, or queer — words so frequently used by kids — than with the objects or subjects of one's dreams.

Surprisingly, even conservative Americans who trumpet family values juxtapose their children with "homosexuals." Of course, they do so in order to oppose them to each other, fighting the threat of homosexuality under the banner of "what's good for children." Yet by doing so, they make the concept of homosexuality central to the meaning of the children they embrace.[9] Needless to say, they do not imagine there are children who are queer. Nor do they imagine that their concept of the child is by definition strange, and getting stranger, in the eyes of the grown-ups who define it.

Estranging, broadening, darkening forms of the child-as-idea are my pursuit, with a keen eye on the ghostly gay child (emblem and icon of children's queerness) as a figure hovering in the twentieth century — and a figure braiding with other forms of children who are broadly strange. (I will show throughout how every child is queer.) Far from a simple, sentimentalized plea for children's rights to come out "gay," this book scouts the conceptual force of ghostly gayness in the figure of the child—this child's subliminal, cresting appearances only *as* a fiction (as something many do not believe in). Such a child makes its own trouble for "gay" precisely by floating about its meanings, whether it knows the word or not, which it well might. The ghostly gay child, as a matter of fact, makes *gay* far more liquid and labile than it has seemed in recent years, when queer theory has been rightfully critiquing it. Odd as it may seem, *gay* in this context, the context of the child, is the new *queer*—a term that touts its problems and shares them with anyone.[10]

Exquisitely rich problems await us. Among them is the matter of children's delay: their supposed gradual growth, their suggested slow unfolding, which, unhelpfully, has been relentlessly figured as vertical movement upward (hence, "growing up") toward full stature, marriage, work, reproduction, and the loss of childishness. Delay, we will see, is tremendously tricky as a conception, as is growth. Both more appropriately call us into notions of the horizontal—what spreads sideways—or sideways and backwards— more than a simple thrust toward height and forward time. *Delay* as central to defining childhood forces us to think of this developmental term as colliding with the (once-dominant) term of theory-speak in literary studies: the philosopher Jacques Derrida's notion of delay as the inescapable effect of our reading along a chain of words (in a sentence, for example), where meaning is delayed, deferred, exactly because we read in sequence, go forward in a sentence, not yet knowing what words are ahead of us, while we must take the words we have passed *with* us as we go, making meaning wide and hung in suspense. What kinds of thoughts about growth emerge when key material issues from childhood (children's legally enforced delays) intersect with theorized notions of words? And not just words but metaphors, which a child may use as a way to grow itself, in hiding, in delay? (Hence the oddity: homosexual seagull.) This book shows that fictions-with-a-gay-child-ghosted-in-them shed light in two directions: on the kinds of corners that childhood scholars haven't looked into; and on corners that some famous theorists (Freud, Lacan, Deleuze, Guattari, Mulvey, Metz, and Bataille, to name a few) haven't explored.

Sharp dilemmas group around these fictions. Why might a child like to contemplate pain or foster his own or others' pain? Is the intellectual life of children (not just "gay" ones) often masochistic, since smart children like to probe ideas of suffering in ways that are emotionally generative and bold? How, for different emotional reasons, do "lesbian" children use their dogs in peculiar ways? How do they use them both metaphorically and materially to fashion a pause: that is, to fashion a crucial delay in expectations being placed upon themselves (and to craft sidelong movements of their own) on the threshold of adulthood? How in the world do pedophiles and animals jointly function as outlets for children's sideways relations? And how, for that matter, do "children's motives" —both a sexual and legal conundrum— relate to their motions? What unfathomable, hazy motives drive the motions of their bodies, motions that can look like sex, seduction, delinquency, or murder? But how does innocence, our default designation for children, cause its own violence? For example, how do children of color display that their inclusion in "the future for our children" is partial, even brutal? And what kind of money, what coin of the realm, do children grasp? Is there an obvious economy of candy, with libidinal pleasures of consumption and destruction? These are selections from questions I address surrounding what I call a ghost and its peers.

We should start again, with the problem of the child as a general idea.[11] The child is precisely who we are not and, in fact, never were. It is the act of adults looking back. It is a ghostly, unreachable fancy, making us wonder: Given that we cannot know the contours of children, who they are to themselves, should we stop talking of children altogether? Should all talk of the child subside, beyond our critique of the bad effects of looking back nostalgically in fantasy?

Fantasy, I find, is more interesting than this. It is fatter than we think, with dense possibilities. In spite of Anglo-American cultures, over several centuries, thinking that the child can be a carefully controlled embodiment of noncomplication (increasingly protected from labor, sex, and painful understanding), the child has gotten thick with complication. Even as idea. In fact, the very moves to free the child from density —to make it distant from adulthood—have only made it stranger, more fundamentally foreign, to adults. Innocence is queerer than we ever thought it could be. And then there are bodies (of children) that must live inside the figure of the child. Given that children don't know this child, surely not as we do, though they move inside it, life inside this membrane is largely available to adults as memory —what can I remember of what I thought I was?—and so takes us back in circles to our fantasies (of our memories). But even fantasy-tinged ghostly memories can spawn complex concepts of the child. One, as is evident, I make central, though not exclusive, to my explorations: the ghostly gay child, who figures as a particular intensification of these problems.

The gay child shows how the figure of the child does not fit children — doesn't fit the pleasures and terrors we recall. And though the gay child can't escape our fancy — that should be obvious — I see this notion figuring children as fighting with concepts and moving inside them, sometimes successfully, sometimes not. And if we take it seriously, it gathers other (concepts of) children in its wake. It makes us see children getting queerer in the century that enshrined and protected the child. In fact, this book immodestly claims that the notion of a gay child spotlights the drama of children's darkness: the motion of their bodies around troubled words; also their propensity for growing astray inside the delay that defines who they "are." Children grow sideways as well as up — or so I will say — in part because they cannot, according to our concepts, advance to adulthood until we say it's time.

Haze, suspense, a fear of growing up: obviously, many "straight" adults will relate to aspects of the gay child and its ghostliness. Conversely, not all so-called gay adults will recognize these feelings, since not everyone called "gay" or "queer" felt such feelings in their youth; nor did all of them even remotely relate to these words when they were children. But for those who did, a telling kind of ghostliness hung about their growth. This is something that childhood studies *and* queer theory have yet to discuss: what I call the gay child's "backward birth," which has piercingly postmortem features.[12] Here is what I mean. Such a child, with no established forms to hold itself in the public, legal field, has been a child remarkably, intensely unavailable to itself in the present tense.[13] The protogay child has only appeared through an act of retrospection and after a death. For this queer child, whatever its conscious grasp of itself, has not been able to present itself according to the category "gay" or "homosexual" — categories culturally deemed too adult, since they are sexual, though we do presume every child to be straight. The effect for the child who already feels queer (different, odd, out-of-sync, and attracted to same-sex peers) is an asynchronous self-relation. Certain linguistic markers for its queerness arrive only after it exits its childhood, after it is shown not to be straight. That is to say, in one's teens or twenties, whenever (parental) plans for one's straight destination have died, the designation "homosexual child," or even "gay kid," may finally, retrospectively, be applied. "I am not straight": "I was a gay child." This has been the only grammatical formulation allowed to gay childhood. The phrase "gay child" is a gravestone marker for where or when one's straight life died. Straight person dead, gay child now born, albeit retrospectively (even, for example, at or after the age of twenty-five). This kind of backward birthing mechanism makes the hunt for the roots of queerness a retrospective search for amalgamated forms of feelings, desires, and physical needs that led to this death of one's straight life. And yet, by the time the tombstone is raised ("I was a gay child"), the "child" by linguistic definition has expired.

Oprah has proven this central point, even in the act of marking our recent cultural shift toward a gay child in the present tense. On a segment of her show in 2005, titled "When I Knew I Was Gay," taglines running under guests' names ("Carson—Knew He Was Gay at Age 4"; "Billy—Knew He Was Gay at Age 8") indicate that Oprah's show is saying that children are often "gay" to themselves (whatever that means) for a long stretch of time, before they come out.[14] In fact, one guest tells of outing herself to her mother at ten. Tellingly, the mother (strategically?) forgot the trauma of this moment by thinking her child was "too young" to know "that." Hence, the "nightmare," in the mother's words, of seeing the "death" of her "dreams" when she learned that her daughter, at the age of seventeen, was gay (again). Guests on the show—none of whom are children—rightly predict that kids will come out now at ever younger ages. But will they come out as "gay," or "queer," or under the banner of some other term? It's too early to say. But the gay child makes us perceive the queer temporalities haunting all children. For no matter how you slice it, the child from the standpoint of "normal" adults is always queer. It is "homosexual" (the interesting problem we have just seen) or, despite our culture's assuming every child's straightness, the child can only be "not-yet-straight," since it, too, is not allowed to be sexual. This child who "will be" straight is merely approaching while crucially delaying (in its own asynchronous fix) the official destination of straight sexuality, and therefore showing itself as estranged from what it would approach. How does any child grow itself inside delay? The question is dramatized, even typified, by the obviously queer dynamics of a gay child, who is put on hold in such intense ways.

Fascinatingly, just now apparent in public discourse, though they have surely and often cruelly been subject to delayed embrace, are "transgendered children." In Barbara Walters's report for the show 20/20, "My Secret Self: A Story of Transgendered Children" (April 27, 2007), children as young as six are "allowed" to "become themselves"—their preferred gender—to family, friends, and the outside world (and to speak on camera). Parents tell about hearing children, even as early as age two, plead discomfort with their "given" gender, and 20/20 takes a decided affirmative stance on acceptance of these children (who, nonetheless, are said to be "diagnosed" with "gender identity disorder in childhood").[15] Strikingly, decisively, no mention is made of object choice, attraction, or sexuality in reference to these children, not even for the teens. And this, perhaps—this absence of any sexual conceptions—is why 20/20 can offer this program. No new segment that interviews self-proclaiming "gay" children—many of whom are clearly transgendered, though at times in complex ways and to degrees—has yet been offered. So, we might ask: How is gender-bending related to a child's and others' perceptions of its ghostly gayness? Isn't bent gender a primary way such a haunting, lurking possibility is perceived by others, whether or not their perceptions are "right"?

Clearly, the gay child is not itself a singular notion. It is not an island of ferment, or torment, as a conception to itself or others. Rather, any notion, any connotation, of a gay child in the last century was already blending and braiding with versions of children we might call—for the sake of grasping them—the child queered by innocence, the child queered by color, the child queered by Freud, and the grown "homosexual" typified by "arrested development" and often rendered as a child (or animal). These are the children that emerge in my reading as blended forms. Here I disentangle them, surely artificially, as strands from a braid, only so as to explain their different, exquisite combinations in fictional texts. Species of strangeness, these versions of children are central to novels and films for a century. And this century was famously named, *before* it began, "the century of the child" by the author Ellen Key in 1900, in audacious anticipation of how historians (at least, predictably, childhood historians and scholars of childhood) would thematize this period. I myself stick with this specific artifice—the discourse of "the century"—so as to show the trouble with "the century of the child" as scholars conceive of it.[16]

Artifice illuminates, especially in the arc of this hundred-year frame that is only fanciful. For this reason, the gay child lights up the problem of History. Lying outside of historians' focus — not yet "in" it — the gay child illuminates precisely what histories have not seen, showing why our notions of history are challenged by the waywardness of fictions. Tellingly, remarkably, in the many history-of-childhood books that claim to cover the history of children from the earliest centuries of "the West," there is no mention of nonnormative sexual orientation in childhood or of children's identifying as "gay" or "lesbian."[17] Homosexuality appears as a topic largely in reference to classical Greece. (This remains the case even for new, twenty-first-century editions of these texts.)[18] So what am I doing when, through my reading of fictional texts, attentive to form, I am producing claims about children, some of whom don't appear in History at all? Am I only crafting a history of the present (with its about-to-emerge gay child) as a kind of fantasy history of the past, finding what I am determined to see? Not exactly. To put it precisely — and, I think, differently from this question — I present this history of these queer children as a matter of fiction, since this history has not taken shape in public ways outside of fiction. Literally, these children — the ones I know from life and the ones I know from reading — lead fictional lives. I can think only beside the terms of History.

Sitting next to History, I use these dynamics to think about how to horizontalize History by putting texts outside of it by its side. My aim is to make History reveal that, in practice, *it* grows sideways and outside itself in at least two ways. The first way is this: there are now ideas (for instance, in fictions) that sit beside histories but in all likelihood will be "in History" sometime in the future. The "gay" child is History's future act of looking back (even if the concept of this child doesn't last).[19] In this way, History grows itself from the side, from what is to the side of it — often in fictions — before it takes this sideways growth, in some form, to itself. Secondly, History, however much it changes, is itself a synchrony, in the largest sense. It is All the Views of Historical Sequence that Exist to Be Read at This Time. Hence, I cannot "go back" to texts, historical or fictional, so as to think their meanings in their own time. No one can. They can exist for me only now as the reader I am, a reader who is using (at this current moment) a raft of ideas from decades of reading so as to read texts that themselves are extremely complex amalgams of various times.[20]

Amalgamated synchronies and glazed complexities not beside the point, the simplest fact remains that whatever hasn't been put into History — my ghostly gay child, who combines with other children—is, by definition, strictly beside it. So I put my readings from the century of the child (that made-up notion) beside the histories of this child-defining century, admitting at the start the artificial borders of "the century" itself.[21] They (my readings and the claims of historians and/or sociologists) often fail neatly to match each other, since fictions frequently don't obey the dictates or contours of their times. For this reason, instead of writing a so-called history, I will make my history the history of my reading a series of fictions, which I arrange. Are we just back, then, to a form of fantasy—namely, my own? I find it too easy and imprecise to say that I saw what I wanted to see in the fictions I read for this book. The thing I would now call "what I wanted"—that I would now say shaped my reading—has been shaped in part by what I started seeing, part of which I didn't see coming at all. I put my reading-in-desire beside the histories that have no place for it, as of yet.

History, nonetheless, surprises, luminesces. I use historical claims about the child—famous, well-established, interesting assertions from the last century—to show how scholars of childhood were turning the child ever queerer, even as they didn't see, or never said they saw, the ghostly gay child (in the fictions) around them. In point of fact, there has been no monograph yet on the queer child—no historically layered, theoretical view of this matter in Anglo-American literature, film, theory, or even cultural studies. One anthology, *Curiouser: On the Queerness of Children*, has appeared with pieces from over the years of queer theory writing, for which I wrote the concluding essay (a précis for this book).[22] And there are now many books on "queer youth," but these focus mainly on gay teenagers and come from the fields of popular psychology, clinical counseling, self-help, parenting, and education studies.[23] Alongside the latter, but often as a contrast, the versions of children talked about here surface in remarkable designs: from Henry James, Radclyffe Hall, Virginia Woolf, Djuna Barnes, and Gertrude Stein (among other thinkers), to Nabokov at midcentury, followed by Capote in the 1960s, to Hollywood movies and independent films (from the 1950s until now)—and also to queer cinema. These are fictions that imagine and present what sociology, Law, and History cannot pierce, given established taboos surrounding children. Novels and films, in their inventive forms, are rich stimulators of questions public cultures seem to have no language for encountering.

Why Speak of Growing Sideways?

There are ways of growing that are not growing up. The "gay" child's fascinating asynchronicities, its required self-ghosting measures, its appearance only after its death, and its frequent fallback onto metaphor (as a way to grasp itself) indicate we need new words for growth. Against the backdrop of crucial arguments made by Lee Edelman, James Kincaid, and Eve Kosofsky Sedgwick, I stake a different kind of claim for growth and for its intimate relations with queerness. Overall, I want to prick (deflate, or just delay) the vertical, forward-motion metaphor of growing up, and do so by exploring the many kinds of sideways growth depicted by twentieth-century texts.

Though the phrase "to grow up" has a long lineage, going back to the Coverdale Bible from 1535 (1 Samuel 2. 26: "The childe Samuel wente and grewe up, & was accepted of the Lorde & of men"), *grow*, according to the *Oxford English Dictionary*, goes back to the Old English *greouue* as early as 725. First used only in reference to plants (since the word *weaxan*—"wax"—is used for animals), *grow* spreads out to mean numerous things: "of a plant: to manifest vigorous life"; "of living bodies: to increase gradually in size by natural development . . . (when said of human beings, the word usually refers to stature)"; "of things material or immaterial: to increase gradually in magnitude, quantity, or degree"; and "of the sea: to swell."[24] Which is to say, growth is a matter of extension, vigor, and volume as well as verticality. And "growing sideways" would likely be an extremely apt phrase for what recent cognitive science recognizes as the brain's growth (throughout a person's lifetime) through the brain's capacity to make neural networks through connection and extension.[25] Hence, "growing up" may be a short-sighted, limited rendering of human growth, one that oddly would imply an end to growth when full stature (or reproduction) is achieved. By contrast, "growing sideways" suggests that the width of a person's experience or ideas, their motives or their motions, may pertain at any age, bringing "adults" and "children" into lateral contact of surprising sorts. This kind of growth is made especially palpable, as I plan to show, by (the fiction of) the ghostly gay child—the publicly impossible child whose identity *is* a deferral (sometimes powerfully and happily so) and an act of growing sideways, by virtue of its *future retroaction* as a child. This child braids with other concepts of the child in play throughout the century, including, quite surprisingly, the child queered by innocence.

It's a mistake to take innocence straight. To believe its benign publicity, as it were. One does not "grow up" from innocence to the adult position of protecting it. This view of innocence—the growing-up view—leaves one open to its peculiar dangers. Innocence, that is, works its own violence on adults and children, and this is a lesson taught by both Kincaid and Edelman. In brilliantly different ways, on behalf of sexuality studies and queer theory, James Kincaid in *Erotic Innocence: The Culture of Child Molesting* (1998) and Lee Edelman in *No Future: Queer Theory and the Death Drive* (2004) have shown the brutality of the ideal of the innocent child.[26] "Erotic innocence" is, for Kincaid, a brutal impoverishment of sexual life by the sexual titillation of innocence. This is diminishment both for children, who are made to be this titillating purity, and for adults who are titillated by it. Kincaid reminds us of the child's exquisite "vacancy" in its guise as spotless, pointing out that innocence and purity are purely "negative inversions" of adult attributes. (Innocence is lack of guilt, sinfulness, knowingness, experience, and so on; the child, in this respect, is "a set of *have nots*.")[27] This kind of emptiness is crucial for the child's role in erotic innocence. "Because [the child's] flatness signifies nothing," says Kincaid, it "does not interfere with our projections," our interest "to discover the erotic . . . in the blank page" (10). Just as importantly, detailed narratives of child molestation, which the press is full of, allow "normal" citizens what they seem to seek: "righteous, guilt-free . . . pornographic fantasies" about the violation of a child's innocence. Under the cover of "outrage" and protest, any adult can read "titillating narratives" of child sex abuse and also block the thought that children's sexuality, in so many contexts, turns out to be "more complicated than we supposed" (5, 12). "We might"—if we let ourselves explore these complications—"find [new] stories that are not fueled by fear" (15).

Fearlessly, Edelman seeks to embrace a different kind of violence, as he seeks to circumvent the violence of innocence. He prefers the Freudian notion of the death drive to the pleasure-killing idea of the child. Actually, for Edelman, embrace of the death drive, its energetic *jouissance*, its open-eyed denial of a person's continuance, could be a tender response to abuse at the hands of the child—the idea of the child to which meaning and the future cling in Imaginary and also pleasure-deadening ways.[28] For Edelman, the figure of the child as the emblem of parents' (impossible) continuity spawns delusional visions. These are visions of the seamless reproduction of oneself, whose future is always represented by (one's) children. Thus "the future" and "our children" are always bound together in a kind of frightening (and hermetically sealed) "reproductive futurism": a "social consensus" that, Edelman laments, has been made "impossible to refuse."[29] And more than that, "the image of the child," he writes, "not to be confused with the lived experiences of any historical children, serves to regulate political discourse" (11). Politics is only done now in the name of, and for the sake of, "our children's future." The brutal result? If in any context there is *"no baby"* and thus *"no future,"* "then the blame must fall on the fatal lure of sterile, narcissistic enjoyments understood as inherently destructive of meaning" (13)—enjoyments dramatically laid at the door of homosexuals. These, of course, are pleasures that Edelman insists upon in his polemic. And he is happy to link these pleasures to the destruction of the social order.[30] Edelman would like to smash this social order and, along with it, the child. Perhaps most importantly for my purposes, even though Edelman makes this point in passing, "the cult of the child . . . permits no shrines to the queerness of boys and girls, since queerness, for contemporary culture at large . . . is understood as bringing children and childhood to an end" (19).

There are other ways to circumvent "the child." One could explore the elegant, unruly contours of growing that don't bespeak continuance. I coin the term "sideways growth" to refer to something related but not reducible to the death drive; something that locates energy, pleasure, vitality, and (e)motion in the back-and-forth of connections and extensions that are not reproductive. These I will theorize as moving suspensions and shadows of growth. To do so, I return to the notion that Eve Kosofsky Sedgwick so profoundly employed in the early 1990s—the "protogay child"—and claim this notion for sideways growth. The child who by reigning cultural definitions can't "grow up" grows to the side of cultural ideals, in ways I examine throughout this book. As for Sedgwick, in her famous essay from 1991, "How to Bring Your Kids Up Gay: The War against Effeminate Boys," she makes her deep-seated focus the widespread cultural "wish that gay people *not exist*" and takes as her more specific target "therapists' disavowed desire for a nongay outcome."[31] As she explains only partly tongue in cheek: "Advice on how to help your kids turn out gay . . . is less ubiquitous than you might think. On the other hand, the scope of institutions whose pro-grammatic undertaking is to prevent the development of gay people is un-imaginably large [:] . . . most sites of the state, the military, education, law, penal institutions, the church, medicine, and mass culture enforce it all but unquestioningly, and with little hesitation at even the recourse to invasive violence" (161). Sedgwick's essay—part imperative, part elegy, as her title indicates—reports on a historical shift barely noticed despite its momen-tousness. In 1973, with fanfare, the American Psychiatric Association decided to drop from the next edition of its Diagnostic and Statistical Manual (the DSM-III) the diagnostic category "homosexuality," thus removing it as a pa-thology. By its next appearance in 1980, the DSM, sleight-of-hand fashion, had added an entry: "Gender Identity Disorder of Childhood," which, Sedgwick tells us, "appears to have attracted no outside attention . . . nor even to have been perceived as part of the same conceptual shift" (155, 157). In essence, the DSM freed the homosexual only to embattle the child. It waged war against homosexuality precisely on a field where a war could be hidden: the proto-gay child.

In this concept "protogay" I see a host of unexplored temporalities, theo-ries of metaphor, moving suspensions, shadows of growth, and oddly *anti*-identity forms of reaching toward "gay," all of which are waiting to be in-vestigated. In fact, one perceives that the protohomosexual child literalizes a concept that Derrida deemed to "govern the whole of Freud's thought": *Nachträglichkeit*, loosely translated by a range of critics as "deferred effect," "belated understanding," "retro-causality," and "afterwardness": a "deferred action," whereby events from the past acquire meaning only when read through their future consequences.[32] Freud developed this view—some-times called "the ghost in the nursery"—as a way to explain how a trauma en-countered in childhood—more precisely, received as an impression—might become operative as a trauma, never mind consciously grasped as such, only later in life through deferred effect and belated understanding, which retro-actively cause the trauma, putting past and present ego-structures side-by-side, almost cubistically, in lateral spread.[33]

Cubist *growth* as a notion lies ahead of us, in the Picasso-infused depic-tions of Gertrude Stein. But in this Freudian context of trauma, one notes how closely the protogay child is made, by the strictures of public discourse, to trace the path of the ghost in the nursery—though in this case, and this point is crucial, the ghostly gay child *may* be fully conscious of its deferred birth.[34] Hence, the Freudian conception of latency doesn't quite fit, though it looks like it fits, ghostly gay children. They may await only (the right to claim) a word, not a mental state of being, withheld from them in childhood. Besides, whatever their grasp of their circumstance, their latency clearly cannot be (re)solved. Since they are "gay children" only after childhood, they never "are" what they latently "were." Obviously, then, I deem children's protogayness a bold and material commentary on Derrida's notion of delay. Derrida argues that "the structure of delay . . . in effect forbids that one make of temporalization . . . a simple dialectical complication of the living present as an originary and unceasing synthesis."[35] Although these dynamics will be utterly changed—and not all to the good—when children can finally come out "gay," here I suggest that the ghostly gay child, to use Derrida's words, "makes us concerned not with horizons of modified . . . presents, but with a 'past' that has never been present, and which never will be, whose future to come will never be a production or a reproduction in the form of presence."[36]

Perhaps this circumstance of the gay child leads the child to metaphor, which itself is a sideways accretion: the act of imagining oneself as something else. In fact, as I argue in chapter 2, which explains time in relation to metaphor, theorists of childhood need to engage literary indirections and linguistic seductions (such as we find in imaginative fictions) that do what children are often shown as doing: approach their destinations, delay; swerve, delay; ride on a metaphor they tend to make material and so imagine relations of their own. My dog is my wife, my dolly is my child. Not uncommonly, children are shown as having a knack for metaphorical substitution, letting one object stand for another, by means of which they reconceive relations to time. How, we should ask, are children depicted as conceiving their relation to the concept "growing up"? Are they shown as (un)wittingly making strange relations ("my dog is my wife") when they anticipate how they will participate in adult time?

Metaphors comically, poignantly approaching and receding from their namings imply something else. These dynamics could suggest that the tag "gay child" is itself, in certain contexts, a possible stricture—even at gay-affirmative hands. When one can say "I was a gay child," one may be in danger of putting to death all the metaphors richly spun out before the word *gay* arrived. All those vehicles sent in search of tenors, moving along their paths of suspension, may be lost as they're parked into "gay." Hence a straight's metaphorical death (marked, I have said, by the phrase "gay child") or a gay child's backward birth (put in motion by a straight person's "death") may be attended by the *death of metaphors*. Unless they are cherished alongside the words *gay* and *homosexual* as an ill fit. Especially in relation to children our law courts do not believe in—overtly same-sex-oriented children—the tendency of metaphor, narrative, and temporal tricks of the camera (or the cinematic image) to reconfigure relations and time will prove why fictions uniquely nurture ideas of queer children. We are in a time that does not officially recognize children as growing sideways instead of up. We are in a time of the historical prematurity of the love of lateral growth. These webbed issues of temporal interval, retrospection, metaphorical death, and the birth and death of metaphors make the cherished category "childhood"—a state of one's being while also delaying a temporal approach to a time it is not (namely, adulthood)—a concept almost foreign to itself.

The child is even defined as a kind of legal strangeness. It is a body said to need protections more than freedoms. And it is a creature who cannot consent to its sexual pleasure, or divorce its parents, or design its education—at least not by law. Even before there were juvenile courts through "progressive" reforms (in most U.S. states by 1915), nineteenth-century rules of criminal responsibility for children made them notably different from adults: children under seven were considered, by law, "incapable" of committing crimes; children between seven and fourteen were also deemed to be "destitute of criminal design," though the prosecution, under a heavy burden of proof, could rebut this presumption.[37] Of course, with greater legal protections of children in the twentieth century came greater legal regulation of them: the state as "parent" of "wayward children." Indeed, the child was not even a "person" in the sense established by the Fourteenth Amendment, until a U.S. Supreme Court case in 1967, *In re Gault*, began to raise the question of whether or not children should be as equal as "people." Or are they "peculiar people," as a law book deemed them?

This peculiarity—not in a broad, watery sense but in a range of precise, if also braided, versions of queer children—is the focus of my book. Later, I return to the question of History and specific claims about historical change. For one may wonder what scholars of childhood histories (and childhood studies) have said — and how a gay ghost sits beside their findings, especially through the dictates of novels and films. First I spell out the versions of children that both histories and childhood studies have underrecognized, oddly conceptualized, or not even seen. In fairness, I myself am offering a set of initial, not exhaustive, suppositions to be pondered. The versions of children I talk about are mobile by dint of being supple ideas, being almost genres of children. These are mobile renditions of children that range *across* the century, as alive at one end as at the other. And, most importantly, they combine, as my book shows.

Central Versions of the Queer Child

THE GHOSTLY GAY CHILD

The first is the ghost, the queer frontier, or the future to avert, depending on your viewpoint: a child with clear-cut same-sex preference, television's long-standing watertight taboo.[38] This queer child stands out clearly, already, in famous fictional texts by Virginia Woolf, Djuna Barnes, and Radclyffe Hall in the 1920s and 1930s. But it emerges in ghostly form as late as the latter half of the 1990s, especially in a range of helping books — manuals for parents, personal stories, and academic interviews — that search for "typicality," strangely enough, in nonnormativity.

Is there a usual, customary freakishness to the gay-child-in-formation or to familial responses to its forms? In the informational *A Stranger in the Family: How to Cope if Your Child Is Gay* (1996), we are told of a "typical pattern" in families' reactions: subliminal awareness, impact, adjustment, resolution, and integration.[39] The first stage picks up a hint of retrospection, implying the family's subliminal awareness of something (some child) "always lurking there in the back of our minds," says one parent — making the later discovery of gayness, says this person, moving into metaphor, "like the chickens coming home to roost" (5). Far more striking in the discourse of the book than lurking children (seen as soon-to-be-roosting chickens) is the frank talk of death. Under the heading "The Bereavement Effect," parents are told that "this phenomenon" of their reactions "has many symptoms in common with those experienced when someone in the family dies. The previously beloved son or daughter suddenly seems to disappear from life and is replaced by a sinister version of the same person. Parents . . . grieve for what they have lost" (21). There is a loss (a metaphorical death) and a "sinister" replacement: the specter of "a stranger in the family," who was often already haunting the family in a shadowy form. ("Sinister": "impending or lurking danger that makes its presence felt indirectly by signs or portents.") As one parent is quoted as saying: "The Carole that I'd known for the previous twenty-four years was suddenly replaced by this woman who was saying she was a lesbian. . . . I got very depressed, very much like I did when my husband died" (20).

Hovering, barely surfacing children, threatening to depress or scare their parents, catalyze family reflections on delay. In a different helping book, with dual retrospections signaled in the title, *Not Like Other Boys: Growing Up Gay: A Mother and Son Look Back* (1996), the *interval* between subliminal "awareness" and conscious "acceptance" is tapped as the source of family pain. It is as if suspension on the path to "growing up" (even "growing up gay") is itself on trial. Not the child's gayness but the interval of family avoidance of the child who was lurking in their minds — even though mother and son both related, secretly, separately, to the lurking child. In her preface to the book, the mother mournfully wonders out loud (but also through ellipsis): "Why didn't I ask him at eleven, or at thirteen, 'Do you think you might be . . . ?' [her ellipsis]. It was an unthinkable, out-of-the-question, horrifying inquiry to put to a boy who might, after all, be heterosexual. . . . Now, when I allow myself to imagine how that question . . . might have saved my son years of desolation, assuaged a childhood and adolescence of torment . . . I become distraught."[40] Indeed, from the son, we learn that at a neighbor's, "while [the mother] busied herself in the kitchen," "I embarked on what I consider my first sexual experience" with her son Ted (10). "Even then, at age five, I knew it felt too good, and knew without being told that it was wrong" (10). Though Ted soon afterward moved away, "the phantom Ted was as close as I came to having a confidant for most of my prepubescent life" (11). Ghostly metaphors continue in his narrative: "By first grade, definable shadows appeared" (13) and "the fear of my parents' finding out followed me like a sinister shadow through my childhood and adolescence" (12). Perhaps not surprisingly, the son, in his preface, states that his goal in writing this book is "to shorten the distance between acknowledgement and self-confidence in others like me" (ix). He ends the preface by surfacing, it seems, from this painful interval: "I'm no longer lost" (x). But is he growing *up*?

The interval of the child's self-ghosting is both measured and explored through subjects' memories in the 1990s, in social-science studies on "sexual minorities"—all in the service (here it comes again) of discovering "the typical developmental histories of gay youths." For example, in a treatise with the title ". . . *And Then I Became Gay": Young Men's Stories* (1998),[41] the researcher Ritch C. Savin-Williams unabashedly seeks (at least in this book) the "normative experiences" of "growing up gay." He even makes it clear whom he excludes in order to find his normative patterns. He refers to earlier studies on gay youth "composed primarily of 'marginal' teenagers such as male hustlers, streetwalkers, homeless youths, and draft dodgers" and then remarks: "only at great peril could anyone attempt to generalize findings from these studies to current cohorts of sexual-minority youths" (11). And so, *through* these exclusions, he lays out a pattern—based on interviews, all retrospective—common to young, homosexual men (age ceiling: twenty-five).[42] The pattern he delineates for going-to-be-gay boys goes like this: not fitting in, same-sex attractions, "the deniable" becomes "undeniable," and "adoption" of "sexual identity or label"—in other words, ". . . and then I became gay." We are given averages for each interval (an average of five years from same-sex attractions to the label "homosexual" for those attractions; almost nine years from attraction-awareness to a "gay or bisexual identity" [15]). And, as one might guess, "the ages at which developmental milestones are reached . . . have been steadily declining from the 1970s to current cohorts of youth" (16). Therefore, the implied-child-in-ellipsis (whatever child predates ". . . and then I became gay") is increasingly coming closer to (or one could say in danger of) community or clinical labels such as "gay" or "homosexual." These have traditionally been more pointed than "strange," "weird," "odd," "clumsy," "The Artist," or even (as one boy reports being voted by his grammar-school classmates) "The Person Most Likely to Own a Gay Bar" (31). Or, to put it differently, their gay "adoption" of their own selves ("I was a gay child") may, in future years, appear ever earlier, sneaking ever closer to a public proclamation, "I am a gay child." What this specific labeling will mean for children's creative occulting of themselves in either metaphors or narrative strings is, of course, anyone's guess. What will get lost through this way of being found?

A confluence of creative occultings appears in the film *The Hanging Garden* (1996), which depicts examples of queer-child-ghosting through the ma-

1. Gay man seeing his ghost-teen self. From the film *The Hanging Garden* (1996).

terializing metaphor of fat. In this acclaimed Canadian film, gay man, fat teen, queer child, and haunted dog all come together to make a picture of sideways growth. The story is retrospective in that a gay man, after ten years away, is returning to his family to attend his sister's wedding. As the film unfolds, viewers see his fat teen self not only as a character-in-flashback (eating, being lonely, being hit by his father, having sex with a boy) but also as the film's primary ghost—since an image of him hanging dead above the garden (from the branch of a tree) keeps appearing to the viewer and to several other characters (also to himself) (figure 1). We see a fat teen hanging from a rope. More intriguing, this primary ghost is made to stand for yet another ghost we glimpse only briefly: a "normal"-looking child (the gay-man-as-a-boy), who we are told didn't want "to play . . . sports, have any fights, [or] have a girlfriend." We see this ghost-child in the kitchen, his hand in the cookie jar, as the gay man tells his mother: "Skinny was the only thing you couldn't make me be . . . it felt good . . . I wasn't going anywhere."

Fat, we find, is a thick figuration and referent for a child (a sexual child) we cannot fully see. Fat is the visible effect, in this instance, of a child unable to grow "up" in his family as his preferred self. So he grows sideways—literally, metaphorically. He is occulted into something to be seen: a visible difference from the film's other boys (he's the only fat teen) that bespeaks a dead or

2. Gay man with "sister" who is his daughter. From the film *The Hanging Garden* (1996).

dying growing up to the stature of straightness. The fat ghost hanging above the garden flowers, which grow and die in time-lapse photography, speaks not only a suicide threat—which the viewer is never sure occurred—but, more powerfully, a moving suspension at the crossroads of adulthood. After being caught having sex with a friend (another young male), the teen is taken by his Catholic mother to a woman paid to take his virginity. Here are two virginities, sequentially lost, both losses leading nowhere ("I wasn't going anywhere"), except perhaps to a hanging in the garden.

And something even stranger. When the gay man "awakens" from this flashback, he can hear his tomboy sister, whom he has just met on this trip, yelling at the dog: "You're dead . . . I hate you, you freaking flea bag." The dog, we realize, though he is old and has lost his sight, can always tell when a ghost is about. He fidgets and whimpers over both ghosts (child and teen) as if, though blind, he can see the unseen—the child and teen both lurking at the thresholds of everyone's consciousness. That the fifth-grade tomboy girl—along with the gay man—is herself bound up with the dog, who is the seer of sideways growth, foretells what we have next to learn. The girl is not the sibling of the now-gay man but actually his child, born of the woman he was sent to by his mother (figure 2). Against his will, he has (re)produced a child. And from all signs, she is a queer child (maybe a going-to-be-gay child, too). *The Hanging Garden* comes to an end when this parent-child duo, acting like siblings and both named for flowers, Sweet William and Violet, head for the city. "Are we running away?" Violet asks her brotherly father. "Yeah, sort of . . . no, we're just leaving," William answers.

The Hanging Garden, one can see, shows the fraught relations of a gay man to what he regards as his gay child self. By the terms of this film, this child is retrospective (he is hidden in time); he is occulted (he appears as a ghost); he is linked with death—metaphorical death (in the image of a hanging); but he gives birth to metaphors. The space of the garden where the fat ghost hangs is aesthetically moving and a treasure trove of metaphors for flowering and growth—though not a growing up, as William's father had imagined.

THE GROWN HOMOSEXUAL

The oddities of this kind of retrospection ("I was a gay child") make a second queer child seen: the grown "homosexual" who is fastened, one could say, to the figure of the child—both in the form of a ghostly self and in the form of "arrested development." This latter phrase has been the official-sounding diagnosis that has often appeared to describe the supposed sexual immaturity of homosexuals: their presumed status as dangerous children, who remain children in part by failing to have their own.

Who, one may ask, still uses this phrase, "arrested development," and who gave it life? Not surprisingly, even now it stays alive largely in certain political and religious rhetoric on the right. As a British evangelical leader states the matter (he calls himself a "former homosexual"): "I don't really believe there is such a thing as a true homosexual"; "it's a name we give to an arrested development, or an immature emotional state where we've got stuck."[43] A voice from the American religious right echoes: "homosexuality is arrested development" and "most gays are stuck in the adolescent courtship stage, or what is called 'sexual liberation.' "[44] Gays even spread their "symptoms of . . . arrested development" to the general population, as is "seen in plummeting birth rates, epidemics of adultery, divorce, out of wedlock childbirth" and so on.

The developmental history of "arrested development" is serpentine and interesting. It happens that contemporary users of this phrase—right-wing fundamentalists—would, if they checked, find themselves in bed with Darwin and Freud. The phrase as it develops is almost always negative, with the intriguing exception of its use at the hands of Freud, who is likely most responsible, nonetheless, for reproducing it and passing it on. But to go back a little, we find that the OED lists sample uses of the phrase by Sir Thomas Huxley (in 1859) and by Darwin in *The Descent of Man* (1871). Huxley is discussing "oceanic hydrozoa" (which are not, he says, "'arrested developments' of higher organisms"). Darwin is discussing what he calls "microcephalous idiots," who illustrate "a difference between arrested development and arrested growth, for parts in the former state continue to grow whilst still retaining their early condition."[45] By this rendering, arrested development is nonnormal growth, but growth nonetheless. And yet the section that follows upon "Arrests of Development" in *Descent* is called "Reversion," where Darwin states: "When a structure is arrested in its development, but still continues growing . . . it may in one sense be considered as a case of reversion . . . the simple brain of a microcephalous idiot, in so far as it resembles that of an ape, may in this sense be said to offer a case of reversion."

Famously, writers on decadent art and criminality—Max Nordau and Cesare Lombroso—pick up "reversion" and showcase it. Nordau scorns: "He who places pleasure above discipline, and impulse above self-restraint, [a decadent artist like Oscar Wilde] wishes not for progress, but for retrogression to the most primitive animality. . . . They confound all the arts, and lead them back to the primitive forms they had before evolution differentiated them. Every one of their qualities is atavistic, and we know, moreover, that atavism is one of the most constant marks of degeneracy."[46] Not just of degeneracy, but of criminality, holds Lombroso (who writes his author's preface to *Crime: Its Causes and Remedies* in the form of a letter to Nordau in 1906). Lombroso emphasizes the "atavistic" origins of human criminality, the features of which correspond to "savages," children, and/or animals. Hence he urges that "born" "homo-sexuals," "who manifest their evil propensities from childhood," "should be confined from their youth, for they are a source of contagion and cause a great number of occasional criminals."[47]

Freud, by contrast, undercuts moralistic judgments against "homosexuality" at the same time that he uses the phrase "arrested development." In a famous letter to an American homosexual's mother, Freud confides: "Homosexuality is . . . no vice, no degradation, it cannot be classified as an illness; we consider it to be a variation of the sexual function produced by a certain arrest of sexual development. . . . It is a great injustice to persecute homosexuality. . . . for a perverse orientation is far from being a sickness."[48] What does Freud mean by "a certain arrest"? That "in every aberration from the normal sexual life [there is] a fragment of inhibited development and infantilism"?[49] Is homosexuality, then, a growing-sideways-only-sexually with no other psychological consequence, since "inversion is found in people who otherwise show no marked deviation from the normal"? What is clear— even if Freud's meaning is not—is that a number of negative slants on "arrested development" are unmistakably continued by conservative, moralizing (and largely American) psychoanalysts writing after Freud. One analyst claims that the homosexual "is ill in much the same way that a dwarf is ill— because he has never developed"; another found "petrified patterns of living" and "atrophied states" among homosexuals. Yet another states that "most . . . homosexuals do not feel like adults. Rather they see themselves as children or adolescents."[50] And so we glimpse how religious fundamentalists have come to have their phrase—through the odd circuits of Darwin and Freud, who craft uses taken over by others with differing views. These are strange bedmates, Darwin and Freud, for Anglo-American fundamentalists.

How fat, then, are the senses of this phrase. And how nicely turned by queer textualities in the direction of sideways growth. *The Hanging Garden* twines its sense of nowhere-to-grow for a queer youth with its depictions of a growing sideways in among the blooms of mums—keeping mum—telling mum. This homosexual cultivates himself, even in the face of a family's arrested willingness to speak about (the ghost of) his developments.

With this crucial cultivation in mind, one can read Gertrude Stein and Sigmund Freud as an odd pair of writers who, side by side, make growing sideways a matter of duration. For example, Freud is publishing his final, gathered form of *Three Essays on the Theory of Sexuality* in 1924, not long after Stein's celebrated story "Miss Furr and Miss Skeene" is published for the first time in 1922. In Freud's *Three Essays*, which itself kept growing over the years to forty pages longer than its first edition, Freud addresses the issues of inversion, perversion, and children's sexuality. ("Inversion," one recalls, was the common nineteenth-century term for what became more commonly denominated "homosexuality" in the 1900s; it had the specific sense of a person adopting the behavior, sexual and otherwise, of one's so-called opposite sex.)[51] Making room, it seems, for an invert child—though perhaps only through adult memory—Freud states clearly that the "trait of inversion may either date back to the very beginning, as far back as the subject's memory reaches" (so that "the person will feel at one with his peculiarity") or "it may not have become noticeable till some particular time before or after puberty." Entering into ghostly terrain, Freud then tries to be more precise: it is "possible to show that very early in their lives [the lives of 'inverts'] a sexual impression occurred which left a permanent after-effect [a ghost?] in the shape of a tendency to homosexuality" (243). But more pertinent to the question of lateral movements and suspensions is Freud's explanation of "perversion" as not just inversion but diversion. Perverts are "diverts," one could say, who *extend themselves* or *linger*. That is to say, perversions are characteristic of people who either extend themselves beyond the normal "path" of "copulation" or linger at midpoints along the way — and both of these diversions appear to be sideways movements or suspensions in relation to the road of copulation to be followed. Here are Freud's words: "Perversions are sexual activities which either a) extend, in an anatomical sense, beyond the regions of the body that are designed for sexual union, or b) linger over the intermediate relations to the sexual object which should normally be traversed rapidly on the path towards the final sexual aim" (247). The problem for Freud is how to distinguish normal lingering (of normal duration) from the kind that spawns a "new sexual aim." For "a certain amount of touching is indispensable . . . so that lingering over the stage of touching can scarcely be counted a perversion, provided that in the long run the sexual act is carried further" (251) — though all of this shows, as Freud concludes, "how inappropriate it is to use the word perversion as a term of reproach," since "the disposition to perversions is itself of no great rarity but must form a part of what passes as the normal constitution" (253, 258). Lingering is pleasurable "for quite a time" and seems for even "normal people" to "find a place" "alongside" getting to the ultimate goal (253).

Lingering lengthens and further deepens in two contexts crossing through each other. Picasso in his paintings and Stein in her stories conceptualize the toggle between the advance of time, on the one hand, and, on the other, the states of lingering that through repetitions give the feel of suspension and duration. For example, in a work from Picasso's cubist period, *Man with a Clarinet* (1911–12), a state of being (of unnamed duration, unfolding in the present) is broken out sideways into horizontal cubes, showing diachronic immediacy (something happening now) as a lateral accumulation of views, making this state both complex and hard to read. Stein, in experiments modeled on Picasso's, creates in her story "Miss Furr and Miss Skeene" (1922–23) a developmental narrative of two women, or even young girls, "cultivating" themselves, after leaving their parents and their homes. Stein draws this portrait as a cubist form of growth, but one building sideways through the repetition of the (code?) word *gay*.

We cannot really know what this word is meant to name. John Boswell, in his study *Homosexuality, Christianity, and Social Tolerance*, has explained that *gay* (which harks back to the thirteenth-century Provençal *gai*, in reference to courtly love and its literature) was used among English homosexuals of the early twentieth century "as a sort of password or code."[52] Stein ghosts the meaning of *gay* in her piece, while making it the word around which the story turns: "Helen Furr and Georgine Skeene lived together then. . . . They were in a way both gay there where there were many cultivating something. . . . Helen Furr was gay there, she was gayer and gayer there and really she was just gay there, she was gayer and gayer there, that is to say she found ways of being gay there that she was using in being gay there. She was gay there, not gayer and gayer, just gay there, that is to say that she was not gayer by using the things she found there that were gay things, she was gay there, always she was gay there."[53]

Steinian syntax is itself an instance of moving suspensions. Meaning is moving and growing in these sentences even while time almost seems to hang suspended. Moreover, not only does *gay* in this context split from itself as it syntactically sits beside itself in a set of appositions (that also temporally follow each other), but it does so so as to make incompatible meanings cohere as inseparables. Here one detects that *gay*, for all its ambiguity in terms of bearing a sexual meaning, can mean as many as four different things all at once: a kind of fundamental orientation ("always she was gay there"); degrees of becoming (being "gayer and gayer" or "just gay"); a state of desire or nondesire ("she did not find it gay"); and a (sexual?) act ("to be regularly gay was to do every day the gay thing that they did every day") (255–56). Stein thus offers combo-cubist formulations that seem impossible only if one doesn't grasp inseparables: "She was not any more gay but she was gay longer every day than they had been being gay when they were together being gay. She was gay then quite exactly the same way" (258). Stein in this fashion makes the idea of gay grow sideways, fattening it up in this four-way spread, even as the pairing of the women (young girls?) endures and changes over time.

The ghostly "gay" child and the grown-"homosexual"-as-a-child: other children shadow these, though perhaps in seeming contrast. For up to this point we've been talking of the dangers of those queer children who will never be straight. But there is a type of dangerous child who, "if all goes well," will be straight, not gay, in a future incarnation, though this child can never be "heterosexual" as a child. The child who answers to this riddle, of course, is the child queered by Freud (our third queer child): the not-yet-straight-child who is, nonetheless, a sexual child with aggressive wishes. From wanting the mother to have its child, to wanting to have its father's baby, to wanting to kill its rival lover, the Freudian child (the child penned by Freud) looks remarkably, threateningly precocious: sexual and aggressive.

Adults, for their part, are suppressed infants, by Freud's implication: "the growth of a civilized and normal individual," Freud informs us, emerges "at the cost of the infantile sexual impulses themselves" (*Three Essays*, 261).[54] For not only is the child a fond practitioner of anality (albeit regarding its feces as gifts, or even as babies); the child is also an avid voyeur (an "eager spectator of. . . . micturition and defaecation") and fully in touch with "the cruel component of the sexual instincts" (since "cruelty in general comes easily to the childish nature") (*Three Essays*, 269). Adults, Freud implies, are encouraged to suppress their childhood love of anality, voyeurism, and aggression. But not their regressions, in some key respects. In Freud's way of thinking, an oddly pedophilic fantasy emerges between "normal" husband and wife, who find they are "a phase apart psychologically." Freud makes this point in his essay "Femininity," saying there: "Even a marriage is not made secure until the wife has succeeded in making her husband her child."[55] And yet Freud regards this pedophilic marriage, in which the husband is his lover's child, as normative, marital "genital maturity." This from the man who pointed out that lesbians ("female homosexuals") — those who seemingly show a "certain arrest of development" — "play the parts of mother and baby with each other as often and as clearly as those of husband and wife."[56]

3. Lying child spying, saying she sees lovers. From the film *The Children's Hour* (1961).

To be sure, the child's lush role in adult relations, combining infantil-
ized postures with strangely knowing (and aggressive) gestures, is intensely
present in Henry James's fiction at the turn of the century and, famously,
in Nabokov's *Lolita* at the middle of the century of the child. This role also
emerges in the cinema, in Hollywood productions, even at a moment when
America is still not sexually revolutionized (or Stonewalled), in a film that
notoriously helped to force the Hays Code to make newly possible "tasteful
treatment[s]" of "homosexuality"—which, evidently, include the suicide at
the film's end.[57] The movie is *The Children's Hour* (1961), a film adaptation
of Lillian Hellman's well-known play (1934). In this film with mainstream
stars (Audrey Hepburn, James Garner, and Shirley MacLaine), a child with
an unnamed aggressive motivation (at times it looks like jealousy, sometimes like resentment over simple discipline), and with the help of a child-
kleptomaniac whom she blackmails into backing her, wrongly and willfully
accuses her school's co-headmistresses, Karen Wright and Martha Dobie,
of being lovers (see figure 3). The school goes under; a libel suit (shades of
Oscar Wilde) is lost by the two accused women; yet one of these, Martha,
confesses that she really did love the other and then promptly hangs herself
in her room. *The Children's Hour*, with its innocent storytime title that signals

a fleeting temporality, ends with suspense as its finality. The time for possibility and clear restoration seems to run out at the end of a rope.

In fact, it appears that a sexual child (or at least a child with sexual knowledge) with aggressive wishes—aimed, it appears, at *in loco parentis*—puts a stop to sideways growth. For until this time, the hyphenated couple of Karen and Martha, running the Wright-Dobie School, were not growing up to marriage and childbirth but were growing sideways in their labors for the school. Martha had no intention of marrying ("I [already] have twenty children upstairs") and Karen's marriage to Dr. Joe Cardin ("I delivered my hundredth baby today," he declares to her) was on hold. The child intervenes in this fertile delay not to straighten this bent trajectory but to bend it further—and in public view. She gets her ideas of lesbian relations from a book smuggled into the school. She then attaches these ideas to a word she overhears spoken by Martha's aunt, describing Martha's "propensities since childhood." (The word is *unnatural*, used in reference to Martha's possessiveness over Karen.)

What stuns viewers potentially in all of this is not the theme of "homosexuality" (not now at least) but the inversion of child/adult conventions. It is not that in *The Children's Hour* innocent childhood is put under threat by adult pathologies. Rather, in the film, adult legal innocence is threatened by quasi-pathological children (a compulsive liar and a kleptomaniac). Or, more intriguingly, adult *perversions* are clearly threatened by aggressive children. In addition, a pupil schools a teacher through the clarifying act of her deception. The pupil's lie reveals to the teacher (Martha) her own feelings, making her pregnant, one might say, with the child's suggestion of her (retrospective) queerness: "You have something in you and you don't know it's there, and then one night a little girl . . . tells a lie and there for the first time you see it. You say to yourself, 'did she sense it?' . . . She found the lie with the ounce of truth."

In fact, one could claim that *The Children's Hour* follows the logic of most Wildean epigrams: the inverse, that is, is always true. What looks like guilt is innocence, but innocence is guilt. Before the child's lie, when they're still considered innocent, Martha and Karen look like a couple (hyphenated, partnered, Martha jealous). When accused of couplehood, they start to look innocent, since they make strong, convincing denials. Still, when Karen presents her innocence to her fiancé, Joe, she thinks he believes her guilty, so she sends him away. This act prompts the serious talk between the two accused teachers, in which Martha proclaims her innocent love for Karen, which, of course, suddenly blooms into rancid declarations of her guilt: "I've loved you like a friend, like thousands of other women have felt; you were a dear friend who was loved, that's all. . . . But maybe I've loved you the way they said! Listen to me! . . . There's always been something wrong. . . . I can't keep it to myself any longer. I'm guilty. . . . I feel so damn sick and dirty I can't stand it." Quite remarkably, after this scene, the lying child's grandmother comes to the women to admit their innocence (the lie now having been discovered as a lie). At the height of Martha's guilt (she is only guilty of wanting sex with Karen), their slate is wiped clean. Now declared innocent, they have a cover for what could become a full-blown affair, since their once-suspicious closeness would now function as the simple sign that they are again their innocent selves. Rather than interrupt this dialectic, the film suspends it. The child slips out of the spectator's view (what becomes of her?) and the "homosexual" hangs postconfession. The jury is hung on two different counts.

THE CHILD QUEERED BY INNOCENCE OR QUEERED BY COLOR

These three models of dangerous children — the ghostly gay child, the grown homosexual, and the child queered by Freud — present us with what for at least two centuries have largely been viewed as antithetical to childhood: sex, aggression, secrets, closets, or any sense of what police call "a past." The child is the specter of who we were when there was nothing yet behind us. Which brings us to the fourth queer child we must consider — the one made famous by so many landmark studies of childhood and by the Romantic poets who, along with Anglo-American legal systems, have so nurtured it. This would be the normative child — or the child who, on its path to normativity, seems safe to us and whom we therefore seek to safeguard at all cost. I am speaking, of course, of the child made strange (though appealing) to us by its all-important "innocence." This is a form of normative strangeness, one might say. From the standpoint of adults, innocence is alien, since it is "lost" to the very adults who assign it to children. Adults retrospect it through the gauzy lens of what they attribute to the child. And adults walk the line — the impossible line — of keeping the child at once what it is (what adults are not) and leading it toward what it cannot (at least, as itself) ever be (what adults are).

What do children queered by innocence share? They all share estrangement from what they approach: the adulthood against which they must be defined. This is why "innocent" children are strange. They are seen as normative but also not like us, at the same time. The contours of this normative strangeness may explain why children, as an *idea*, are likely to be both white and middle-class. It is a privilege to need to be protected—and to be sheltered—and thus to have a childhood. Not in spite of privilege, then, but because of it, the all-important feature of weakness sticks to these markers (white and middle-class) and helps to signal innocence.

In surprising ways, the complex poem "The Little Black Boy" (1789) in William Blake's *Songs of Innocence* turns upon this point and highlights dynamics for the child queered by color in the twentieth century—matters that are central to my last chapters. This particular poem hits the wall of interpretive dilemmas because it gives us children of two different colors. The narrating black boy announces at the start his rather mixed relation to central terms:

> My mother bore me in the southern wild,
> And I am black, but O! my soul is white;
> White as an angel is the English child:
> But I am black as if bereav'd of light.[58]

Strange to say, what he, this little black boy, is bereaved of, come to find out, is the weakness of whiteness, which is so central to the sign of innocence (and, by extension, to privilege and childhood). The black boy, quite simply, is not weak enough to come across as innocent. He is a paragon of strength and experience. How do we know? What signals this experience? His black skin. Or so his mother tells him. He has experienced, intensely on his skin, the burning rays of God's own love. He's burned black. And so his blackened skin is the sign of "bearing" God, which of course requires (and also fashions) strength. Or, as his also blackened mother narrates:

> "And we are put on earth a little space,
> That we may learn to bear the beams of love,
> And these black bodies and this sun-burnt face

Is but a cloud, and like a shady grove.
For when our souls have learn'd the heat to bear,
The cloud will vanish."

If the angel metaphor excludes the little black boy ("White as an angel is the English child") — or just eludes him — the blackened boy participates in tropes of cloud and shade.

No wonder this poem has no companion in William Blake's subsequent *Songs of Experience*.[59] There is no need. It *is* about experience. No wonder that critics who war with each other over the poem's ultimate meaning largely agree that the poem is too complex for *Songs of Innocence*, that its ambiguities are deepened, not resolved, by Blake's illustrations, and that the poem is "so elaborately about learning through suffering that the black boy seems oddly superior to the white boy."[60] What he actually is is stronger and thus less privileged.

And thus I say to little English boy:
When I from black and he from white cloud free,
And round the tent of God like lambs we joy,
I'll shade him from the heat till he can bear
To lean in joy upon our father's knee.

Freed from their color clouds, one boy still seems too advanced for innocence. The boy formerly known as the black boy serves and protects the weak boy formerly known as the white boy (actually, the "English boy," whose nationality stands for his whiteness) so that the white boy can bend toward the father and bear God's love. And though they meet in the metaphor of lamb, we likely sense a dominant color (the color of lambs we see in our heads). Besides, this is a journey — for the black boy — from the womb of the mother to the knee of the father, from her blackened skin to his golden tent. The white boy, by contrast, seems boldly self-continuous in his neatly unfolding leaning.

In the 1990s there are echoes of this problem. In fact, it is echoed not just for children queered by their color but also for children whose families are not financially well-endowed. Experience is still hard to square with innocence, making depictions of streetwise children, who are often neither white nor middle-class, hard to square with "children." One solution to this problem (of children lacking the privilege of both weakness and innocence) is to endow these children with abuse. As odd as it may seem, suffering certain kinds of abuse from which they need protection and to which they don't consent, working-class children or children of color may come to seem more innocent. To take just one example, in the feminist film production (1996) of Dorothy Allison's *Bastard Out of Carolina* (written in 1993), directed by Angelica Huston, the working-class protagonist, a child named Bone, is raped on-screen at agonizing length while being forced to sit, then forced to move, on her stepfather's lap. Why was this scene, and another more head-banging rape of this child, allowed to be shown? (The Adrian Lyne film of *Lolita* [1997] was nearly banned from American theaters due to its depictions of a sexual child.) The *Bastard* scenes are permitted, perhaps, because their brutality, showing the child's need for protection and her weakness in these moments, confirms the child's innocence. But innocence of what? Not of sexuality; the child sadly knows what is being done to her and she is bearing it. Rather, she is innocent of any consent. Unlike Lyne's and Nabokov's Lolitas, there is no sexual countermotion on Bone's part. No erotic pleasure in her own world, and no mystery surrounding her motives. Knowingly, and fully unambiguously, Bone does not consent. Evidently, this equal-opportunity innocence for the underprivileged, which requires their being brutalized, is worthy of our sight.

WHEN VERSIONS BRAID

Finally, in conclusion to these versions of the queer child—speculative, after all, and incomplete—we should grasp the intertwining nature of these strands. Their critical, intricate braiding allows for such unexpected portraits of queer children. For example, the film *The Hanging Garden* intertwines all at once, and in one character, the ghostly gay child, the grown homosexual, Freud's precocious child, and the child queered by innocence (the latter evoked by the gay child's abuse at the hands of his father). No wonder this film can say so much. It is deftly combining children the film is literally teaching us to see.

A different illustrative instance of braiding is one that shows how the innocent child and the Freudian child, who seem like polar opposites, can come together in the same child, in a dramatic sideways growth—really the kind of arrested development Freud associated with homosexuals. This combination surprisingly emerges from a conventional sentimental source, Steven Spielberg, in *A.I. Artificial Intelligence* (2001), appearing at the start of the twenty-first century. Based on the Brian Aldiss story "Supertoys Last All Summer Long," from 1969, and emerging from a project begun by Stanley Kubrick, *A.I.* tells of a "robot-child." It is a kind of millennial reflection (at least as Spielberg shapes it) on the status of children's relations with their parents. The story takes place in the unhappy future of human history, in the "years after the ice-caps had melted because of greenhouse gases," with Amsterdam, Venice, and New York "forever lost." This is the time of the reign of "legal sanctions to strictly license pregnancies," thus making "robots, which were never hungry and did not consume resources, . . . so essential and economical." Wed to this market-driven robot-child, who is worth his price, is something priceless: a "love that . . . never end[s]." In the case of this new "mecha" (short for "mechanical"), "with neuronal feedback," "love will be the key by which [he] acquire[s] a kind of subconscious never before achieved — an inner world of metaphor, of intuition, of self-motivated reasoning, [and even] of dreams." In fact, this artificial child, David, is the quintessential innocent child in the film's terms, because he is wired for unconditional, undying love and supreme obedience, which later make him fragile. ("Would you like me to sleep now?" David asks; "I can never go to sleep, but I can lay quietly and never make a peep.") Or as the designer who creates him (played by William Hurt) expresses it: "Ours will be a perfect child, caught in a freeze-frame, always loving, never ill, never changing . . . a little mecha [who] will open up a new market and fill a great human need."

This both priced and priceless child is bought by parents, Monica and Henry, who have lost their only biological child of the same age (eleven years old). More precisely, their "deceased" son is being kept on ice in a cryogenics lab, for the day when he might unexpectedly awaken. Expectedly, he does. And if the robot-child is the innocent child, by contrast the "natural" human child (normally Spielberg's paragon of wide-eyed innocence, wonder, and hope for the future) is conniving, rivalrous, and blatantly cruel. In an early scene, he sends David off on a "special mission" ("I want a lock of Mommy's hair") with a promise bound to be alluring to David: "Then I'll go tell Mommy *I* love you and then she'll love you too." David, sensing a breach of obedience, wistfully answers: "I can't, Martin, I'm not allowed," though he feels he must obey Martin's wish, so he cuts the lock — and it goes

4. The robot-child, suspended in liquid, endlessly longing. From the film *A.I.* (2001).

badly. (Monica awakens to scissors near her face and worries that David might be violent.) This bold contrast between these children (one robot, one human) is our first jolt, underscored by the parents' feeling that David's intensity of unblemished love is almost creepy (itself underscored by David's being played by Haley Joel Osment of *The Sixth Sense*). Our second jolt arrives when the innocent robot's tacitly sweet, unblinking devotion to the mother (the father seems a mere pleasant afterthought to David) becomes a Freudian fixation of Brobdingnagian proportions. Spielberg has somehow succeeded in combining two versions of children (the innocent, the Freudian) that are opposed in the minds of most Americans, and also in his own.

David is soon abandoned by his mother. She leaves him in the woods after he has innocently (to avoid a stabbing at the hands of Martin's friends) dragged Martin into a backyard swimming pool where Martin almost drowns. The camera's image of David floating, arms outstretched, at the bottom of the pool, as if he were stranded in a watery grave, is iconic for the film (see figure 4). This is his constant posture in relation to a mother that eludes him. This is his gesture of encompassing arrest. And since it occurs in the middle of the film, his outstretched yearning can only grow with time. No amount of wild adventure can redirect its spread across the story and the screen. The "flesh fairs" that threaten his very existence (festivals of robot-destruction that resemble a Kid Rock concert crossed with a tractor pull); his friendship with robot Gigolo Joe (Jude Law) that pairs him with blatant sexuality to which he stays oblivious (Joe: "We are the guiltless pleasure for lonely human beings—you're not going to get us pregnant, or have us to supper with mummy and daddy: we work under you, we work on you, we work for you"); and their trips to Rouge City and half-sunk Manhattan: none of these events shakes his single-minded focus. Not even his eventual discovery of other robot-clones of himself—a row of Davids—which he aggressively smashes as he shouts: "You can't have [my mother]. She's mine. I'm David. I'm unique. I'm special."

Indeed, David ends up stranded underwater one last time—this time, however, for two thousand years—arrested in staring at the Blue Fairy (who resembles a Madonna) from Coney Island (now that the park is submerged in the sea). Found post–ice age by nonhuman life forms, David is no less focused on his mother. In order partially to grant his wish to see her, these beings resurrect (really, reconstitute) the long-dead mother from the lock of hair that David had once clipped from her. But she is restored to him only for a day. Now the massive time frame of the film funnels to one intense point. David, through his memory, goes back and to the side of his former child-life to grow a perfect day that he has never lived. He looks the same as he has throughout the film—not one bit taller, or older, or sadder—and so does his mother. Looking like lovers, complete with a scene in which they bed down, mother and son are joined in bliss. Or as David puts it: "No one else [was] in her mind—not Henry [David's father], not Martin—just David." He goes to sleep and, shadows of Freud, finally dreams. (Yet, for the viewer, the screen goes dark.)

This book offers numerous braidings. In fact, every chapter will stress its own combination of these children, for it is the manner in which they braid that makes for striking takes on growth: portraits of sideways relations, motions, and even futures that tip to the side. Moreover, these portraits horizontalize History, in a manner of speaking, making History broaden itself by growing outside and beside itself, or so I claim. But if these versions of queer children would sit beside, would get beside, the histories of the child and childhood studies, we need to know the shape of these studies as conceived.

Horizontal History, or Sitting beside the History of the Child

With fiction as my witness, read with my fantasies fully engaged, I could say that I believe the century of the child is the century of the fictions of the ghostly gay child and its queer companions, among whom I include the "normative" child—all growing sideways more than up. This is my book's most basic claim, surrounded by four realizations that extend it:

(1) *those who fetishize "delay" for the child must believe in sideways growth*

First of all, importantly, childhood commentators, as we will see, are always trying to get their concept of delay to come out right. Exactly how and for how long, they seem to be asking, does one attempt to delay the child's inevitable, encouraged, but hopefully-not-too-rapid arrival at adulthood? In highly telling ways, even in these thinkers' ideal views of growth, children would have to be growing sideways while on delay, since these thinkers make delay a central factor for children's growth.[61] Finding the Goldilocks solution to just the right amount of delay proves elusive, however, for these writers, giving rise to paradoxes that surround the child and that appear in childhood studies, even if obliquely:

(2) *evidently, we are scared of the child we would protect, and*

(3) *in the century of the child, the child is feared to disappear (just as the gay child appears to be emerging)*

The chief paradoxes for childhood studies in the last century seem to be twofold, in my view. Just as children are deemed more vulnerable by their guardians in the 1900s (and thus are deemed more in need of protections, many in the form of laws), they are constructed as more problematic, as presenting adults with more and newer problems, even dangers to face.[62] A second paradox that shows up in commentaries, not so obliquely, is the observation that the century of the child turns out to be the century in which the state of childhood itself is shrinking, even disappearing, as children advance "too quickly" to adulthood.[63] Sexual precocity, as one would imagine, aided by both the media and the Internet, is high on scholars' list of factors causing children to "grow up fast" and thus disappear. These same factors, scholars could point out—though they don't point out—are making the concept "gay" more available to children who, from early ages, are feeling queer. Yet will the public emergence of the "gay" child aid in accelerating children's disappearance? Or will the marker "gay" be desexualized in the public discourse on childhood? Surely the current sex-predator hysteria taking place now on cable television participates in these paradoxical developments (as James Kincaid, I am certain, would suggest). In this current version of the pedophile wars, law enforcement officers pose on the Internet as virtual children—often as the sexually talkative, willing, provocative youngsters the law, fundamentally, can't believe in (since the law says that a child can't consent to sexual contact with adults, given the child's extreme vulnerabilities). This child voice that police send out to "pedophiles" in order to "catch" them is the voice of childhood that the law denies—yet must believe the public, especially parents, feels increasingly endangered by. Adult accusations of adult pedophilia are a way to disbelieve the voice of this child.

(4) furthermore, children are vulnerable (and dangerous) as much by means of money as by means of sex

What may be children's greatest vulnerability, according to the fictions I read for this book—also their greatest danger to adults—involves not sex but money. If children were to have more economic power, would they be less vulnerable, even less sexually vulnerable to adults, in some contexts? Or would they be more vulnerable? Being speculative, it is hard to say (though the fictional Lolita has an answer). What changes so dramatically for Anglo-American children in the early 1900s, according to all historians of childhood, is their economic role. Through labor laws, children, who were once working bodies in the labor force, cease to work for wages. How, then, are children made unique and strange by money? Among other ways, by not bringing money in the form of incomes into their families; by receiving, instead, an "allowance" from their parents; by spending money on toys and consumer choices driven by media targeted at them (and later sexually aimed at them). Fictions particularly and uniquely address this child queered by money, along with its obvious appetite for media.

Where am I taking these four realizations? With my intention, my almost cubist project, of putting certain fictions next to childhood studies, even to draw attention to their mismatch or only near-match with each other, my main aim is to broaden the child through a set of broadening questions. But am I displaying what Carolyn Dinshaw calls "a queer desire for history," a need to "feel historical," as Chris Nealon has so beautifully put it in Foundlings: Lesbian and Gay Historical Emotion before Stonewall?[64] I wouldn't say so.

But if this need seems to haunt my book or me or my readers, which I know it might, this need to "feel historical" can only be enacted by a being-fictional I claim for children throughout the last century.[65]

Why, though, tangle with History at all? This is something Lee Edelman asks in a roundtable essay on "Queer Temporalities." Wondering why "we're obliged to keep turning time *into* history," one that would offer us "the promise of sequence as the royal road to *consequence*," Edelman speaks against the notion of a "historical procession obedient to origins, intentions, and ends whose authority rules over all."[66] He would remind us that "we're subjects . . . of the real, of the drive, of the encounter with futurism's emptiness, with negativity's life-in-death." Or, as he later states, "we're never at one with our queerness; neither its time nor its subject is ours." As a counter, Dinshaw cautions against our setting up "'history' as a straw man, in a form in which none of us actually practice it." She goes on to say: "Thinking nonlinearity over and against linearity is hard enough, but figuring out the criteria by which different nonlinear temporalities might be meaningfully brought together—figuring out how to make heterogeneity analytically powerful—is exponentially harder." Edelman, still, will countenance only "an encounter with what can't be assimilated to any systematic understanding, what doesn't conduce to the logic of periodization or identity"; "call it the queerness of time's refusal to submit to a temporal logic."

It could be I am doing what Dinshaw says, while thus confirming what Edelman claims. But if what Edelman claims is the case, why not have the pleasure of pursuing the thoughts, illusory or not, that Dinshaw seeks? Pleasure cannot harm the work of negativity if, as it does in Edelman's thinking, it works against pleasure-killing mainstream pieties. That is to say, making use of fictions, why not figure out certain "criteria" for the ghostly gay child's nonlinearities, which collide with other children's nonlinearities, which confirm "we're never at one with our queerness"?[67] Besides, no matter what anyone claims for History as a record of origins, ends, authorities, and identities, even orthodox historical practice shows that we are in each moment simply adding to historical *spread*—adding more documents, findings, arguments, to the so-called files of every period—so that our view of sequence, which is daily changing, is unbounded on both "ends" (and in between them). History will just keep getting fatter. Something, then, about the "practice" of History (Dinshaw's word) fits key aspects of Edelman's descriptions.

It is time to sample some historical claims, and three kinds of studies help fashion my selection. First, from the study that birthed "childhood studies" — *Centuries of Childhood*, written by Philippe Ariès and translated into English in 1962 — come the field-defining questions: What makes a child? What conditions are needed historically for there to be creatures who are called "children"?[68] A second, closely related ring of studies seeks to explain the changes for childhood in the last century: what new conditions, from the early 1900s to the late 1990s, contribute to children's so-called uniqueness during the century of the child? Among these studies are Anthony Platt's *The Child Savers* (1969), a study of juvenile delinquency and the rise of juvenile justice in the last century, and Viviana Zelizer's *Pricing the Priceless Child* (1985), about changes in children's labor in the twentieth century — both of which are landmark works. And, finally, there are gay, lesbian, and queer studies (for example, the essays in *Queering Elementary Education* and the study *The New Gay Teenager*) that are revealing, in my view, of problems for any nonfictional study of the "gay" child.

It cannot surprise us that childhood studies, when it first becomes an entity, finds its starting point by arguing that children as a concept are conceived at a certain point in time. Exploring the family not as a reality but as "an idea," Ariès explains why there was "no place for [the concept of] childhood" in the Middle Ages and thus how childhood as an idea evolved "from immodesty to innocence" only in the middle of the seventeenth century (33, 110). Ariès's thesis, as well as those of writers who later extended it, turns on the axes of literacy, education, legislation, and shame.[69] For the child to be born as a cultural idea, adulthood must be seen as a wholly different state, as something the child initially does not possess and therefore must acquire in the place of innocence. Adulthood must be something a child approaches gradually, legally, as it takes on by degrees adult linguistic codes. With the changing conditions of literacy (the appearance of the printing press dividing children from literate adults), with the changing conditions of education (the increasing emergence, first in Scotland, of a graduated curriculum), and with the changing conditions of censorship (what is thought essential to withhold from children — sexual knowledge heading the list), "the child," conceptually, begins to take shape, as Ariès and later scholars explain. It is a creature of *gradual growth* and *managed delay*, bolstered by laws that ideally will protect it from its own participation in its pleasure and its pain. For if the child is innocent, it is also weak. "Weakness" and "innocence," Ariès claims, are the twin pillars (are seen as the pillars) of children's "reflection of divine purity," requiring of their keepers both safeguarding measures and strengthening help (113).

Help comes boldly in the twentieth century. Measures that are aimed at safeguarding children, historians tell us, are one of the earmarks of this era, even though fictions are depicting the paradoxes I presented earlier: we seem to be scared of the child we would protect; and the child is vulnerable and dangerous through money. As for these fictions, along with the matter of children's intelligent involvement with pain, the perilous, murderous child-homosexual—not a figure recognized by Ariès or others[70]—figures distinctively in several of my texts, even in *In Cold Blood* and *Elephant*, in which implied homosexuals appear. This child's motives are exceptionally mysterious, captured in a series of filmic experiments in movement and parallel-track narration. And as a curious prelude to these portraits, especially the puzzle of juvenile motives, there is *Lolita*. Through a set of metaphors (dolly, dog, and car), and even through a car chase that takes place as a comical chase between literary genres, one genre actually tailing the other (as strange as that may sound), *Lolita* reminds us of the difference money makes for the child's sexuality. Children's inability to be self-propelling *and* self-sustaining (the latter in a financial sense) makes them either a kind of 1950s wife (demanding of allowances for services rendered) or a prototypical "wayward" child whom the state can confine, provided the child is not good at escape (though Lolita surely is).

These are not the matters that historians explore, at least not in this way. Nor do sociologists writing social history cover this ground. The fascinating workings of children's masochism; the shape and intricate movements of their motives that the law does not believe in; and their creative maneuvers around or between their wifeliness and their waywardness: these are not stories these scholars tell us, by and large. Nor do they outright state that we are scared of the children we protect. But a sense of the child's growing strangeness is implicit in their studies—for example, in the history of juvenile justice. This is a story about the child's queerness in criminal matters (these are my words), really the creation of a new kind of child: a "delinquent," a *pre*-criminal person, who must be protected from his own propensities and from the environment that could set them off. Paradoxically, then, progressive efforts to safeguard children at the beginning of the twentieth century, to honor children's innocence, so we are told, *create* their delinquency — and so, ironically, as fictions explore, create the child from whom we seek protection. Anthony M. Platt's study of the origins of juvenile justice, if it doesn't quite offer the pairing of protecting and fearing the child, does at least capture the paradox of adults harming and stigmatizing children while protecting them, an irony he foregrounds in his study's title: *The Child Savers: The Invention of Delinquency*. In this treatise, which trails Ariès by roughly seven years but precedes Michel Foucault's *Discipline and Punish* (1975/1977) by about six, Platt explains how, early in the century, reformers with concerns for "purity," "salvation," "innocence," "corruption," and "protection," who sought to "rescue" those children "less fortunately placed," created "special judicial and correctional institutions for the labeling, processing, and management of 'troublesome' youth."[71] (Humbert warns Lolita she'll be sent to such a place, if she dares to think about calling the police.) And these were efforts that despite reformers' "benign motives" "diminished the civil liberties and privacy of youth" (4). Nonetheless, considered "one of the greatest advances in child welfare that has ever occurred," the first official juvenile court was established in 1899 in Illinois, followed by Illinois's Juvenile Court Act that became a model for other states and countries (9).

How did protection and harm for the child — or as fictions tell it, protection and fear of the child — come together in the Illinois founding of the juvenile courts? Platt cites a commentator's explanation that "the critical philosophical position of the reform movement was that no formal, legal distinctions should be made between the delinquent and the dependent or neglected" (138). This collapsing of distinctions, putting them in jarring apposition to each other, making for a strange combination indeed, was certainly a change from the nascent criminology of the nineteenth century, from 1870 to 1900. That criminology, rooted in the theories of Charles Darwin, Herbert Spencer, and Cesare Lombroso, held to the inborn nature of the criminal. Breaking with these views around 1900, according to Platt, reformers reasoned that "delinquent children" were most often "neglected children." Even so, they were "the criminals of the next generation" and must be stopped "from pursuing" their "careers" on the criminal path (45). That is to say, by implication, the criminal-in-child-form must be arrested in its development for the civic good.

One imagines this view of a child's precriminality allowed the term *delin-quent* to be used by reformers without their believing they were stigma-tizing children. Indeed, Platt cites the Chicago Bar Association from 1899 as saying "that the State, acting through the Juvenile Court, exercises that tender solicitude and care over its neglected, dependent wards, that a wise and loving parent would exercise with reference to his own children under similar circumstances," leading to the state's "wide discretion" in addressing the problems facing children (138). (In a phrase Foucault would be likely to pounce upon, Platt cites a juvenile judge as saying, "We must reach into the soul-life of the child" [143].) In practice, this paternalism meant that "delinquency" referred not only to the kinds of criminal acts adults com-mit but, more profoundly, to "violations of vaguely defined catchalls—such as 'vicious or immoral behavior,' 'incorrigibility,' 'truancy,' 'profane or in-decent language,' 'growing up in idleness,' 'living with any vicious or disrep-utable person,' etc.—which indicated, if unchecked, the possibility of more serious misconduct in the future" (138). The law could see itself looking back in future times to find a (ghostly) criminal. Furthermore, inside Platt's own "etc.," one can only guess, also lie behaviors deemed to be prehomosexual. (One thinks of Lolita being schooled by "little Lesbians," as Humbert puts it, before he ever touches her.) To be sure, under its Juvenile Court Act, the state of Illinois could even issue penalties for what it called "pre-delinquent" behavior (making for a pre-pre-criminal child?). For, ultimately, in the words of Platt, "a child was not accused of a crime but offered . . . guidance; judicial records were not generally available to the . . . public; and hearings were conducted in relative privacy" (137).

What did these safeguards lead to in consequence? Often they led to insti-tutional confinement and the *"non-person"* status of children and teens, inso-far as constitutional guarantees did not apply to them. Platt points out that "the basic tenet of the child-saving philosophy"—which largely was aimed at children of lower-class and immigrant families—was "commitment" of delinquents to so-called special "schools" or reformatories, which were pre-dictably overcrowded and more like prisons than like schools (140). Records from that early juvenile court in Illinois indicate that "one third of all juve-niles charged with delinquency [and "almost two-thirds of . . . 'delinquent' girls"] were sent to the John Worthy School, the state reformatory, or trans-ferred to the criminal courts" (140). (Girls were committed to "state and local institutions.") Platt asserts that when he is writing his book in 1969 "little has changed in the institutions for delinquents" (152).

One thing had changed by Platt's time, as we learn from legal history: a juvenile's right to due process procedures. For over half the century, juveniles had no such guarantees. For example, since "a child's case" was "not a legal case," it was thought unnecessary for children to have lawyers—never mind to have timely notice of their charges, a right to cross-examine, or the right to remain silent in custody. *In re Gault*—a Supreme Court case from 1967—changed these circumstances. In fact, the landmark aspect of this case involving Gerald Gault, a fifteen-year-old charged with making lewd phone calls, was the U.S. Supreme Court's ruling that juveniles, too, are entitled to due process rights guaranteed by the Fourteenth Amendment. The court opinion famously held that neither the Fourteenth Amendment nor the Bill of Rights is for adults alone. And though Platt ends his book with the prediction that *Gault* will do little to change the bigger picture of juvenile justice—since the "views of lawyers about the rights of children differ quite fundamentally from those expressed by the Supreme Court and academics" (167)—there have been other cases (for example, *Tinker v. Des Moines*) that have raised the question of juvenile rights, as did the 1989 United Nations Convention on the Rights of the Child.

"Children's liberation," then—but from what and whom?—proves to be a checkered matter in the century of the child. The view from key historians looks like a pattern of constraint and escape: parents attempt to constrain their children who often elude them. The fictions I explore put this all a bit differently, perhaps just more specifically. They see empowerment for children strongly tethered to their *enthrallments*, their almost slavish rapture in the face of their diversions, which can lead to no escape, no exit, in the end, though after captivating fireworks of struggle.

But first the view from History, from a key historian summarizing twentieth-century developments. In his end-of-the-century essay "Historical Perspectives on Twentieth-Century American Childhood," in *Beyond the Century of the Child: Cultural History and Developmental Psychology* (2003), Peter Stearns argues that, in the last century, "adult constraints on children were more detailed and demanding even as children's outlets through consumerism expanded," and that "this central tension—constraint and release—was the most important new twentieth-century framework."[72] Stearns goes on to specify that "most of the leisure fare offered to children" in this era "escaped" their parents' concern or "control" (97). Hence, while earlier rhetorical patterns of describing children as innocent and vulnerable continued in this century, "new key facts" surrounding children emerged: the disappearance of their labor, the enforcement of schooling (even for lower classes by the 1920s), the increasing emergence of child-rearing manuals (which sought to *heighten* parental anxiety), and, quite importantly, the "targeting" of children as new consumers. Or as Stearns puts it: "echoes of hoped-for innocence lingered [but] confidence declined"; "the result was a . . . more problem-focused approach to children, with expert definitions and parental responses increasingly stressing difficulties" (101, 104). But if these anxieties led to constraints (more parental supervision, more intense moralizing, and more scheduling of children in some contexts), the child's consumerism ("the pattern opening up around 1900") made children increasingly "define themselves," throughout the century, "in terms of acquisition and spectatorship" (106). Comic books emerged in the 1920s, signaling a trend toward children's choosing (apart from adults' choosing for them) their toys and entertainment, making newly possible fantasy worlds unfamiliar to their parents and causing, argues Stearns, "children's affections to center around the toys with which they . . . lived and played" (105). (*Heavenly Creatures*, as we will see, shows fantastic uses of toy clay figures, which become heterosexual props for seeming lesbian romance and sex. Barbie and Ken, no doubt, have played queerly in similar ways.) The simple emergence (again, in the twenties) of children's "playrooms" (and, later, "rec rooms") increased their "interaction with media" and offered "spaces where children could be alone" or with each other (106–7). One can imagine, though Stearns never mentions it, how crucial these trends turned out to be for children who thought they were gay or pursued sexual interests with each other.

Fictions, as I say, may shift this picture for us, bend it toward darkness, because they are putting more detail before us—and because they may import ideas from different times. Whatever the reason, the fictions in this book make a slightly different case for "constraint" and "release." Here the option of children's empowerment—their freedom from parental and state constraints—comes, paradoxically, tied to their enthrallment to spending money and escaping through, but being bound to, media. It is a signal aspect of *Lolita* that Lolita "Dolly" Haze is in thrall not to Humbert but to any roadside ad that asks its readers to spend money. "If a roadside sign said: VISIT OUR GIFT SHOP—we *had* to visit it," Humbert laments. "The words 'novelties and souvenirs' simply entranced her by their trochaic lilt. If some . . . sign proclaimed Icecold Drinks, she was automatically stirred, although all drinks everywhere were ice-cold. She it was to whom ads were dedicated: the ideal consumer, the subject and object of every foul poster." That this particular Dolly's rebellion comes by means of the automobile, in which she is closeted but which acts as a mobile TV (as if you could drive a TV while watching it), is only fitting: Dolly will escape with a different pedophile, who will lead her nowhere, by a complicated, convoluted car chase Nabokov invents as a chase by both a detective and a ghost. No less inventively, Peter Jackson shows us, in *Heavenly Creatures* (1994), how a dramatic sexual attraction between two girls is a class attraction of an intricate sort, a falling-in-love with two parents who have money, but an in-loveness that makes the girls project themselves as royal starlets on the Hollywood screen. Here a child's enthrallment to money (and class) joins up with her escape through visual media, although these escape artists (these two girls) suffer a crash when they commit murder.

Social historians or sociologists might explain that what allows for these developments, even in fictions, is the profound shift in children's social roles in Europe and America: the end of their positions as legal wage-laborers. This end comes in the twentieth century for children of all classes in "developed countries." Nonetheless, what doesn't end—as my texts show—is the role labor plays in the child's imagination and relations with adults. Henry James, for instance, depicts the machinations of man/boy love as a labor relation, a context rarely given for so-called pedophilia; never mind labor as a masochistic bond between adult and child, and adult masochism, through the lens of labor, especially a teacher's pedagogical labor, as mirroring a child's fascination with pain. James presents these revealing depictions of sideways relations.

As for social scientists writing social history, no one has told the story of children's changing work-life with more curiosity than Viviana Zelizer, in her *Pricing the Priceless Child: The Changing Social Value of Children*. Writing late in the twentieth century (1985), Zelizer asserts that "the emergence of [the] economically 'worthless' but emotionally 'priceless' child has created an essential condition of contemporary childhood."[73] Not only "worthless" but also "expensive," children come to be "expected to provide love, smiles, and emotional satisfaction, but no money or labor" (aside from a few odd hours of housework, often performed for a weekly allowance and seen more as "character-building" than as work) (3). This development, Zelizer tells us, was a major change from the eighteenth century, when the birth of a child in rural America would signify "the arrival of a future laborer and security for parents" (5); it was also a change from the nineteenth century when, as middle-class children's labor decreased, working-class children's labor rose (by one million workers) from 1870 to 1930. (Even as early as 1820, children were 55 percent of the workforce in certain New England textile mills.) The year 1900, according to Zelizer, marks the beginning of middle-class reformers' agitations against children's labor: the first Child Labor Committee is formed in 1901, followed in suit by the national version in 1904; in 1907, *Cosmopolitan* magazine ranks children's work with "bull-baiting, witch-burning, and all other execrated customs of the past" (62). More specifically, reformers deem children's labor an "inexcusable 'commercialization of child life'" by parents who "coin shameful dollars from the bodies and souls of their own flesh and blood"—all leading to the "new cultural equation," in Zelizer's words, that "if children were useful and produced money, they were not being properly loved" (70–72). Of course, the fiction of Henry James counters, as I'll explore in depth, that even priceless children, admitted to be priceless, could be neglected—and dragged into dramas of other people's labor, which are dramas of sexual intrigue involving these children.

As for Zelizer, she wants to grasp how the change she chronicles was accomplished. She asks how children's labor began to disappear, against the vigorous voices supporting it as a necessary supplement to working-class incomes, fallback income if a father fell ill, a valuable protection against "child-idleness," and even a way of keeping children "out of mischief." Given the battle, lengthy and heated, that ensued in the courts and in public debate (only by 1938 was there definitive, federal regulation of children's labor), Zelizer concludes that the change in children's work was not due simply to economic causes (such as the demand for educated laborers, the institutionalization of the family wage, stricter compulsory education laws, and competition for children's jobs from immigrants). Rather, she explores how "expulsion of children from the 'cash nexus' at the turn of the century . . . was also part of a cultural process of 'sacralization' of children's lives," such that they became sentimentalized as a "separate non-commercial" locus in a quite commercial world (11). She examines how three phenomena in particular—children's insurance, compensation for the accidental death of a child, and the adoption and sale of children—came to terms with (put a price on) children's new sentimental value. The conclusion she draws is that "this exclusively emotional valuation had a profoundly paradoxical and poignant consequence: the increasing monetization and commercialization of children's lives" (15). That is to say, "today, bereaved parents receive cash compensation for the loss of their child's love and companionship; adoptive parents are willing to pay as much as $40,000 to buy an infant's smiles and tenderness"; and "thus, dollar values are routinely assigned to affection and pain, extending the market into supposedly unquantifiable sentiments" (15). One is left to wonder about the so-called contrast between the sacred child—priceless, useless, and expensive, says Zelizer—and queer life depicted by conservatives: hedonistic, arrested, and, especially, wasteful.

A last group of studies compels our attention, moving us from money back to sexuality—and to the couplings of the terms *gay* and *child*. These studies show how queer child issues are starting to break into childhood studies, beyond the realm of provocative fictions. In addition, they offer a set of startling ironies, which their authors do not themselves present, though they give us the means by which to see them. First comes the irony (not put forward in this way by its authors) that no one believes more firmly in "gay" children than do other children—most especially children of a prejudicial sort, who "out" any children they believe are acting strangely or any boy or girl whom they happen to dislike. Then there is the thought (not offered by its author) that just as "gay" children are starting to appear (while childhood is shrinking), gay teens are disappearing—or just disavowing that "gay" is a meaningful concept to them. Both of these ironies come to us via disquisitions on queer youth, largely from the fields of educational studies, educational psychology, and social-science research on developmental issues.

With no eye for irony, *Queering Elementary Education* (a compendium from 1999) strikes a stance for fairness, respect, diversity, and openness in school curricula and classrooms. It advocates acknowledging children of gay and lesbian parents, on the one hand, and children who themselves may feel sexually different, on the other. From this decidedly liberal group of essays emerge several insights. First of all, a fair amount of gay-child ghosting goes on even here, with authors speaking of "eventually emerging sexual selves," "children who develop into gay . . . people," those with "evolving affectional preferences," and "students who may grow up to be gay," as these authors try (perhaps out of carefulness) never to assume any child is already "gay" to herself.[74] Even so, they relate how Jamie Nabozny, "a Wisconsin middle-school student," who "was kicked unconscious and urinated upon" by fellow students, was warned by his principal "to expect such treatment if he chose to be openly gay" (8).

The authors also tell us that "that's so gay" has "become the mantra" of young "school-children" (one senses this has been true for some time) and that "eight-year-olds already know that 'gay' equals 'bad'" (ix–x). One author quotes a child who says of another child: "It doesn't matter what he says; he's still gay," making "gay" less of an orientation than "a boy's marginalized culture and status" (53, 56). And yet, for those children who do take this word to themselves for themselves, *closeting*—a word almost never used of children—is a feature of their schooling. Or, as one of the authors puts it: "Today's queer youth still experience the feeling of being 'the only one in the world'" (3). One has to imagine that this peculiar feeling has already changed for children at the start of this new century, with so many gay people on TV (a trend that began in 1997, when Ellen DeGeneres came out on her show). Whereas it might have happened for a child growing up any time before the 1990s that college could be the first occasion for encountering another gay person, children now in the twenty-first century, while they are still children, will at least see and quite possibly know queer, including transgendered, people. Certainly, they will meet these people in fictions—in movies and books and on TV—by a very young age. Increasingly now, gone will be the circumstance, so prevalent for queers in the 1900s, that was rarely lived by a black or Jewish child (or any "minority") in the last century: the sense that somewhere blacks, for example, must exist; you've heard they do exist; you hope someday to meet someone who openly says they are black, since you (a child) think you are too, though your family doesn't know it has a black child. We are on the cusp of this dynamic disappearing.

What is already at this moment dissolving, according to the study *The New Gay Teenager* (2005), is the gay teen who develops from the child. The social scientist Ritch C. Savin-Williams wrote this book, he who in 1998 wrote the study "*. . . And Then I Became Gay.*" Now Savin-Williams puts the matter in new terms, which seem fulfilling of his personal wish: "I hope that contemporary teenagers are bringing the sexual identity era to a close," since "new gay teens have much less interest in naming [their] feelings or behaviors as gay"; "their sexuality is not something that can be easily described, categorized, or understood apart from being part of their life in general."[75] The researcher continues: "I celebrate this development because my lifetime professional dream—that homosexuality will be eliminated as a defining characteristic of adolescence, a way of cutting and isolating, of separating and discriminating—is within reach" (ix–x). And so he announces: "I write for 'pregay' young people, in the hope that they will never have to 'act gay' or mold themselves into a stereotype" (x).

These remarks are striking for a social-science scholar of historical bent. Moreover, whatever Savin-Williams thinks of children (at one point, he concedes that "the childhood of same-sex attracted individuals has . . . been ignored" [93]), his fascinating statements make "pregay" youth into figures of future ex-gay teens, perhaps in such a way that "gay," he imagines, never will come to settle upon them (even as adults are still coming out as gay). But there is something telling in Savin-Williams's wordings. One notes these lines: "the new gay teenager is in many respects the *non*-gay teenager"; "perhaps she considers herself to be 'postgay,' or he says that he's 'gayish'" (1). One could conclude from lines such as these that "non-gay," "postgay," and "gayish" are ways that "gay" does attach to these "new gay teens"—not just because these phrases all have "gay" inside them. Rather, "gay" may stick to these teens because it is not just they who control the way in which the word detaches *from* them. Other teens and people must grant these detachments.

Beyond this major wrinkle, there are gender differences in Savin-Williams's discourse that may change his picture. It seems persuasive that teenage girls enjoy the emotional and sexual liquidity "postgay" implies. "Gayish," however, still smacks of subtle or less oblique closeting. One finds it hard to see how *gay* for teenage boys isn't still a land mine, even at this moment, that they have to mind in their teen world. Therefore, to say, as one boy does, that "'gay' has been annexed and spandexed!," "it's been so bent out of shape that it don't exist no more" (1), seems both to recognize the massively growing public acknowledgment of "gay" life *and* to ignore the extent to which "gay" for men (and for teens, in spite of what they say) still operates as the border for their manliness. Given that Savin-Williams's research on these youth is (understandably) based on self-report, one must interrogate what such trends in self-reporting indicate. Perhaps the "disappearing gay adolescent" is, at the moment, as of yet, only female, or largely so. The author, in some respects, concedes this differential. As he says at one point: "We'll know that change has truly taken hold when thirteen-year-old boys who are best buddies, spend all their time together, draw hearts with their names in them, and profess their friendship and love forever are deemed as normal as thirteen-year-old girls who do the same" (20).

This is a concession to the not-yet status of nongay teens. These teens are clearly not yet nongay. Many of these teens, Savin-Williams believes, were pregay children—whose ghostly gayness, if the author gets his wish, may never get birthed. His concession, furthermore, to this not-yet status is indicated by the "I hope" language that permeates his book: "It is my hope," he ends his introduction, "that in the future, all books on the subject of 'gay youth' will be history books" (22). For Savin-Williams, we dramatically discover, we hope for no future as "gay" people. We hope for retrospections that will not haunt our present. Death to the ghost, Savin-Williams implies.

Now in a series of concentrated ways, focused on works from the century of the child, we can find out what imaginative writers were making of children in their minds. We can discover, through imaginative reading, the kind of conceptions that could not have been forged or given any form outside of fiction. It is time to turn to fictional children who may be the History of the future that has passed.

The Queer Child, in Short

This book has the look of chronology. It appears to flow from a Henry James novella from the 1890s, titled The Pupil, to a queer turn by Johnny Depp as Willy Wonka in Tim Burton's Charlie and the Chocolate Factory (2005), based on the book by Roald Dahl. Despite this look of bookends, I take the century in between them as a synchrony in the simplest sense, noting that all these texts and their ideas still exist to be read. To read this way does not put a stop to the pleasure of hunts for diachronic patterns, sequence, influence, contexts, or authorial circumstance—I will participate in these enjoyments—it just restores these hunts to their place in the textual spread before us, at this current moment, which allows tremendous "latitude" for how we arrange our fictions in our heads, going back and forth between them and among them, whether or not anyone "lets" us, in some official sense.

My book freely, but I think importantly, conceptualizes three realms of growing sideways: sideways relations, motions, and futures. Where do children go, to whom do they turn, when they cannot relate to their presumptive peers? What are their substitute sideways relations? This is a matter of great concern to children who secretly, even perhaps unknowingly, relate to the meanings surrounding *gay* or any of its cognates. Kids may feel least comfortable coming out to peers, at least when they are children—or so it has seemed until recent times. But this feeling of fearful self-disclosure may concern any child who feels out of sync with the children around her or feels repelled by the future being mapped for her. She may prefer growing sideways in relations that are not the standard connections to peers in the act of growing up. Still, the role of "pedophiles" and animals in nurturing a child's growing sideways may surprise us, as it appears in fiction. Then there's the issue of bodily motions and what they may signal about children's motives. What moves children to act as they do and what do their actions say about what drives them? The notion of "children's motives" in the realms of sex and crime is often not a publicly available concept. The law has virtually made the idea of children's motives oxymoronic. What kind of sideways growth, therefore, is the motive of the child, and how does it illuminate the problem of the concept of motive for anyone, whether one is an adult or a child in the eyes of the law? By extension, how does Freud make the matter of motives always already a question of children ghosting our lives, especially our distorted, sexualized dreams? As for dreams, of course, our futures grow sideways whenever they can't be envisioned *as* futures—due to forceful obstacles, forms of arrest, or our wish to be suspended in the amplitude of "more," as in our simply wanting more time, more pleasure, more leisure, more luxury, even more destruction (as odd as that may sound)— just "more." As we see in my conclusion, color and money are critical components of so-called futures that turn on their sides.

Relations, motions, and futures are simply the general means by which I limn my texts. Now, more specifically, let me sketch them. The first two chapters form one set. Together, each braiding four versions of the queer child, they respectively introduce two remarkably distinctive forms of growing sideways for boys and girls, especially for children who have often not found it safe to express their "same-sex" longings to their peers without the fear of being ostracized or bullied. In the first chapter, "The Smart Child Is the Masochistic Child: Pedagogy, Pedophilia, and the Pleasures of Harm," against the recent backdrops of the Foley scandal, NAMBLA debates, and TV shows like *To Catch a Predator*, I start my book with Henry James in relation to Edward Carpenter's "Affection in Education" (1899), an essay that celebrates aspects of age-differential relations for men and boys who are side by side in the labor of learning, in the setting of school. I do so to show how "man/boy love" has been thought, by certain texts, to function as a substitute lateral relation for men and boys—especially if they both feel saddled by society's dictates of delay, unable to see their sexual dreams as anything but suspended in uncertainty. Moreover, via case studies by Krafft-Ebing and the famous novel *Venus in Furs*, I read James's novella *The Pupil* through the lens of masochism, with the latter's preference for erotic delay (as we will be reminded) rendered through James's linguistic suspensions. This odd focus adds a new element to (what goes under the name of) pedophilia. I find in James, in his story *The Pupil*, the sideways bonding that pain allows for a man and a boy who make the most of their painful delay, who find the promise of a love growing sideways, at least for a time.

My second chapter, "Why the (Lesbian) Child Requires an Interval of Animal: The Family Dog as a Time Machine," offers a different sideways relation for our consideration. This one turns around canine connections, making animal/child bondings, especially for girls attracted to girls, an outlet for feelings they long to express. The animal in novels by Virginia Woolf, Djuna Barnes, and Radclyffe Hall is a different kind of peer in the game of delay. It is at turns a witness, confidante, rebel, protector, and pretend lover. As such, the animal allows girls to run a gamut of emotions from ecstatic commitment to bewildered sorrow to determined pause in the face of a future not careful of their pleasure. More interesting still, the dog is a figure for the child herself, growing aside from the concept of a future altogether, since animals do not grow in human generations. And so, in part in contrast to Deleuze's and Guattari's notion of being-and-becoming animal in *A Thousand Plateaus*, I seek to theorize a new view of metaphor, one grasped not solely in terms of translation (a girl as a dog) but also in terms of transport and time, a transport inside a kind of hung time (a girl who is moving through an interval of animal). This makes a metaphor a moving suspension.

Chapter 3, "What Drives the Sexual Child? The Mysterious Motions of Children's Motives," picks up this thread, as it ties together in the fictions of *Lolita* (the novel and films) pedophiles and animals, which are both critical to these texts. So begins my foray into matters of motive, tying together chapters 3 and 4. Is the child an author of her motions and emotions? Nabokov makes an answer through obliquities in metaphors, even though the metaphors themselves are rather bold. Making Lolita (the Freudian child who braids with "innocence" and ghostly "gayness") resemble both a dog and a car, Nabokov shows the outline of Lolita's motives emerging through her motions, even as described by an unsuspecting pedophile. In this canny way, he gives the child a sidetrack, which only sharp-witted readers can perceive if they read for metaphors. Lolita, in this respect, has much in common with the "little Lesbians" (Humbert's phrase) who precede her in fiction. Their hidden movements through the metaphor "dog" teach us how to read secret motions in *Lolita*, in Lolita "Dolly" Haze. The child's sexuality runs alongside and moves against this pedophile, who, in this case, very much like the law, is blind to the child. He cannot see the mysterious motives of the child hiding in a dog or a car. Curiously, an investigation of the imbrication of "motion" and "cause" in the "Western" philosophical tradition (extending from Plato to Aristotle to Newton to Locke)—a conversation happening in education theory—backlights the genius of Nabokov's metaphors. But so does a treatise this field does not engage: *The Expression of the Emotions in Man and Animals*, by Charles Darwin. Darwin does not know that, courtesy of fiction, a dog beside a girl (as discussed in chapter 2) might express the feelings of the girl by its side. Nor does he address what *Lolita* will show us: that locomotions, not just postures or facial expressions, of human beings—on their legs or in their vehicles—might indicate specific emotions, even motives.

As I next argue in chapter 4, "Feeling Like Killing? Murderous Motives among Queer Children," the law makes the intrigue of children's motives conceptually off-limits. Never mind sex, can a child mean to murder? How hazy are the motives of a murderous child? Are these murders actually dreams spun off in wrong directions, destined to be spoiled at the moment of murder? *Lolita* (1955) teaches us to read for glancing motions to the side of our own as the signs of Haze—where there's Haze there's fire. Truman Capote (in *In Cold Blood*, 1965) and Peter Jackson (in *Heavenly Creatures*, 1994), converging on the fifties through two different murders on two different continents, each makes a model of motive growing sideways. For each writer, a motive accumulates, is itself a lateral spread of feelings, desires, and physical needs from different temporalities, but, *as* a motive, is birthed backward at the point of murder as the cause of killing. In fact, both artists write inside a legal problem on their own aesthetic terms: how "motive" as a concept differs from "intent" in judicial language and legal theory (which I analyze in two legal treatises that bring together British, American, and New Zealand law). Both of these artists, thinking through children, thinking *as* children in some important ways, through imaginative backbends, show why the "homosexual" child and the queerly "innocent" child reveal the conceptual dilemmas of motive, in general, for the legal field. Final thoughts on *Elephant* (Gus Van Sant, 2003) take motive (in) to school.

Heading into chapter 5, "Oedipus Raced, or the Child Queered by Color: Birthing 'Your' Parents via Intrusions," we discover portraits of futures on their sides, an issue implicit in all my texts, often in non-utopian fashion, but perhaps intensified when color and money are brought to the fore with the ghostly gay child. Though my destination is two famous films on American race, I enter this chapter via the recent Hollywood film on Sierra Leone, the movie *Blood Diamond* (Edward Zwick, 2006). Looking back to chapter 4, we discover in this film a unique short-circuit of the path from the queerly "innocent" child to the dramatically murderous child—*without* any motive, at least at first. I am referring to the movie's depiction of "child soldiers" in the diamond wars of 1999. Abducted from their families, these boy children are forced to be killers by other boy children and by older teens (with a few adults above them) who train them and "raise" them. In essence, these children, who are trying to stay alive, are "given" their motives by the children beside them—other child soldiers who now wish to kill, though these children also were supplied with motives from the children who were killing by their side. These are dramatic sideways relations and sideways futures at the end of a gun. And this is also a forced family of children side by side who are broadly horizontalized—in this context, to frightening effect.

For all this trauma, I want to visit an imaginary threat for some white Americans, even, remarkably, for some liberals. This imagined threat is the child-intruder who wants to be family, to marry their daughter or be a sibling to their children, even though his color marks his status as outsider. Like a "gay" child, the child queered by color has a backward birth to manage: in this case, however, that of his new parents. He must create new parents who want him, who will now *become*—birthed backward from this moment—the liberals they say they have been all along. This is the challenge in the liberal films *Guess Who's Coming to Dinner* (1967) and *Six Degrees of Separation* (1993). In the former film, "interracial marriage"—between the white daughter of a liberal family and a "Negro" doctor (played by Sidney Poitier)—is the film's crisis, especially for the father (Spencer Tracy) of the daughter. Will he approve of this unforeseen materializing of his liberal views? In the later *Six*, which explicitly thinks through *Guess* and its dilemmas, a black queer hustler, who turns tricks for money, intrudes upon a family, seeking companionship (later, adoption), by pretending he is friends with the white parents' children and is Sidney Poitier's son. Both of these films about race relations are haunted by the issues—really, the specters—of "gay" children. *Six Degrees of Separation* simply makes explicit what now, from the standpoint of contemporary struggles (surrounding gay marriage, gay adoption, gay childhood), retrospectively looks like the spectral presence of homosexuality in *Guess Who's*, as I will establish. These reversed births, of parents by children, theorize, therefore, an Oedipus raced, as I proceed to show. Braiding strands of the child queered by color, the ghostly gay child, the grown homosexual, and quite dramatically the Freudian child, they reconfigure Freudian thought through fictional inventions responding to color. Just as importantly, they revise aspects of architecture theory—Beatriz Colomina's "domestic voyeurism"—by showing black intruders immodestly aiming to be someone's child.

Speaking of immodesty: Warhol is my segue into my conclusion, "Money Is the Child's Queer Ride: Sexing and Racing around the Future." In his own person, "Raggedy Andy," as he was called, exquisitely gathers my versions of children and gives me a chance to follow the money threads that draw together quite distinct portraits of sideways futures. In fact, I conclude by discussing two films that will seem a strange pair: *Hoop Dreams*, from the 1990s, and *Charlie and the Chocolate Factory*, from the start of the twenty-first century (2005). They are completely divergent in form: one is an urgent, highly acclaimed, gritty documentary, following the hopes of two black boys for a five-year period, as they dream of the NBA as their explicit future; the other is a fiction feature film depicting children dreaming of chocolate (based on the book by Roald Dahl from the 1960s, later revised to remove its references to black pygmies), here updated by Johnny Depp, who plays Willy Wonka as decidedly queer, seemingly in both its broad and narrow senses.

My reading of *Hoop Dreams* (1994) will stress two remarkable aspects of this film: the poignant disappearance of a child's face, along with his future, as he dreams for years, making his face recede, sink down into his body and the motion of his limbs, as if the face is read from the boy's hands and feet as he runs around a court; and the fervent dream of becoming a shoe, as a boy dreams of endorsement deals and moneyed success (for instance, via Nike). In a particularly ironic twist on Laura Mulvey's theory of visual pleasure and bodily motion, the motion of the body, which in this film is increasingly beautiful, puts a painful stop to the face. The boy is drained of the signs of his dreams and replaced by the shoe beside his bed. "That's me," one of the boys tells his brother, as he points to a sneaker he fails to become. As if it over-turns *Hoop Dreams'* documented, serious sorrows, *Charlie and the Chocolate Factory* is the manufactured white child's dream of the factory (he might run) that manufactures dreams. Like other children, Charlie dreams of chocolate in the mysterious economy of candy. How this desire has libidinal force; how it is something like sex for children on sexual delay; how it offers versions of "Bataille for Kids," complete with the pleasures of near self-destruction; how it concludes in an unexpected elevator that moves children fancifully sideways *and* can shoot them up to the sky; and how it leaves us with a queer child, Willy himself, taking the figure of the innocent child under his wing to learn the secrets of "making chocolate" as his future: this is the final growing sideways I unfold.

PART I   Sideways Relations: "Pedophiles" and Animals

CHAPTER I The Smart Child Is the Masochistic Child

Pedagogy, Pedophilia, and the Pleasures of Harm

Television won't let you *not* catch a predator. At least now, every day on cable, and even on *Dateline NBC* with its series *To Catch a Predator*, we are asked to think of adult-child relations almost first and foremost in the guise of harm. Or potential harm, if adults and children who are not related are allowed close contact without supervision. And these suspicions were underscored a while ago (in September, 2006) by the "Foley scandal," involving Congressman Mark Foley (R-Florida), who was mentoring congressional pages aged sixteen. When he "harmed" these "children" by talking with them about sexual pleasure, his and theirs, it became more evident what "harm" is, according to the public: anybody's pleasure, an adult's or the child's, that comes to children (even to their ears) before it is time. *Harm* is any form of premature ejaculation (a "sudden . . . utterance," says the dictionary) involving children.[1]

[THE PUPIL] MADE THE FACTS SO VIVID AND SO DROLL, AND AT THE SAME TIME SO BALD AND SO UGLY, THAT THERE WAS FASCINATION IN TALKING THEM OVER WITH HIM.
—HENRY JAMES, *THE PUPIL*

Henry James Instead of Television

If we would circumvent what TV is telling us at the start of the twenty-first century, we must begin in the 1890s—and, most importantly, with Henry James. With James's help, one cuts a path, a distinctly different path, through the field of children's harm and thus raises questions that television, with its current focus, fails to see. First, we can ask: are we as an American society much less troubled by children's pain (for example, their economic suffering) than we are troubled by their sexualized pleasure, even though we cite their possible pain as our rationale for delaying their pleasure?[2] Laws, we should notice, at least in the United States, are better designed to catch a child predator than put an end to childhood poverty. Second, we might wonder: given that children and teens have not found it safe by and large to express their same-sex longings to peers (without the fear of ridicule, rejection, or bullying), to what extent has man/boy love, at least for a century, in some contexts, functioned as a substitute lateral relation for men and boys? — especially if each of them has been publicly trapped in delays, with the dictates of arrested development and ghostly gayness thrust upon them. Or to meld these questions: has what is called man/boy love found surprising outlets in mutual pain, giving men and boys ways to meet *inside* delay?[3] As we know, delay is the crux of so many matters that touch upon children, girls and boys.

Speaking of Children Delaying Relations

Delay is seen as a friend to the child. Delay is said to be a feature of its growth: children grow by delaying their approach to the realms of sexuality, labor, and harm. The point of delay as a boon to growth is to shelter children from these domains.

But the act of sheltering is a kind of dancing on the knife-edge of delay. How can children be gradually led by degrees toward domains they must not enter at all as children? In the broadest sense, children are protected by laws that blanket them from harm, to be sure, but also from agency in their own pleasure. (Age of consent laws are a clear example.) Indeed, the paradox I put before us in the introduction is the possibility that we fear the children we would protect. We sense they are vulnerable and dangerous through pleasure, whether this pleasure comes through money or through sex. Labor, I have said, long after it is outlawed as a child's moneyed engagement with the world (because it is thought a harmful engagement), still is a force, often for pleasure, in the child's imagination ("what will you be when you grow up?"), though sometimes in unimaginable forms, especially if the child is precocious or clever.[4]

The problem, therefore, is delay's infidelity. It has relations with relations it stalls. (Labor relations, for example.) Moreover, as is obvious, we know how sexual delaying sex can be. Sexual delay as an active arrest ("I am delaying my sexual activity") is a way, we say, of "maturing" sexually—a sexual growth to the side of sex—raising the question of when does the child, when does each child, actively enter into delay? Talking, of course, can be a delay, even itself a sexy delay. It's a delay since it often isn't sex (it is talking, after all), but it can be greatly suffused with pleasure, even a highly sexualized pleasure, even if the topic of the talking is pain.[5] Talking about one's battles with parents or their neglect can be a sexy bond among teens. Talking can even be a kind of whipping: a verbal (and imaginative) painful enjoyment.

Confessing none of this, ours has been a culture (especially in America, even quite currently) obsessed with how adults talk to children, never mind how adults prey upon children.[6] In fact, to talk "about" the child in certain ways—even in oddly democratic ways, as we're about to see—is predation in the minds of many people. Unless you are NAMBLA and talk in these ways.

NAMBLA is not subtle. It well knows that pedophilia still, in the twenty-first century, is a bogeyman in public depictions of gay men as teachers or gay men with children. Yet, knowing this, the North American Man/Boy Love Association stirs the pot with slogans like "Smiles Imply Consent."[7] Even so, NAMBLA has serious intents. The murkiness of children's smiles aside, NAMBLA advocates for a child's agency, insisting that adult pedophilic love for children is not about molestation or harm. The child is a companion to his male lover, not some verbal or sexual prey, in NAMBLA's view.

All of this is surely provocative enough for most people's tastes. And, indeed—this story is familiar—many gay communities continue to ostracize NAMBLA from their ranks.[8] But there is something we might find more provocative, at least conceptually. This provocation comes to us from Henry James, from his novella *The Pupil*, from 1891, around the time of the entry of the word *homosexual* into English. With the stroke of his pen, one could say, James revises our conceptions of children, their talk with their teachers, their teachers' labor (as a scene of pain), and the love of a boy for a man and vice versa, all in the context of *enjoying harm*. James reveals how the budding intellectual is a masochistic child. This is someone whose verbal delights attach themselves to talk of pain and whose masochism, even more remarkably, leans on the masochism of a pedagogue whom he loves, pursues, and admires.

These last claims—about enjoying harm and the child's mirroring of his teacher's masochism, as if he were catching a lateral pass—are the heart of this chapter. It is also pertinent for the start of my book that James's story displays the outlines, in the 1890s, of four (or even more) versions of children who are intertwining: protogay child, adult queer child, innocent child, and child whose fascinations with aggressions would catch the interest of Freud.[9] For here in *The Pupil*, a child who might be called a "homosexual," if we could see his future unfold, is practically given to his tutor by his parents. The tutor himself is a quasi–queer child in that he is fastened to the future of a child he himself has not fathered and appears delayed, to put the matter mildly, in his own approach to normal couplehood. More than that, we watch the tutor learn to love the boy for how the boy defeats the assumption of his innocence, showing instead a remarkably savvy sense of what is sex in James: money, family finance. James turns the screw of what could look like same-sex pedophilia in the direction of brotherly masochism: man and boy side by side in a contract that lateralizes boy and man, though it does not at all equalize them.[10]

In fact, in *The Pupil*, in taking revenge on the world of parents, James has his cake and eats it too. It's as if a certain kind of man/boy love—the masochistic kind—is a reply to parental abuse. That man and boy pleasure themselves with their words *about* abuse (to them it's a thrill to rehearse how they are "beaten") is James's clever portrait of a pleasure he himself perhaps knew as a child: a cyclical, syntactical rehearsal of shame that he intellectually embraced and enjoyed.[11] But this is getting ahead of ourselves. We should start again with a general provocation to our imaginations.

The Child, the Adult, and the Scene of Pain

It would be striking to hear of a case coming to court in which an adult is accused of allowing a child to beat him (to thrash him, for example, with a riding whip). Or of allowing a child to spank him while both are fully clothed. Or of allowing a child to seduce him into monetary ruin. Could an adult be said to be guilty of letting a child render him this pain?

Not even NAMBLA has asked this kind of question. Their stated fantasies (emphasis on "stated") are more directly modeled on questions of pleasure and the language of equality in a standard vein. In fact, from the fantasies of NAMBLA comes a principle, in their estimation: the gay pedophile is drawn not only to the child, they would say, but also to its agency. That is to say, in NAMBLA's view, the presumed dominator of an innocent child (namely, the pedophile) is, by contrast, fighting like a lawyer for the child's legal rights, for the child's freedom to appear to the law as something other than an innocent. So NAMBLA argues for the child's legal right to design its education; to divorce its parents; to choose its pleasures.[12]

But here is where their fantasies of democratic pleasures can't escape an irony. For to what extent is the object of pedophilic attraction — that is to say, the child — a *product* of the law? To what extent does the pedophile need the law to produce the figure of the child, and thus need the juridical measures that so curb the childhood agency he would undress? (Otherwise, how is he undressing a child?) And what about the law's own cherished fantasies? In the way it makes the child into an innocent, a body more in need of protections than of freedoms, the law has produced the child as queer (odd, strange) even as the category is produced as normative. The child is a species of legal strangeness in its position as judicial teacher's pet: literally so, after what is called "the Mary Ellen Affair," taking place in 1874 (four years past the publication of the novel *Venus in Furs*, the most well-known of all masochistic texts). In this legal case, a New York social worker found to her dismay that no laws existed that would make it illegal to abuse a child. After this discovery, she took a clever tack. She persuaded the Society for the Prevention of Cruelty to Animals to prosecute the parents of her abused client according to the terms of the existing cruelty-to-animals law, armed with the logic, successfully presented, that children belong to the animal species and therefore should enjoy an animal's right not to be treated cruelly by anyone, including one's parents.[13]

But to make this more complex: What about the *right* to be treated cruelly; the right to be beaten according to one's wish at the hands of adults; or, as a child, to inflict such pain? (We know from case studies, even from the 1880s, that masochists, for instance, had these thoughts as children.) Do such rights belong to the child? Adult masochistic relations, of course, are to a point protected by the law. But can children, who cannot legally consent to their sexual pleasure with adults, consent to the giving or receiving of pain with them? Generally, not—if there is any hint of erotic pleasure tied to it. Courtesy, that is, of most state statutes, these would be "indecent liberties" that the adult would be taking with the child.[14]

As a devil's advocate—from another planet—one might argue otherwise. For insofar as masochism often is not sexually penetrative; and insofar as masochism is itself a preference for a sexual delay (suspended states of erotic contemplation, as we will see); and insofar as masochism generally stands hierarchies on their heads (making a woman, for example, the torturer of a male masochist); and insofar as masochism may itself imagine a new symbolic order, as we will explore, might not the child who agrees to give pain, and the adult who agrees to receive it, be guilty only of *playing* at remaking laws without really breaking laws?

Masochism's Child and the Masochism Not Appearing Here

Believe it or not, these kinds of questions pertain to James's novella. Yet despite my focus, here there will be no *Venus in Furs*, at least not exactly: no tableaux of the masochistic kind—paintings or statues—assisting a dreamy young man stopping time in contemplative states, mostly nocturnal, so as to imagine a beautiful woman dressed only in furs, a woman he teaches to take up his torture, to whip him unconscious again and again in accordance with a contract established between them. Instead, almost barricaded by a large lady who draws her gloves through a fat jeweled hand, we will find a smart child. Pursuing him, a tutor, caught on the horns of loving the child precisely for this young boy's brightness, for the linguistic seductions surrounding this student's secrets, making for every true pedagogue's dream: the pupil whose knowledge might challenge or defeat us. As for this pupil, he is well endowed with ears. With "big mouth and big ears," he seems to be fashioned with "intercourse" in mind—the kind of talk that, even so, runs along a spectrum of "refinement and perception." He is a scholar whose "sallies were the delight of the house"—even if he always was "as puzzling as a page in an unknown language." "Unconscious and irresponsible and amusing."[15]

James is a central figure, in my view, if we would understand how masochism comes to be regarded as a mental state more than a visual sexual act. But what does James imagine for the child in this transition, from the whip to the mind, the fur to the word, that has all of us accusing ourselves in common parlance of being masochists (at one time or another)? One should recall for a moment the particular masochistic paradigm — the sexy kind — for which most readers have some kind of image: a beautiful woman armed with a whip delivering a blow to a willing man, according to a contract both have agreed to. As for *The Pupil*, masochism is a distinctly mental matter (no whips, no furs) and offers a distinctly verbal pleasure, allowing James to look as if he turns the physical features of masochism toward psychological and verbal intrigues.

His other move is more stunning still. *The Pupil*'s masochism, as I've been suggesting, weds a young man's pain to a child's. For in James's story, a tutor makes a pact not to take on a woman but to take on a pupil — a boy (age eleven) with a weak heart but a mind so sharp that the tutor fears the child might be smarter than himself, even though the promise of the child's linguistic prowess is precisely a lure. Oddly, at the moment of the tutor's pledge to take the job, the child comes out with a puzzling cry — the narrator describes it as "the mocking, foreign ejaculation 'Oh là-là!'" (3). The boy's ejaculation over the contract (by this I mean his outburst over the agreement) is the first indication of the child's wry sense of family secrets, especially his parents' history of making torturous contracts with their employees, which cause *him* pain. This is juicier than it sounds. As the tale unfolds, the tutor who's a masochist to his teaching contract is torn between his wish to escape his employment, on the one hand, and, on the other, his desire to be verbally seduced by a child, whose mouth and ears are so alluring (for all that they catch and then convey). In one of the central man/boy scenes, talk turns into and out of blushing before it ends with a playful discussion of spanking and beating.

If one adds to this the pleasure of discussing the depravity of his employers with their son (the pupil in question), one has a recipe for an oral intercourse, one kept in motion by the teacher's masochism and the boy's verbal play. In this important way, the story addresses man/boy love not in the context of sexual illegality, nor in the context of physical domination, but, by contrast, in the context of employment. For the child is both the receiver of a service (the tutor's instruction) and a representative of the employer (in this case, the family who is shafting the tutor). Also, as one might expect in James, the boy as the tutor's conduit to torture is also being not so subtly impoverished by the parents, making boy and tutor together the sufferers of a masochistic scene, before the pupil's death from a violent joy (as cryptic as that sounds).

This chapter offers, then, one peculiar version of children's embrace of their delay: their desired role in dramas of pain, which may emerge in relation to labor, even as laws around 1900 emerge to protect them from waged work.[16] No wonder *The Pupil* comes into better focus through Leopold von Sacher-Masoch's German novel *Venus in Furs* (from 1870), along with the Austrian Richard von Krafft-Ebing's sex case studies from the 1880s (in which confessing masochists tell of their masochistic fantasies from childhood) and the English-born Edward Carpenter's essay "Affection in Education" from 1899. Yet James's novella crafts a different picture from those of the texts I put beside it. And there is another context more telling to begin with, which is from the other end of the century. This is a context that tells us why we're not allowed to mix pain with pleasure in speaking of the child.

Congress Insists That the Child Must Be Harmed

Importantly, just about a century later than Henry James's novella, a protest breaks out in the 1990s surrounding abuse: "child sexual abuse," to be specific. The focus of ire is a scientific study that finds — one might have thought rather happily — that "self-reported reactions" to child sexual abuse, reported by male and female college students from fifty-nine studies, "indicated that negative effects were neither pervasive nor typically intense, and that men reacted much less negatively than women."[17] Hence, the study's three authors conclude that "basic beliefs about CSA [child sexual abuse] in the general population were not supported" (22). Two other findings are central to the study. First, it is found that "poorer adjustment" could not be attributed to CSA because "family environment (FE) was consistently confounded with CSA" and thus "explained considerably more adjustment variance" than did child sexual abuse (22). Second, and this point is seen as more scandalous, the authors claim that "the construct of CSA, as commonly conceptualized by researchers, is of questionable scientific validity" (46). Why? For this reason: "Overinclusive definitions of abuse that encompass [on the one hand] willing sexual experiences accompanied by positive reactions and [on the other hand] coerced sexual experiences with negative reactions produce poor predictive validity" (46). "To achieve better scientific validity," the authors say, "a more thoughtful approach is needed" (46). In fact, they suggest that researchers might adopt the phrase "adult-child sex," "a value-neutral term," for "a willing encounter with positive reactions" in distinction to "child sexual abuse," which could be reserved to indicate "harm" (46). The authors, probably sensing political objections, end their article by stating that a behavior's "lack of harmfulness does not imply lack of wrongfulness" (47). Indeed, they point out, the "moral codes of a society with respect to sexual behavior need not be, and often have not been, based on considerations of psychological harmfulness or health" (47).

What the authors Rind, Bauserman, and Tromovitch didn't know when they placed this study, in 1998, in the prestigious academic journal *Psychological Bulletin*, published by the American Psychological Association, was who their audience would turn out to be: NAMBLA, Dr. Laura, Tom DeLay, and the full United States Congress, among many others. In fact, the study would cause "the political storm of the century for the field of psychology" just eight months after it appeared, leading to the charge (by "many in the media, politics, and grassroots organizations") "that failure by the APA to re-nounce the study was tantamount to condoning pedophilia."[18] For the first time in the public domain, the APA was pressed to defend their process of publishing articles and thus the process of peer review itself.

Here in brief is how it all happened, according to Ellen Greenberg Garri-son and Patricia Clem Kobor in their article "Weathering a Political Storm," written for *American Psychologist* three years after this storm broke. First, as they relate, NAMBLA touted the study on its website under the cheerful head-line "Good News!" Then, NARTH (the National Association for Research and Therapy of Homosexuality), a group that asserts that homosexuals with the right therapy can go straight—and a group that clearly reads the NAMBLA website—picked up word of the study *from* NAMBLA and began claiming that the APA, because it had published the study in question, had an agenda to normalize pedophiles. Dr. Laura Schlessinger, cued by NARTH, then began attacking the APA for their "junk science" and their seeming embrace of pedophilia (166). In spite of an APA press release that explained the asso-ciation's "long history of advocating for expanding child abuse prevention" and that reminded anyone listening that articles it published were not its own policy statements, Dr. Laura kept inciting protest. Only weeks after she began attacking, a resolution was introduced in the Alaskan legislature (H. J.

Res. 36, 1999), "rejecting the conclusions in a recent article published by the American Psychological Association" (166). The state legislatures of California, Illinois, Louisiana, and Pennsylvania soon followed suit. Next, as Garrison and Kobor chronicle, Tom DeLay (R) of Texas issued a release, which he headlined "DeLay Is Appalled by American Psychological Association," prompting the organization to send a "Letter to Congress" that concluded: "No responsible mental health organization, including the APA, endorses pedophilia or denies its negative effects on children" (167). And though the APA asked the American Association for the Advancement of Science (AAAS) and the National Academy of Sciences to be its allies in this fight, neither organization issued any public comment.

About two months after all attacks began, Representative DeLay with two other congressmen held a press conference, flanked by NARTH and the Family Research Council, with Dr. Laura joining in by satellite. Here they announced they would introduce a bill to the U.S. Congress that would require the APA to renounce the findings of Rind et al. As both Garrison and Kobor point out: "We know of no other prior instance in which a specific scientific article has been singled out for censure in a congressional resolution or a scientific organization chastised for publishing it" (168). The APA's response to this unique circumstance, along with its efforts to explain "that science is a self-correcting process [and] that peer review is the gold standard for scientific publishing," was to try to get a less extreme resolution put before Congress (169). To that end, the APA sent a letter to DeLay that, among other things, "promised that the APA general counsel would prepare materials that could be used to counter any potential court argument claiming that the Association had put its imprimatur on efforts to 'normalize' pedophilia" (171). They got their (partial) wish. The final bill "no longer denounced the APA or the *Psychological Bulletin* for publishing the Rind et al. article" — only the findings of the study were condemned (172). The resolution passed in July 1999 by 355 to 0.[19]

Garrison and Kobor conclude that the battered APA, having weathered this political storm, is better prepared to fight future battles. For example, they tell us that the "new media and congressional challenge" to another article — "Deconstructing the Essential Father" — that "concluded that fathers do not make a unique or essential contribution to child development" and "that there are potential costs to father presence" did provoke the upset of the bipartisan Congressional Task Force on Fatherhood Promotion but did not result in another resolution (173).[20]

Congress, it would seem, has acted only once to resolve against science: in order to say that children must be harmed.

Violent Affections and Affectionate Humiliations: The Joys of Delay

But to return to earlier contexts, we may find that the piece that most puts *The Pupil* into focus, largely by contrast, is Edward Carpenter's essay "Affection in Education," published eight years after *The Pupil*.[21] Carpenter and James were born one year apart. Born in Brighton but schooled at Cambridge, Carpenter, though himself of the bourgeoisie, became a pioneer of the British Labour Movement and an emulator of Whitmanian poetics in his volume *Towards Democracy*. He even eventually declared his thoughts on homosexuality and settled down with his working-class lover, a younger man, in 1891 — the year *The Pupil* appeared in print. Suffice it to say, Carpenter has been considered to be more political than James, more radical than James, specifically more concerned with labor than James, and surely far more sexually open about himself (and male-male love) than Henry James. It would even appear that Carpenter sensed a queerness about himself in childhood: "There was that other need . . . that of my affectional nature, that hunger which had indeed hunted me down since I was a child. I can hardly bear even now to think of my early life . . . the denial and systematic ignoring of the obvious facts of the heart and of sex."[22]

One might suppose that this "affectional nature" that seems to be a rather violent "hunger" (it "hunts [him] down" after all) is a code for sexual desire — especially since what are denied are the "obvious facts of . . . sex" that are joined to the "heart." How striking, then, to find that his essay "Affection in Education," which addresses this "affectional nature" in a pedagogic context, is so much tamer — if that is the right word — than James's edgy novella *The Pupil*, which gives a masochistic spin to pedagogy in its scenes of man/boy love. James, I suggest, out-Carpenters Carpenter, even on the score of democratic brotherhood, as we will see. But first, a few of Carpenter's thoughts on education may prove useful, especially his sense that "affection" has a "profound influence" on "the building up" of the body and the brain, especially if occurring between "an elder and a younger school-mate, or — as sometimes happens—between the young thing and its teacher."[23] Carpenter continues: "That such feelings sometimes take quite intense and romantic forms few will deny"—and, indeed, two paragraphs into his essay he quotes from a letter written by a younger boy (age sixteen) about an elder one (age unspecified).[24] (Carpenter says he has another letter from a boy age eleven to a man of twenty-five—nearly the age spread of *The Pupil*.) Among phrases cited in the boy's letter are phrases that link affection to violence but split the "facts of the heart" *from* sex. Here's the young boy speaking of the elder: "I would have died for him ten times over. My devices and plannings to meet him . . . were those of a lad for his sweetheart, and when I saw him my heart beat so violently that it caught my breath. . . . [I] thought of him night and day . . . [and wrote] him . . . veritable love-letters. . . . The passion violent and extravagant as it was, I believe to have been perfectly free from sex-feeling. . . . It distinctly contributed to my growth."[25]

Carpenter presumably begins with this letter because it so aptly contains the logic he presents throughout his piece, which goes like this if we compress it: These are "attractions." They are "absorbing," "violent," and "intense." The elder has no motive except that he is "touched." The younger often starts these attractions out of "worship" and "thrills with pleasure at [the] words of the elder." All of this resembles the man-boy relations of ancient Crete, he says, which were largely contractual relations between man and boy "side by side in battle."[26] Now in modern times such friendships have been stifled or been overtaken by "the disease of premature sexuality" (Carpenter's phrase). For there is "a simple physiological law," Carpenter tells us: to arrest growth is bad for boys, but growth only comes by arresting sex, delaying it, soundly suspending it.[27] Even more intriguingly, Carpenter claims that a kind of nonsexual homoeroticism is the *sign* of sexual delay, as if the violent same-sex hungers he describes boys talking about are precisely a kind of treading water to the side of sex itself. These strong hungers are a purifying treading, even more strikingly since they are the sign that "no furtive desire has crept in," the sign that the "sacredness of sex" has been preserved, the sign that "premature" talk ("morbid" talk) has not yet begun.[28] Violent same-sex longings talked about are, by this logic, a maturing kind of talk.

It is instructive to hold for the moment this question of talking, this plea for delay, this image of persons side by side in battle, and this sense of emotions absorbing, intense, and even violent (if we believe the letter). Now sliding over to *Venus in Furs*, we find these elements making the amalgam that becomes "masochism." As for the author, Sacher-Masoch, he was ten years older than both James and Carpenter; unlike them, of Slavic descent; the child of a father who was chief of police and so a child who witnessed (through his father's labor) prison scenes and riots, which had profound effects on him; a person who later in life was concerned with labor relations in rural contexts, especially the organization of communes and struggles of peasants; and someone who was himself a pedagogue, professor of history at Graz, in Austria. After he became a well-known novelist, Sacher-Masoch was dismayed to find that a famous psychiatrist—this was Krafft-Ebing— had used his name (Sacher-Masoch) to name the perversion we know as masochism.[29]

One thing to know about *Venus in Furs* is that the novel's arc is spare. (We will see this spareness in *The Pupil*.) It starts with a dream and ends with the end of a cycle of sufferings—a cycle that stops when the sufferings become *too much* for masochism. Specifically, the narrator of *Venus* at the start falls asleep while he is reading (Hegel, no less) and dreams of Venus, the Goddess of Love, cruel in her furs. Then after waking, he meets Severin, who gives him a manuscript (Severin's book) about his relations with Wanda von Duna-jew, a wealthy widow he meets at a Slavic health resort. Unable to persuade her to marry him, Severin starts the game (the alternative plan—the second-best option) of being her slave, which he continually persuades her to accept. So begins their strange adventure that intermittently overwhelms Severin but to which he continually recommits—until Wanda lets a beautiful, virile Greek man whip an unconsenting Severin severely, without warning.[30] This excessive cruelty ends their seemingly endless cycle of relations. "It was as though I were awakening from a . . . dream," Severin confesses.

Here are three fragments of the *Venus* paradigm, highlighting violence, devotion, and stamina:

[Severin says:] "The first thing I remember is when I saw blood dripping from my hand, and asked her in a flat voice: 'Did you scratch me?' 'No [she said], I believe I bit you.'"[31]

"Do not look so miserable," [Wanda said,] "you are making me sad. For the time being you are my servant . . . [but] you have not yet signed the contract, and you are still free to leave. . . . You have played your part to perfection. . . . But are you not tired of it? Do you not find me abominable? Come now, speak. . . ."

[Severin answers:] "I am more in love with you than ever. Even if you abuse my devotion I shall only adore you the more fanatically." (213)

"A month has gone by in the gray monotony of hard labor." (224)

These selections are what one would expect, since they picture physical suffering, the role of the love-slave, and duration. But one should recall just how much of this book is given over to talking, on the one hand, and to delay, on the other. Wanda and Severin talk and talk (then talk some more)—a lot about pain but also often about the kinds of topics that will make Severin suffer. Talking is mental whipping in this text: Severin is exposed to a host of cruel thoughts (often his own). But talking is often a form of delay, and delay itself (sometimes in the form of elaborate waiting games in which Wanda plays neglectful parent) is a major source of painful pleasure.

Two other postures supplement these. Aside from scenes of physical whipping, Severin finds lustful excruciation in playing the roles of employee and child. Dressing up in livery at Wanda's request, Severin pretends to be first employed as her domestic servant ("to pant along behind her, loaded like a donkey"), then to be her slave ("I can escape but I do not want to . . . I am ready to endure anything as soon as [Wanda] threatens to set me free")— all while being financially dependent upon both his father's and Wanda's wealth. At other times, Severin is scripted as a child — Wanda's "plaything" — who "stood in a corner like a child waiting to be punished" by a parent. And, indeed, striking to recall in all of this: Severin depicts his lustful wish for punishment as stemming from his childhood, as being an active, conscious lust *in* childhood. This is a depiction he shares with his author, Sacher-Masoch. For in 1888 (three years before *The Pupil*), Sacher-Masoch writes a childhood memory that reflects upon his novel.[32] First he makes it clear that he found an outlet for his desires in childhood through the act of reading: "When I was a child I showed a predilection for the 'cruel' in fiction; reading this type of story would send shivers through me and produce lustful feelings. And yet I was a compassionate soul who would not have hurt a fly. I would sit in a dark secluded corner of my great-aunt's house, devouring the legends of the Saints . . . and the torments suffered by the martyrs" (273–74). (Who

could object to the legends of the saints as a boy's purifying form of delay?)
Then at age ten, at his aunt's house, he, in a game of hide-and-seek, hides
in her closet, from which he sees her beating her husband, after which sight
he becomes the object of her whip and ire (as punishment for spying). "This
event," he says, "became engraved on my soul as with a red-hot iron" and he
"both hated and loved the creature" who had beaten him (275).

In Krafft-Ebing's cases from the 1880s (that is to say, in this Austrian psychiatrist's compendium called *Psychopathia Sexualis*), the theme of masochism going back to childhood is quite prevalent—though, predictably, none of
his patients are themselves children. Still, they often recount their memories
(from ages six, seven, and eight) of being or seeing children being punished
or debased at school (sights not remotely forbidden to children); of seeing
horses being whipped in the streets in the course of daily labors; and of reading novels—like *Uncle Tom's Cabin*—which produced erections through its
scenes of whipping, and wanting themselves to be humiliated. Case studies
run like the following one, which makes a childhood punishment (perhaps a
childhood longing now put into motion) the absolute prerequisite for adult
sex—sex that is inseparable from harsh talk:

> **Case 66.** Aged thirty-eight, engineer. . . . Visited periodically a prostitute
> who had to enact, previous to coitus, the following comedy. As soon as
> he entered her compartment she took him by the ears and pulled him
> all over the room, shouting: "What do you want here? Do you know
> that you ought to be at school? . . ." She would then slap his face and flog
> him soundly, until he knelt before her begging pardon. She then handed
> him a little basket containing bread and fruit, such as children carry with
> them to school. He remained renitent until the girl's harshness produced
> orgasm in him, when he could call out: "I am going! I am going!" and
> then performed coitus. It is probable that this masochistic comedy may
> have arisen from some scenes enacted during his schooltime.[33]

Indeed, many cases refer directly to childhood scenes and children's longings:

> **Case 51.** Technologist, twenty-six years old. . . . At the age of seven he
> took part in a general fight between the pupils of the school which he at-
> tended, after which the victors rode on the backs of the vanquished. This

impressed [him] considerably. He thought the position of the prostrate boys a pleasant one, wanted to put himself in their place, imagining how by repeated efforts he could move the boy on his back near his face so that he might inhale the odor of his genitals. These thoughts, coupled with pleasurable feelings, often recurred to him afterwards. (131)

Case 52. Man of letters, aged twenty-eight. . . . At the age of six he had dreams of being whipped in the nude by a woman. Upon awakening, intense lustful excitement; thus he came to practice onanism. When eight years old he once asked the cook to whip him. (133)

Case 57. "Even early in my childhood I loved to revel in ideas about the absolute mastery of one man over others. The thought of slavery had something exciting in it for me, alike whether from the standpoint of master or servant. That one man could possess, sell or whip another, caused me intense excitement." (137)

There is something even more telling for *The Pupil* in Richard von Krafft-Ebing's sexual studies, and that is this: the mental component of masochistic practice. It is key to note how often Krafft-Ebing stresses the imaginary and verbal elements of masochistic scenes:

Case 50. [Mr. Z, aged twenty-nine] recognized that flagellation was subsidiary, and that the idea of subjection to the woman's will was the important thing. . . . When he had the "thought of subjection" he was perfectly successful. At times of great excitability it was even sufficient if *he told stories of such scenes* to a pretty girl. He would thus have an orgasm, and usually ejaculation. (129–30, emphasis added)

In a particularly striking version of this pattern, a masochist attached to his torturer's "pretty shoes" must think "cruel thoughts about the shoes" in order to be potent; more specifically, "he was forced to think with delight of the death agonies of the animal from which the leather was taken" (164). In yet another case, "the mere mention of the words 'rattan cane' and 'to whip' caused . . . intense excitement" (179). And in one of the oddest case studies, a man sneaks into a housemaid's room with the intent to drink her urine, which he finds an alluring thought, but then finds the act too disgusting to perform (132). This distinction between thought and action occurs frequently in Krafft-Ebing, sometimes taking the form of disappointment: the acts are a letdown compared to painful thoughts. Here are the companions to a Jamesian twist, though James more dramatically turns the physical components of masochistic sufferings in the direction of mental and verbal excruciation.[34]

There is one last link in this chain of lateral texts before we turn to James.[35] From the start, we have talked about the kind of masochism that does not appear in James: A man sits dreaming of Venus as a statue or a sumptuous painting; her cold, suspended form comes to life; she holds a whip above his head, almost frozen in delay; when it cracks upon him, it marks his skin with the sign of their relation. No penetration, only surface bruising.[36] This insistent image does not appear in James. What do appear in *The Pupil* even so, in singular fashion, are what Gilles Deleuze in his "Coldness and Cruelty" deems the central features of Masoch's masochism. First and foremost is the masochist's (in James's novella, the tutor's) *initiation* of a contract with a torturer. This is a contract he not only seeks but also, in pedagogic fashion, oversees, instructing his torturer through the contract. By being beaten according to its terms, the masochist pays up front for his attachment. He shows himself attached to delay, since he waits for pleasure that is bound to be late, that contractually cannot follow until the pain that ensures it has been suffered. Perhaps not surprisingly, he fears the torturer's canceling the contract that guarantees beatings *and* delays (even repetitions of beatings and delays).

What is surprising in Deleuze is the masochist's break with patriarchy by hiding the figure of the father *in himself*, him who is beaten. This break with fathers and all that they stand for exactly reverses the Freudian model of male masochism, in which the figure of the father is presumed to be "hidden in" the woman who is doing the beating. By Freud's reckoning, the masochist's self-punishment results from his guilt over his wish to usurp the father's place. Freud sees the woman as a cover for the father (in her role as punisher) because she keeps the masochist from seeming homosexual in his wish to be beaten by a man. Woman-as-cover also allows the would-be usurper (that is to say, the masochist) to plead with his father: "'You see, it is not I who wanted to take your place, it is she who hurts . . . and beats me'" (58).

Deleuze takes exception to this interpretation. First of all, he argues, masochism cannot be viewed as part of an S/M whole. It is not aggression turned back upon the self. Actually, by contrast, it is *a special way of pursuing a pleasure that comes on delay.* For this important reason, the masochist does not seek relations with a sadist, whom he would be unable to instruct. Equally important, masochism does not seek to overtake the father but rather to humiliate the father and his law. Deleuze: "The masochist feels guilty, he asks to be beaten, he expiates, but why and for what crime? Is it not precisely the father-image in him that is thus miniaturized, beaten, ridiculed and humiliated? What the subject atones for is his resemblance to the father and the father's likeness in him. . . . Hence the father is not so much the beater as the beaten" (60–61). The result of masochism, according to Deleuze, is the masochist's keen disavowal of the world as we know it, a disavowal accomplished through highly formalized aesthetic contemplation. Hand in glove with this disavowal is the masochist's suspension of laws by his making absurd contracts with them — especially the sexual laws conventionally mapped for men and women. In other words, by his submission to the law, the masochist undoes it. Whipping ceases to punish erection. Rather, it produces it. Moreover, when the masochist through his punishment literally atones for his resemblance to the father, he seeks in its place a maternal symbolic, both nurturing and cruel.

Thinking Past NAMBLA with Henry James:
Man/Boy Love and Embrace through Abuse

Perhaps we can see the effect James achieves by making his masochism turn around a child. To begin, it's as if the Jamesian masochist, literally a pedagogue, disavows the world not only of conventional sexual relations but also of adult relations to the child. Consenting to suffering through his contract with the parents, the tutor buys a pleasure that is wedded to delay (so fitting for his love of a pre- or protohomosexual child). He frees a space for himself *and* the child, in which the "beatings" he suffers do not punish seductions he feels at the hands of a boy. Rather, his pleasures are the product of this contract — here, a teaching contract. As this arrangement breaks the tutor's likeness to the pupil's father, as we will see, the tutor's embroilment with his pupil allows him to seek a *fraternal* symbolic that would lateralize (though not equalize, not equate) adult and child. Each pursues a masochism that would tilt in the other's direction.

These are large claims. As we move to scenes supporting them, we can see how the story's masochism revises the usual tropes of childhood: the child's presumed inferior grasp of education, money, sex, and shame. The story's first lines, to which we now turn, make contract the issue and even make the getting of a contract a torture and a matter of delay. The story begins:

> The poor young man [the tutor, Pemberton] hesitated and procrastinated: it cost him such an effort to broach the subject of terms, to speak of money. . . . Yet he was unwilling to take leave . . . without some more conventional glance in that direction than he could find an opening for in the manner of the large, affable lady who sat there drawing a pair of soiled *gants de Suede* through a fat, jewelled hand and, at once pressing and gliding, repeated over and over everything but the thing he would have liked to hear. He would have liked to hear the figure of his salary; but just as he was nervously about to sound that note the little boy came back—the little boy Mrs. Moreen had sent out of the room to fetch her fan. (1)

From the first sentence, the would-be pedagogue (age twenty-six) is hung on the hook of uncertain terms—monetary terms that are perhaps improper for a boy to hear, or so the tutor thinks. But two circumstances immediately undercut Morgan's (the boy's) virginal relation to the scene of contract: his blasé cynicism and his role, which he grasps quite well, as his tutor's meal ticket (his quite more than imaginary role in his tutor's labor).[37] In fact, in this scene we are told that Morgan "came back without the fan, only with the casual observation that he couldn't find it" and that "as he dropped this cynical confession he looked straight and hard at the candidate for the honour of taking his education in hand" (1). Pemberton's hand has been forced by money, and his forced entry into his tutoring has a faint sexual ring to it: the fact that his "University honours had, pecuniarily speaking, remained barren"; barren from "putting his tiny patrimony into a single full wave of experience" (2, 4). "He had had his full wave, but couldn't pay his hotel bill" (4). And so his teaching contract is not his first option for pleasurable living and actually sets the stage for excruciating tangles with the boy and parents.

In this first installment of their struggles, the mother supplants the pupil's father, who in this scene as in many others remains offstage, yet whose authority hangs over the story as a patriarchy boy and tutor would divert. (The father, we are told repeatedly, mockingly, fancies himself "a man of the world," detached, above the fray; indeed, what he does in the world we never learn.)[38] Intriguingly, the feel of this struggle with the parents (always over money) is rendered as dreamlike right from the start, though from Pemberton's backward glance. In fact, the whole experience is considered strange: "Today, after a considerable interval, there is something phantasmagoric . . . in Pemberton's memory of the queerness of the Moreens. If it were not for a few tangible tokens—a lock of Morgan's hair, cut by his own hand, and the half-dozen letters he got from him when they were separated—the whole episode and the figures peopling it would seem too inconsequent for anything but dreamland" (6). Nothing, however, looks "inconsequent" as this "dream" unfolds. Not the "tokens" of man/boy affection: a lock of hair and letters, which in an Austen novel would mark the man and boy as potential future lovers. And not the death of the boy himself, which will end this "episode" of the tutor's masochism, not to mention the novella itself.

Pemberton is right, though: the family is queer: a pack of "Bohemians who wanted tremendously to be Philistines" (8), "living one year like ambassadors and the next like paupers" (27), according to Morgan. In fact, one of their oddities is how they elevate Morgan himself, precisely for his being the voice of deflation (cynicism, irony, piercing wit), as if the child's ability to talk derisively (even of them) is a sign of distinction for the family. Indeed, for all his otherworldliness—he is an "angel," a "mystic volume"—the pupil could resemble a worldly dandy (and homosexual?) from 1891: Oscar Wilde's Lord Henry Wotton from *The Picture of Dorian Gray* (from around the time of *The Pupil*). For in James's novella, the pupil is "supernaturally clever" with "a sharp spice of stoicism" (9); he has a "range of refinement and perception," making him "unconscious and irresponsible and amusing" (9–10); he is one who "liked intellectual gymnastics and who, also, as regards the behaviour of mankind, had noticed more things than you might suppose" (10).[39] As Pemberton says: "One would think you were *my* tutor!" (28).

Here lies the rub that will lead to masochism for the tutor who will teach him. The family clearly can't grasp Morgan, their queer child. Morgan is too smart for them and too unlike them, making his family "rather afraid of him" — and so they are eager "to wash their hands of [Morgan]" by "forc[ing] a constructive adoption on the obliging bachelor" (namely, Pemberton), whom they know they can get to stay for free. How do they know this? They believe firmly in their child's seductiveness and in the man/boy attraction before them.

And, undeniably, their boy's powers as "a little prodigy" are Pemberton's bind: the tutor's wish *not* to escape his painful financial engagement with this pupil who so appeals to him: "[Pemberton] was partly drawn on and partly checked, as if with a scruple, by the charm of attempting to sound the little cool shallows which were quickly growing deeper. When he tried to figure to himself the morning twilight of childhood, so as to deal with it safely, he perceived that it was never fixed, never arrested, that ignorance, at the instant one touched it, was already flushing faintly into knowledge, that there was nothing that at a given moment you could say a clever child didn't know. It seemed to him that *he* both knew too much to imagine Morgan's simplicity and too little to disembroil his tangle" (26). Pemberton doesn't know how to stop himself. And the parents wouldn't want him to. Here we see syntactically that the tutor's "scruple" in the first sentence fashions a pause in the sentence itself, as if the scruple *will* "check" the act of Pemberton's being "drawn on." But then the syntax runs past the "scruple" to "the charm of attempting to sound the little cool shallows which were quickly growing deeper." What are these "shallows" ("little cool shallows") a metaphor for, in this sentence? What would it mean, moreover, to "sound" them? They may sound sexual while also sounding simply intellectual: in other words, the metaphor of sounding little shallows, whatever it means, makes this rendering safe for the reader (and for Pemberton) to receive and contemplate. But we next see the tutor himself "try[ing] to *figure* to himself the morning twilight of childhood, so as to deal with it safely" (my emphasis). What worries Pemberton? What would not be safe? Talking *and* ignorance *and* knowledge all at once, or so it seems: for "ignorance, at the instant one touched it, was already flushing faintly into knowledge, [so] that there was nothing that at a given moment you could say a clever child didn't know." And "touching" and "flushing" (as just mental matters?) both seem dangers of some sort.

Indeed, they are features — curious ones — of a striking scene that takes us back to the battle of labor:

At Nice once, toward evening, as the pair sat resting in the open air after a walk, looking over the sea at the pink western lights, [the pupil] said suddenly to his companion:

"Do you like it—you know, being with us all in this intimate way?"

"My dear fellow, why should I stay if I didn't? . . . I hope you don't mean to dismiss me. . . ."

"I think if I did right I ought to."

"Well, I know I'm supposed to instruct you in virtue; but in that case don't do right. . . ."

"Do you like my father and mother very much?"

"Dear me, yes, they're charming people. . . ."

"You're a jolly old humbug!"

For a particular reason the words made Pemberton [the tutor] change colour. The boy noticed in an instant that he had turned red, whereupon he turned red himself and the pupil and the master exchanged a longish glance in which there was a consciousness of many more things than are usually touched upon, even tacitly, in such a relation. It produced for Pemberton an embarrassment; it raised, in a shadowy form, a question (this was the first glimpse of it), which was destined to play . . . an unprecedented part in his intercourse with his little companion. Later, when he found himself talking with this small boy in a way in which few small boys could ever have been talked with, he thought of that clumsy moment on the bench at Nice as the dawn of an understanding that had broadened. What had added to the clumsiness then was that he thought it his duty to declare to Morgan that he might abuse him (Pemberton) as much as he liked, but must never abuse his parents. . . . He thought it the oddest thing to have a struggle with the child about. He wondered he didn't detest the child for launching him in such a struggle [with the parents]. . . . but to know [Morgan] was to accept him on his own odd terms. . . . Against every interest [the tutor] had attached himself. . . . Before they went home that evening, at Nice, the boy had said, clinging to his arm:

"Well, at any rate you'll hang on to the last."

"To the last?"

"Till you're fairly beaten."

"*You* ought to be fairly beaten!" cried the [tutor], drawing him closer. (10–12)

Ending with obvious talk of beatings, the scene begins with a kind of tableau, the aesthetic freezing that is prelude to the whip. The pair is at rest in the "pink western lights"—a clear anticipation of the surface suffusion of a mutual blush. Just as talk will color them, will make a material mark upon the skin, talk is their suspension and even their lash. The pupil snaps the relation in motion, wrapped in an "us" that ties boy and tutor together to the parents ("Do you like it . . . being with us . . . in this intimate way?"). The tutor seems stung—though perhaps only playfully ("My dear fellow, why should I stay if I didn't?" he replies). Whatever the tutor's tone may be, his words voice the masochist's fear of dismissal, just as the boy's sound reluctance to proceed. As if on cue, the tutor then plays the masochist pedagogue, schooling the offspring of the torturers to persist (in what is deemed "a struggle"): "I know I'm supposed to instruct you in virtue; but in that case, don't do right." The tutor even seems to instruct the child in blushing. Feeling the effects of their verbal play and wearing it on the surface of his skin ("the words made Pemberton turn colour"), the tutor seems to lateral his blush to the boy, turning their prior disequivalence in the direction of mutual exchange ("pupil and master exchanged a longish glance"), one in which the syntax lets the man and boy converge on a single verb and object, even on "a consciousness."

Then there is metaphor. A phrase such as "touched upon"—"a consciousness of many more things than are usually touched upon . . . in such a relation"—seems metaphorical (a way of saying "talked about"). But what is talked about looks as if it has quite materially touched a face and flushed it red. (A blush, after all, is blood that is drawn to the surface of the skin.) Even the question that is said to be "raised, in a shadowy form" seems plausibly material—as if this is a question that one might catch a glimpse of (as the reader does, precisely on the page). The sentence that contains this question ends with what is quite material: the tutor's "intercourse with his little companion." For "intercourse," of course, has two different meanings, both of which refer to material actions: "communication," on the one hand, and "coitus" on the other.[40]

Indeed, intercourse clearly seems material (you do it with another—here it's a bodily action on a bench) when adult suggestiveness spills its guts in the sentence on talking: "Later when he found himself talking with this small boy in a way in which few small boys could ever have been talked with, he thought of that clumsy moment on the bench in Nice as the dawn of an understanding that had broadened" (11). Here the boy has gotten smaller ("this small boy," "few small boys"), upping the ante of man/boy talking while James presents it (through the tutor's memory) as a first intercourse that prepared for others. From this first one taking place at sunset comes "the dawn" (a metaphor) of "an understanding" that shapes their highly material talk.

With any first intercourse there is "clumsiness," but just when the tutor's duty enters in to make him seem older ("he thought it his duty to declare to Morgan," 11), the tutor skillfully becomes the masochist ("to declare to Morgan that he might abuse him [Pemberton] as much as he liked, but . . . never . . . his parents," 11). The child is the cause of the struggle with the parents, as if he is part of what tortures Pemberton; and somewhere within and beside the contract with the parents are the tutor's "odd terms with Morgan." At any rate, their last exchange is clearly if playfully masochistic. In these lines that end with a reference to a beating ("*You* ought to be fairly beaten!" cried [the tutor]), the pupil's position as the torturer both remains ambiguous and even tilts, in lateral fashion, toward his tutor's position as the beaten. To the pupil's taunting in relation to stamina ("you'll hang on to the last": a staple trope in *Venus*), the tutor's reply about beating the pupil only reminds us of his own abjection. It is teachers who beat pupils in the more usual pedagogic setup; pupils and their parents do not beat teachers. But the tutor's answer does something else (two things, actually). The boy's ambiguous sense of Pemberton's getting "beaten"—is it financial? or psychological? or more broadly metaphorical?—is turned physical by the tutor in the terms of his retort. And the tutor turns his *talk* of spanking Morgan into physically "drawing him closer."

From the metaphorical-material wobblings of this passage, we should be struck by how James's words are transforming something like literal punishments into a still material masochism of linguistic relations. The fetishism so dependent on sight in Sacher-Masoch's masochistic novels (tableaux, female beauty, the nude body veiled by fur) is not in operation here. Rather, fetishistic stasis and delay are accomplished by the elegant syntactical suspensions and linguistic textures that carry James's trademark. Here they become the tutor's drawn-out shadowy sessions of oral intercourse with a boy, an intercourse all about the family abuse of man *and* boy, making them "conscious," as the narrator puts it, of a "democratic brotherhood" established with each other (and others in need), one in which the pupil "might pass for [the tutor's] . . . sickly little brother" (14).

What is so notable about these dynamics is how they repeat in cyclical form: the tutor wants to leave because he's not paid; the parents continue not to pay the tutor, knowing he will stay; the tutor does stay out of love for the boy, who looks ever shabbier through neglect; and the boy and tutor talk about these "beatings," so "that Pemberton stuck it out . . . for [this] purpose": "Morgan made the facts so vivid and so droll, and at the same time so bald and so ugly, that there was fascination in talking them over with him" (29), even though Pemberton wonders "how far it was excusable to discuss the turpitude of parents with a child" (17). All of this continues. In a "blow-out . . . with his patrons," announcing to them his "impossible position," "that he couldn't go on," Pemberton "was exasperated to find that Mrs. Moreen was right, that he couldn't bear to leave the child" (14–16). This "illuminating flash" "descended upon Pemberton with a luridness which per- haps would have struck a spectator as comically excessive, after he had re- turned to his little servile room" (16). "He had simply given himself away to a band of adventurers"; "the idea, the word itself [*adventurers*] had a sort of romantic horror for him — he had always lived on such safe lines" (16). The tutor even thinks to himself at one point, "Morgan, Morgan, to what pass have I come for you?" (as if he is some kind of Christ on a cross), though the boy keeps urging him to flee the situation: "You can't go on like this"; "You ought to *filer* [go away] . . . you really ought" (18). The only longer lull in this action — as Morgan turns twelve, thirteen, and fourteen — is Pemberton's one attempt to take on a pupil (the only other one he can seem to find) in a different country. At the point of leaving, Pemberton "jokes": "'You'll marry [when I'm gone]!' . . . as high, rather tense pleasantry would evidently be the right, or the safest, tone for their separation" (36).

It is Morgan's heart that brings them back together. Sickness is the pretext for this story's climax. The boy's weak heart — the story's ultimate materi- alizing metaphor — pushes the question: After or beyond the length of this struggle, is there a form to hold boy to tutor in something other than their imagination? Actually, this question breaks the masochistic frame — maso- chists, after all, suspend all finalities and prefer delay. Which is to say, no one is a masochist to the very end. Not Severin, not Pemberton.

In fact, as the tutor begins to expect the parents' impending financial crash, the narrator informs us: "Pemberton waited in a queer confusion of yearning and alarm for the catastrophe which was held to hang over the house of Moreen, of which he certainly at moments felt the symptoms brush his cheek and as to which he wondered much in what form it would come" (43). The pupil's way of wondering takes a more decided form: "He talked of their escape (recurring to it often afterwards), as if they were making up a 'boy's book' together" (41). Here is another of James's deft jokes, or so I presume. The "boy's book" adventure imagined by the pupil turns again toward Austen. Man and boy, in the pupil's plan, are not going to sea but are setting up house. Moreover, the pupil's transition from a child to something much more akin to a wife is what makes the tutor fear for his pleasure. Earlier, the tutor had wondered to himself: "He (Pemberton) might live on Morgan; but how could Morgan live on him?" (33). Now this thought intensifies: "For the first time, in this complicated connection, Pemberton felt sore and exasperated. It was . . . *trop fort*—everything was *trop fort*. . . . He saw what the boy had in his mind; the conception that as his friend [the tutor] had had the generosity to come back to him [in his illness] he [the pupil] must show his gratitude by giving him his life. But the poor friend didn't desire the gift— what could he do with Morgan's life?" (43).

Intriguingly, the changing terms of their relation are, in the tutor's estimation, "too strong" (the literal meaning of *trop fort*, which can also mean "too clever" or "too loud"). The tutor finds his lot too hard for his pleasure, just as the boy is most fully joining him in humiliation. (Learning of his parents' crash, Morgan "blushed to the roots of his hair," showing tears of "bitter shame.") Even more pointedly, the parents' giving of their son to his tutor, in something between an adoption and a marriage, officially breaks the tutoring contract. It also, so importantly, breaks the grand suspension of man/boy relations in the masochistic field. Now delay and its pleasures are rushed toward a "violent emotion" that ends these relations:

> "Do you mean that he may take me to live with him—for ever and ever?" cried the boy. "Away, away, anywhere he likes?" . . .
>
> Morgan had turned away from his father—he stood looking at Pemberton with a light in his face. His blush had died out, but something had come that was brighter and more vivid. He had a moment of boyish joy,

scarcely mitigated by the reflection that, with his unexpected consecration of his hope—too sudden and too violent [—] the thing was a good deal less like a boy's book. . . . The boyish joy was there for an instant, and Pemberton was almost frightened at the revelation of gratitude and affection that shone through his humiliation. When Morgan stammered "My dear fellow, what do you say to *that?*" [Pemberton] felt that he should say something enthusiastic. But . . . [Morgan] had turned very white and had raised his hand to his left side. . . .

"Ah, his darling little heart!" [his mother] broke out. . . .

Pemberton saw, with equal horror, by Morgan's own stricken face, that he *was* gone. . . .

"He couldn't stand it, with his infirmity," said Pemberton—"the shock, the whole scene, the violent emotion." (46–47)

This scene really is too violent for masochism. Does Henry James want us to wonder: Is there a form to hold boyish joy (here, quite dramatically, a violent joy) at the thought of being given, by one's parents, to a man? The pupil dies from a strain of joy that has no recognized form to hold it. In fact, the parents positively cannot read it:

"But I thought he *wanted* to go to you!" wailed Mrs. Moreen [to the tutor]. [The father, not the tutor, answers this wail:]

"I *told* you he didn't, my dear," argued Mr. Moreen. He was trembling all over, and he was, in his way, as deeply affected as his wife. But, after the first, he took his bereavement like a man of the world. (47)

In these final lines, the lines that close the story, the father is more than unable to see joy (to see the "gratitude and affection that shone through his [son's] humiliation"). He is unable to claim his own sorrow. (He is, after all, "trembling all over," "as deeply affected as his wife.") The eccentric phrase "took his bereavement like a man of the world" sounds like he takes some kind of beating he denies with a pose. This strange posture of the patriarchal figure is our final image.

This story, therefore, allows rare sights. Among them, this one: James presenting two motifs that are made famous years later by NAMBLA—the child's right to design its education and its privilege to divorce its parents—without James's having to debate a man's love for a boy, or vice versa. Even the typical NAMBLA profile described by one member profiles the tutor: "overeducated," "underemployed," and "not [very] sexually active."[41] Such clever touches show James outreaching and outradicalizing his contemporary Edward Carpenter on "Affection in Education."

And yet, the very notion of the masochistic child as the quintessential pupil should not surprise us, should be familiar to any intellectually minded adult, especially to so-called gay adults, who know that pain and unfairness in employment are pleasures to discuss. From which I conclude: we are James's pupils and perhaps have taught, or more likely been, his kind of child.

CHAPTER 2 Why the (Lesbian) Child
Requires an Interval of Animal
The Family Dog as a Time Machine

Children are flooded with animal figures. In the stream of stories expressly told to them, in the toys and movies directly aimed at them, there is an obvious abundance of animals. Dogs chief among them, some of them memorably impressed upon the screen for major stretches of the twentieth century.

Lassie, for example, was an elegant diva from 1943 to the re-release of *Lassie Come Home* in 2005. She went on the radio in 1946, then on television in 1954, where she has since remained a fixture, beloved by children.[1] Rin Tin Tin, the famous German shepherd who preceded Lassie's fame, made twenty-six pictures for Warner Brothers before he died in 1932 and is said to have been "credited with saving the studios from financial ruin" during the era of silent films.[2] Each dog, in fact, has its own website, an indication of both dogs' longevity with scores of children. On Rin Tin Tin's, we find this dog's "biography, fan club information, appearances by his descendants, children's activity section, gifts and collectibles." His home page, moreover, announces him to be "a living legacy since 1918" and proudly displays his star on Hollywood's walk of fame; we even learn that his owner's wife filed for a divorce, naming the dog as corespondent, "saying [her husband] loved the dog more than her."

These famous dogs and the lore of their roles are not aside

WHEN I WAS A
YOUNG CHILD I
SLEPT WITH A DOG.
. . . NOW IT IS A
GIRL'S HEAD THAT
LIES ON MY ARM.
—DJUNA BARNES,
"LULLABY"

from the points at hand. One must grasp the ample, surprising role of animals in the child's delay, the child's supposedly slow approach to the realms of adulthood, coupledom, and parenthood. Strangely enough, like man/boy love, or so I will show, animal/child affectionate bondings can offer opportunities, queer as they will seem, for children's motions inside their delay, making delay a sideways growth the child in part controls for herself, in ways confounding her parents and her future.[3]

And yet even animals are not for human beings just what they seem to be. The family dog, for instance, is not just a pet. It is a metaphor for all that is loyal, familiar, familial, and family-photogenic. Or as Leo Bersani said in the late 1980s, before there were many gays on TV: "The family identity produced on American television is much more likely to include your dog than your homosexual brother or sister."[4] This was true—and false. Lassie was never such a simple companion as she seemed. She was never just a figure devoted to the ordinariness of family life. Rather, the dog is a living, growing metaphor for the child itself, as we are going to see, and for the child's own propensities to stray by making the most of its sideways growth. The dog is a vehicle for the child's strangeness. It is the child's companion in queerness. As a recipient of the child's attentions—its often bent devotions—and a living screen for the child's self-projections—its mysterious bad-dog postures of sexual expression—the dog is a figure for the child beside itself, engaged in a growing quite aside from growing up. Doggy style, dead dog, dog tired, a dog's life, going to the dogs, let sleeping dogs lie: the dog has a habit of taking on meanings, not all of which can appear in *Lassie*. But they emerge in other texts. The principle of Lassie is even quite abstract, as we're going to find out, making the family dog a time machine, so fitting for the modernism of Virginia Woolf and, especially, Djuna Barnes.

Animal Pause

Returning for a moment to where we have been, we have seen the child as managed delay. This is the notion that children should approach all things adult with caution and in ways that guarantee their distance from adulthood. In many respects, the adults who surround the managed child—supremely its parents—are the ones who hold on behalf of the child the visions of approach, since children, while approaching, are thought unable to see these visions. Henry James's perspective in *The Pupil* turned these visions on their side. From a masochistic pupil in the mind of Henry James we learned new tricks in the realm of delay. Masochism, pursued by man and boy, became a special way of pursuing a pleasure that comes on delay, a way of agreeing to pain up front as the promise of a pleasure bound to follow in its wake. Pleasure in *The Pupil* rode astride the back of pain. It came disguised as pain, so that two parents couldn't see a boy's climax that occurred before their eyes. Masochism and its fateful ending offered *forms* for joy, even forms of metaphors that became material: a truly bursting heart.[5]

Sorrow suffuses the present chapter. Again the child battles parents' projections of its future that run against its pleasure. This is sorrow, sometimes frustration, met with canny determination and the child's resolve to control its own delay. Specifically, these children are girls in three of the most famous women's novels ever written: Virginia Woolf's *Mrs. Dalloway* (1925), Radclyffe Hall's *The Well of Loneliness* (1928), and Djuna Barnes's *Nightwood* (1936). These are works from the 1920s and 1930s when the sexual love of women for each other, and more generally women's autonomy, were still a public impossibility (hence the banning of Hall's *The Well of Loneliness* in 1928). Now we consider lateral relations and sexual movements in delay that are, if anything, stranger than *The Pupil*'s, because they are not human.

Experimental metaphors. Active pause (even animal pause) on the threshold of adulthood. Sexual kids and their sideways growth through the figures of their dogs. A same-sex lover *as* a child and a dog. I will make animal abstractions explicit, showing how the densities of modernist works—especially their experiments with animals and metaphors—shed their light on the childhood issues crucial to this book. In the last chapter, via Henry James, we found four versions of childhood queering emerging in fiction from the 1890s. Now in this chapter, we learn that famous works from the twenties and thirties were already braiding versions of the queer child—*Nightwood* most complexly—as they made animals central markers of queer child time. *Nightwood* is only the most lavish rendering of problems shared by Virginia Woolf and Radclyffe Hall in shaping plots of sideways growth.

To begin, we should recognize that metaphors in some respects are something growing sideways. They "grow" meanings ("increase [them] in quantity, size, and degree") by putting people and things rather oddly beside themselves. A metaphor is an "implied comparison," the dictionary tells us.[6]

So when ministers say, for example, drawing on the Gospels, that "Christians are sheep," we compare their features.[7] We put a sheep body next to a Christian and "find" the Christian inside the sheep, growing, expanding the meaning of a Christian by putting "Christian" beside itself in a figure for itself (putting the concept of "sheep" by its side). Such a move is so familiar, fattening up a concept through the use of metaphor, we may not notice its reliance on both strangeness and time. That is to say, while in the act of domesticating meaning—making meaning more familiar and accessible—we often use a strangeness. When we say "Christians are sheep," we almost seem perverse as we make a sacred point. Yet we are willing to suffer this strangeness because sheep take us somewhere to a more important point about Christians. This is why a metaphor is said to have a "vehicle" (a figure of speech—"sheep," in this instance) that takes us to a "tenor" (a metaphor's meaning). "Sheep" as a "vehicle" takes us for a ride. It conveys us to some new meaning as it moves us across the distance between two different concepts ("Christian" and "sheep"). And it takes time. There is an interval—sometimes it is long, sometimes it is short—between every vehicle and its tenor: the time it takes, of course, to arrive upon a meaning. This makes a metaphor a moving suspension. Meaning is moving and growing in a metaphor even while time seems to hang in a delay.

Nightwood (1936) famously and perplexingly, especially in its ending that has been read as crassly sexual, offers us the metaphor of a haunted dog—not unlike the dog from the film The Hanging Garden (1996), which we encountered in my introduction, though here the dog is both more bizarrely and more intensely rendered:

> Down [Robin] went [we read in Nightwood, on the novel's final page], until her head swung against [the dog's]; on all fours now, dragging her knees. . . . Backed into the farthest corner, the dog reared as if to avoid something that troubled him to such agony that he seemed to be rising from the floor. . . . He let loose one howl of misery and bit at her. . . . Then she began to bark also, crawling after him—barking in a fit of laughter, obscene and touching. The dog began to cry then . . . and she grinning and crying with him. . . . until she gave up . . . her face turned and weeping: and the dog too gave up then, and lay down, his eyes bloodshot, his head flat along her knees.[8]

Here is a woman playing with and as a dog. Throughout the novel's length, we find this grown "homosexual" woman also relentlessly figured as a child. Her access to her childhood, through her female lover who acts like her mother, is reaching her on linguistic delay. Now she is a queer child when she is not a child.[9] We seem to be watching her tunnel back in time to where she is suspended in sideways growth. For until this famous ending, she is, throughout the novel, like a sleepwalking child, a child Sleeping Beauty, yet to be awakened to vitality and life.[10] In loving her, her lover tries to grasp a wayward child. To complicate matters in a way that almost outdoes Freud, before this queer "child" finds her lover, she herself becomes a mother, the process of which triggers, so it seems, her sudden desire to sleep with one. Rounding out our knotted sense of childhood, this queer child births a boy whose innocence, as a sickly holiness, makes him fully strange — and estranged from adults.

There is something more. Even though Nightwood's most central metaphor should sound familiar — lesbian lovers as mother and child — this worn trope, well worn by Freud, becomes in the hands of Djuna Barnes an intricate metaphorical skein. Barnes seems to take the Freudian notion that "female homosexuals play the parts of mother and baby" and embroider it.[11] She does so with reason. First, it can symbolize the impossibility of lesbian love in the public's eyes at the time she is writing. Painting these women as mother and child, she shows these lovers as doomed by (their) time. Theirs is a time that can never arrive: the time when mother and child can be lovers in the public's embrace; or when mother and child will inhabit the same generation. These are clear impossibilities, akin to waiting for night to be day. They are also impassabilities, akin to the historical prematurity of queer love in the 1930s, in a world so clearly not ready to receive it. (The Well of Loneliness had been banned through public trial, showing in the figures of Radclyffe Hall and her protagonist, Stephen Mary Gordon, the "look" of lesbians and modern women to the public at large.)[12] Simply, time is out of joint for the woman who loves other women and so cannot "grow up" in this relation. Secondly, this metaphor of mother and child leads to the novel's extremely strange ending, where the one lover who is figured as a child gets down in the dirt with her lover's dog, barking, howling, and biting, as if she, too, is a canine — as if she could be her lover's dog and thus legally belong to her lover. Stressing the relation of metaphor to children, I will show the queer child entering into an "interval of animal," as I coin it, and therefore creating a moving suspension, one both touching and active on the child's behalf.

Oddly, this relation has a legal precedent, showing the force of an animal metaphor. This legal case is the one briefly mentioned in the last chapter: what is called "the Mary Ellen Affair" (1874), which famously led to the founding of the New York Society for the Prevention of Cruelty to Children (the first such society in the nation), making this case a landmark moment in the rise of child protections.[13] In this case, a New York social worker, absent any laws that made child abuse illegal, cleverly prosecuted one child's parents by using the law against cruelty to animals. The social worker argued that children belong to the animal species and, therefore, by the terms of established law, could not be abused. Why is this significant? If, in this Mary Ellen Affair, the animal comes to the aid of the child in need of safe space, it does so creatively. It becomes a metaphor—actually, a metaphor claimed to be material—where the child can legally hide. Undercover as an animal, the child can have its day in court as something other than itself.

This is a development that the French philosopher Gilles Deleuze and the psychoanalyst Félix Guattari might appreciate, given their reflections on being-and-becoming animal in *A Thousand Plateaus*.[14] However, in their treatise, in which a "plateau" could be conceived as a sideways growth as I have been defining it—an increase in magnitude, quantity, or degree—Deleuze and Guattari emphasize the material side of being-and-becoming animal. For these theorists, a "plateau" is a state of "intensity," leading to "irreducible dynamisms . . . and implying other forms of expression" (237). One such plateau is what they call "becoming-animal": an "alliance" between human and animal that "traverse[s] human beings and sweep[s] them away." Such an alliance is "anti-Oedipal"—has "nothing to do with a sentimental or domestic relation" or "filiation" (244). Rather, it is "an unnatural participation" of the human with the animal (240). Quite importantly, this becoming-animal is "a question . . . not of development or differentiation but of movement and rest, speed and slowness" (255). Deleuze and Guattari speak of "transport" in this context. Children are particularly "moved" by animals in this way and "continually undergo becomings of this kind," leading Deleuze and Guattari to note (in rather general terms) "the assemblages a child can mount in order to solve a problem from which all exits are barred him" (257, 259, 260).

Dalloway's Dog: Am I Becoming My Mother's Kind of Lesbian?

Girls mount these "assemblages" in the form of dogs in Woolf, Barnes, and Hall. Of course, such a strategy on the part of girls would be striking if it surfaced in any one novel, a kind of clever sidestep of expected plots. But that this pattern, never noticed by critics, of girls-with-dogs should reach across this trio of well-known novels and over to *Lolita* (in my next chapter), and with increasing sophistication, is fully telling.[15]

Woolf, it appears, contemplates these matters in her brief portrait of queer child with dog, coming to these issues so crucial to Barnes a decade earlier, in *Mrs. Dalloway* (1925). This is not a lesbian novel per se. It is a novel with sapphic threads. These threads connect the mother, Mrs. Dalloway, and her sapphic memories of when she was eighteen, to her only daughter, who, at seventeen, is "falling in love" with a female tutor old enough to be her parent.[16] (When Michael Cunningham crafts these relations anew in *The Hours*—Woolf's *Mrs. Dalloway* in the age of AIDS—he makes the mother an out-and-out lesbian and he makes her daughter enthralled not with a tutor but with a queer theorist.)[17]

One formal project of this novel is delay. Mrs. Dalloway, if she could, would make time hang.[18] She works to create suspended states that make one's flow with time less terrifying ("she feared time itself," the feeling of "being . . . [swept] out to sea," 44, 11). Pause, exquisite in itself, prepares a woman for exquisite transport, though what we often see is the pause: "So [Clarissa Dalloway] . . . felt often as she stood hesitating one moment on the threshold of her drawing-room, an exquisite suspense, such as might stay a diver before plunging while the sea darkens and brightens beneath him, and the waves which threaten to break, but only gently split their surface, roll and conceal and encrust as they just turn over the weeds with pearl" (44). The action of Mrs. Dalloway's dive may be hung upon the threshold, but, while it hangs, the ongoing threatening motion of the waves, given to us in metaphoric suspension, continues to roll toward its climax in "pearl." The metaphor actually moves the "diver" to safety and pleasure before there is any literal plunge.

The novel's sapphic material also comes in on a pause, with Clarissa's rendering of something orgasmic, in a rush of metaphors, as a suspension that is also a flowing, a moving pause: "She could not resist sometimes yielding to the charm of a woman . . . confessing, as to her they often did, some scrape, some folly. . . . She did undoubtedly then feel what men felt. Only for a moment; but it was enough. . . . a tinge like a blush which . . . , as it spread, one yielded to its expansion, and rushed to the farthest verge and there quivered . . . swollen with some astonishing significance . . . which split its thin skin and gushed and poured. . . . Then, for that moment . . . a match burning in a crocus" (46–47).[19] The pleasures of suspension next intensify with Clarissa's extended memories of kissing Sally Seton at age eighteen—her most erotic pause before her plunge into marriage: "Then came the most exquisite moment of her whole life. . . . Sally stopped; picked a flower; kissed her on the lips. . . . [S]he felt that she had been given a present, wrapped up, and told just to keep it, not to look at it—a diamond, something infinitely precious, wrapped up" (52–53). Now Mrs. Dalloway, thinking back in memory, rides a jeweled vehicle (in the diamond metaphor) that conveys her to Sally's kiss that was a pause: the metaphor of diamond pointing toward Sally and away from any engagement to a man ("they spoke of marriage always as a catastrophe," 50). Sally is not her lesbian lover, though Sally smokes cigars, runs naked on a path, and cuts the heads off flowers. She is the future Mrs. Dalloway's delay. "If it were now to die 'twere now to be most happy" (51), thinks Clarissa, with the aid of Shakespeare.[20]

Strikingly, however, Woolf lets Clarissa see herself repeated in another generation, as she watches her daughter's relations with the older tutor—"the woman who had crept in to steal and defile" (266), according to Clarissa; a woman old enough to be her daughter's mother. What is so intriguing, even so puzzling, is Clarissa Dalloway's upset over her daughter's kind of love—she hopes it is "a phase"—that Clarissa still worships as an interval: that magical sideways time-out-of-time with Sally Seton. The worry is not "my child is queer," but "is my child being queer in my way?" Evidently, what matters is the *kind* of sapphic relation that ushers one's daughter into womanhood. ("But why with Miss Kilman?" "She was over forty. . . . She was poor, moreover. . . . She had . . . to take whatever [work] she could get," 16, 186–87.) Woolf uses money to mark Mrs. Dalloway's incomprehension of her daughter's choice of pause.[21] For Woolf insists that an obvious interval separates a mother from her child; the mother cannot deliver her daughter into a future that is her own past. This—the mother's future, which she's already lived—is precisely no future for her child. The child cannot be in mother-time.

Which is how the dog comes into play. The dog is a sign of playful rebellion, a sign that Clarissa's daughter, Elizabeth, will not assimilate into her mother's sense of future—a growing up to knowing the right shoes and gloves.[22] Elizabeth, we are told, "cared not a straw for either of them [shoes or gloves]. . . . [She] really cared for her dog most of all. . . . Still, better poor Grizzle [the dog]," thinks Clarissa, "than Miss Kilman ['Elizabeth's seducer']" (15, 266). One gets a sense of the dog as delay—the dog as pause—as marking Elizabeth's space for suspension and lateral movement on the threshold of adulthood, which makes the dog a safer choice than Miss Kilman (at least in Clarissa's eyes) but also an ally in schemes of resistance. The dog may specifically defend the child from metaphors of a particular, damaging sort. These are the kinds of figures of speech that carry (truly, hand over) the girl to conventional plots: metaphors culturally shared and repeated in a kind of fixed chain. "It was beginning. . . . People were beginning to compare [Elizabeth] to poplar trees, early dawn, hyacinths, fawns, running water, and garden lilies; and it made her life a burden to her . . . and she had to go to parties, and London was so dreary compared to being alone in the country with her father and the dogs" (204). And later: "(She was like a poplar, she was like a river, she was like a hyacinth, Willie Titcomb was thinking. Oh how much nicer to be in the country and do what she liked! She could hear her poor dog howling, Elizabeth was certain.)" (287).[23] In at least three passages, mention of Elizabeth's loveliness by others is set beside her attention to her dog.

Even at last, on the novel's final page, amid a father's delight at seeing his daughter "come out" as a lovely young woman, the dog appears to undercut the daughter's disappearance into Oedipal pride: "Richard [Dalloway] was proud of his daughter. . . . He had looked at her, he said, and he had wondered, Who is that lovely girl? and it was his daughter! That did make her happy. But her poor dog was howling" (296).

The Metaphor That Licks You: The Child as Dog in Loneliness

Mrs. Dalloway's dog-as-pause swells to almost absurd proportions in Radclyffe Hall. In *The Well of Loneliness* (1928), animals and "inverts" talk to one another in "a quiet language" outside of English. They exchange vows. They pledge devotion. They create a contemplative space in which the invert, the girl named Stephen, rehearses her exclusion from a world that won't accept her.

The future is her problem, since it holds no form that her growth would like to take. Thus "[Stephen] would shrink from what might be waiting in the future," "repelled" by the thought of forward advance.[24] Indeed, this repulsion appears at birth. For the "little tadpole of a baby . . . yelled and yelled for three hours without ceasing"—the novel calls it "howling"—"as though outraged [to be] ejected into life" (13). Moreover, in what is possibly the first named portrait of an "invert" child—a "queer child," "queer fish," "queer kid," as she is called throughout the novel—*The Well of Loneliness* shows her ghostliness.[25]

She is "like a soul that wakes up to find itself wandering, unwanted, between the spheres" (35). At seven, Stephen is "already . . . struggling to get a grip on life," subject to "small fits of dejection" and "a dim sense of frustration"—"and Stephen was often conscious of this sense, though she could not have put it into words" (14). In fact, she is conscious of being inarticulate—of having "longings for something that she wanted yet could not define" (36)—and this lag in speech (words will later come) is exactly the sign of her not fitting in: "Her relations with other children were peculiar, she thought so herself and so did the children; they could not define it and neither could Stephen, but there it was all the same" (46). Her clothes also speak what she cannot seem to say, literally figuring her ill-suitedness, "that indefinable quality in Stephen that made her look wrong in the clothes she was wearing, as though she and they had no right to each other, but above all no right to [her mother]" (27).[26] For "the [mother's] hand would be making an effort to fondle, and Stephen would be conscious of that effort" (15). Thus, with no words, at least not on this score, but with a consciousness, "the inarticulate Stephen" (15) is precisely like the novel's treasured animals: smart but "dumb": that is, perceptive but also in possession of "very few words" except "small sounds and many small movements, which . . . meant more than words" (59).

One "small sound" and one "small movement," one might say, are enough to make Stephen at the age of seven "first become conscious of an urgent necessity to love" a woman (16): a twenty-year-old housemaid who sweeps Stephen's stairs: "Stephen had seen Collins sweeping the stairs for two years, and had passed her by quite unnoticed; but one morning, when Stephen was just over seven, Collins looked up and suddenly smiled, then all in a moment Stephen knew that she loved her — a staggering revelation. . . . [Collins] had always said: 'Good morning, Miss Stephen,' but on this occasion it sounded alluring — so alluring that Stephen wanted to touch her, and extending a rather uncertain hand she started to stroke her sleeve" (16–17). Here is age-differential love again: Stephen "wanted Collins," "tried to woo Collins," "pictured them living alone in a . . . cottage," "a very intimate picture, full of detail" (18, 27, 25) — fed by the fact that (Sally Seton–like) "Collins suddenly stooped and kissed her" (18). Again, Stephen has "no name" for these feelings. Even if others *would* have names, the specific movements of Stephen's joy — the motions of her love — do not likely signify clearly to others her attractions: "The thought [of seeing Collins] would set her splashing in her sitz-bath, and tearing the buttons off her clothes in haste, and cleaning her nails with such ruthlessness and vigour that she made them quite sore in the process" (19). Nor would someone know that her "torment" of her dolls — or her "orgy of prayer" — meant that she was in love (20, 21).

This love is not returned. And though this frustration in another kind of novel would be merely comic, this childish impasse of an unrequited crush is the first sign of impossible love: impossible forward advance to the future. From here, therefore, the novel moves in unusual ways, since its plot can only topple sideways: Stephen remains often figured as a child but begins also to be figured as a dog; as an adolescent, she "marries" a horse, then meets a woman by attending to her terrier. That is to say, Stephen starts taking shape as the grown-homosexual-as-a-child. When she asks her father at age eighteen, "Father, is there anything strange about me? . . . I was never quite like other children," her father thinks to himself: " 'Stephen, my child, my little, little Stephen.' For now in his pity she seemed to him little, little and utterly helpless again" (106). At other moments, Stephen feels "shamelessly childish" and speaks "as a child who wants comforting" (163). But mostly the novel, through its many characters, sees her early on as a dog, "like a little dumb creature that had somehow got itself wounded" (28), her mother also being "puzzled by this creature" (32) who "fidgeted under [her] nurse's rough fingers like a dog in the hands of a trimmer," "her flanks as wiry and thin as a greyhound's and even more ceaselessly restless" (37). Much later, at age seventeen, in Stephen's loneliness, it is said that "her eyes would grow . . . apologetic, like the eyes of a dog who has been out of favour" (76).

Presumably, this lonely animality makes Stephen seek new relations with her animals, her form of substitute relations with peers. Stephen enters into the "lure of horse-flesh": "She grew to adore the smell of the stables; it was far more enticing than Collins' perfume" (39). And so Stephen, "laying her cheek against [the] firm neck" of her horse, says to him: "You're not *you* any more, you're Collins!" (40). We are not surprised, then, when Stephen veritably weds a horse, who, like this one, "trembles with pleasure" between her knees: "It was love at first sight, and they talked to each other for hours . . . not in Irish or English, but in a quiet language. . . . And Raftery said: '. . . . I will serve you all the days of my life.' And [Stephen] answered: 'I will care for you . . . all the days of your life.' . . . And Raftery was five and Stephen was twelve when they solemnly pledged their devotion" (59). (Later, a man disturbed by Stephen's looks "would stare at Stephen as though she were a horse whom he strongly suspected of congenital unsoundness," 183.)

Nonetheless, a dog, rather than a horse, leads to Stephen's first real love. Stephen moves to save a woman's dog from being killed, making this woman extremely grateful: "'I don't know what I'd do if it weren't for Tony [her terrier] . . . I'm kind of thrown back on my dog'" (133). The dog is a sign of the woman's bad marriage—and, as it happens, her availability to Stephen's love. (In a note inviting Stephen to lunch, she ends flirtatiously, "Tony says *please* come Stephen!" 143.) In two different senses, Tony sits in Stephen's place: first, in proximity to this woman's body ("Stephen wanted to [take] her hand and stroke it, but unfortunately it was now stroking Tony," 139); then, in proximity to her husband's rage: "'It's all this damned animal's fault that you met her!' He would kick out sideways at the terrified Tony, who had lately been made to stand proxy for Stephen" (152).

In short, the world of horses and dogs offers girls—here young-women-who-are-not-seeking-men—what they can't easily or otherwise discover: a lateral community that understands, affirms, and offers sorrow for unsupported choices. And so when Stephen enters her most important love affair, which is eventually broken by the weight of the discourse of futurity — Stephen cannot see a future for her lover, which she thinks her lover needs — a dog comes into this sorrowful picture: "a clumsy and inarticulate fellow," "one more desolate creature who had followed [Mary, Stephen's lover] home" (335, 332): "David [the dog] sat watching with luminous eyes in which were reflected [Mary's] secret troubles. . . . He nearly broke his own heart. . . . he wanted to lay back his ears and howl with despair to see her unhappy. He wanted to make an enormous noise, the kind of noise wild folk make in the jungle — lions and tigers and other wild folk that David had heard about from his mother. . . . But instead he abruptly licked Mary's cheek — it tasted peculiar, he thought, like sea water" (335–36). With this young woman's troubles in his eyes, and with the lateral breaking of his heart, the dog, inseparable from his howling, is truly a figure for what it means to be beside oneself with sorrow. Yet as a figure for Mary-beside-herself, the dog is in some respects a metaphor that licks her, tasting her tears. He even thinks in similes ("it tasted peculiar, he thought, like sea water").

The dog, to be sure, renders not only someone-beside-herself. Because he himself cannot grow generationally in human time (though he has a mother), the dog is a figure for lateral growth. Like the queer child who will never be straight, who puts the goal of socially-sanctioned couplehood on perpetual delay, he grows sideways in relation to his mistress. Further, if the dog marks a space for the child the women between them cannot produce, he is at least compensation for a sorrow: sorrow for the historical prematurity of the love of lateral growth: "And this sadness mingling with that of the house, widened into a flood that compassed Mary and through her David, and they both went and sat very close to Stephen on the study divan. As the twilight gradually merged into dusk, these three must huddle even closer together — David with his head upon Mary's lap, Mary with her head against Stephen's shoulder" (394).

A clear lap-lover, the queer lovers' dog, the messianic David, finally stands as witness to the novel's overarching lament over interval: "How long? How long?" This is the novel's economical phrase for historical impasse. And so in a very strange close of its own, Hall's novel ends with its invert, Stephen, just having permanently parted from Mary, being watched by David, their beloved dog—a figure for her loneliness ("there was only a dog . . . called David," 436). As it happens, he is watching his mistress being haunted by historical prematurity: haunted by the ghosts of unborn going-to-be-unacknowledged children, along with the ghosts of dead queer friends, pleading for their right to existence: "Oh, but they were many, these unbidden guests. . . . The quick, the dead, and the yet unborn. . . . In their madness to become articulate through her, they were tearing her to pieces. . . . They were everywhere now, cutting off her retreat. . . . At the cry of their suffering the walls fell and crumbled: 'We are coming Stephen . . . and our name is legion—you dare not disown us!' . . . They possessed her. Her barren womb became fruitful— it ached with its fearful and sterile burden. It ached with the fierce yet help- less children who would clamour in vain for their right to salvation" (436– 37). So Hall's novel, rooted in nineteenth-century realist and sentimental fiction, ends with an almost gothic depiction of the impossibilities of queer love and invert childhood in Hall's time. Stephen is now the metaphorical mother of melodramatically occulted queer children ("they possessed her," "her barren womb became fruitful"). And though the dog sees her suffering from these ghosts—"they were tearing her to pieces"—David, the dog, as a savior still to come, can only crouch and tremble, with eyes of amber struck by anguish.

Getting into Mother's Lap: Nightwood's Haunted Dog

Nightwood, too, ends with "The Possessed," a fitting title to its final chapter in light of Well's conclusion. It seems as if a woman has been suddenly pos- sessed by her lover's dog and the dog possessed by her: "Down she went . . . on all fours now. . . . The dog reared as if to avoid something that troubled him to such agony. . . . He let loose one howl of misery and bit at her. . . . Then she began to bark also, crawling after him—barking in a fit of laugh- ter, obscene and touching. The dog began to cry then . . . and she grinning and crying with him. . . . until she gave up . . . her face turned and weeping: and the dog too gave up then, and lay down, his eyes bloodshot, his head flat along her knees." Can the dog this time, in contrast to The Well, serve not just as anguished witness to historical impasse but also as a vehicle (a metaphor's vehicle) by which two women are transported to each other? Can the dog facilitate a moving delay?

Nightwood's readers may be forgiven if the novel's final scene overruns their sympathies. Scholars of the novel are themselves a kind of study in how to skirt a dog. Some imply that *Nightwood* does not really end here, that it has ended with the scene before, making the dog scene merely an "epilogue." Others substitute gossip surrounding the novel's author for a reading of the end, stressing that Barnes, though she did intend revenge against her lover Thelma Wood, did not intend the ending to seem bizarrely sexual. Still others say that attempts to make meaning from the ending reveal a reader too attached to meaning-making, in a novel that thwarts it. And yet any reader of *Nightwood* I have known still wants to know what to do with the dog.[27]

It is tempting, to be sure, to lean on Barnes's biography for clues to *Nightwood*'s oddities. Barnes's early life was just as perverse as her novel might suggest, making her writing, according to the biographer Phillip Herring, tied to acts of "vengeance against [her] family."[28] As many readers of *Nightwood* will know, it has been a matter of great speculation—by critics and biographers—whether Djuna Barnes was sexually involved with her own grandmother, who was a philosopher of free love. (As Barnes herself once famously stated: "I might be anything; if a horse loved me, I might be that," xix.) It is clear Barnes felt betrayed by her grandmother with whom she slept for fifteen years. However, this feeling could have had many causes. As Herring tells us, Barnes's father Wald, who was a "dilettante," "polygamist," and "polymath" and essentially deserted Barnes's mother by bringing another woman home, was "indulged" by Djuna's grandmother (Wald's own mother) from his childhood (24–25). Even more unusually, Herring suggests that Zadel, as she was called, acted as "procuress" for her son's appetites by "binding young women to him with her charm" (26), making the bohemian Barnes family known to their neighbors as "the Mormons," funnily enough.

Given Barnes's mother's displacement through these arrangements (through her father's attachment to Fanny, the other woman, whom Barnes slandered via metaphor as having "the broad butt of a librarian looking for a good book on a low shelf," 30), it's not surprising that Djuna reported: "I loved Zadel as a child usually loves its mother" (52). This strong bond produced a set of letters that has seemed sexually suggestive to critics, along with the pair's naming of their breasts and Zadel's drawing of breast cartoons. Herring tells it this way: "Most of [Zadel's] surviving letters to her adolescent granddaughter carry sexually explicit messages. From Djuna's side, the only reference to this aspect of the relationship is at the bottom of . . . [a] torn [page], [where] one can make out Djuna's thoughts on sleeping for fifteen years beside Zadel and playing with her breasts, here called 'Red-lero' and 'Kedler.' . . . [Djuna's] breasts were 'Cuddlers.' Zadel's breasts, also called 'Pink Tops', . . . are the subject of cartoons at the conclusion of most of her letters to Djuna" (54–55). One letter written when Djuna was thirteen "shows a sketch of Zadel with her breasts stretched out of shape to look like penises" (one is named for a town on Long Island, the other is named "New York City," 55). Yet another letter "shows Zadel's nipples as eyes, read-ing one of Djuna's letters" (55) and other letters speak of the passion the grandmother's breasts have for Djuna: "Pink Tops are simply gasping with love!" and "I'm huggin' you close to the Pinknesses, and they is cortlin' tre-mendous" (55). As one can imagine, interpretations abound of these materi-als, ranging from grandmother-granddaughter incest (a fifty-one-year gap between them) to "good-natured fondling" to just "bawdy talk."[29] Barnes never spoke of exploitation between them, though she may have felt that Zadel had betrayed her by pushing her to marry, before she turned eigh-teen, Fanny's brother Percy (her father's lover's brother), who was fifty-two. (They lasted two months.)

In any case, the biographical context most germane to *Nightwood* is of course Djuna Barnes's eight-year lesbian "marriage" which began around 1921. Thelma Wood, the lover, nineteen years old, was said by twenty-nine-year-old Barnes to resemble her grandmother; and by all accounts, including Barnes's own, Thelma was "a wonderful wild creature" (159). In fact, Barnes later commented, "I was a (truly) virgin yokel looking for lost sheep, and mistook her wolf's blood" (157). Emily Coleman, the modernist author, fig-ured Thelma in stranger terms: "Thelma [was] like an old greyhound . . . like a polyp . . . like a stuffed mushroom . . . like an amoeba" (161). Suffice it to say, they had an ugly breakup over Thelma's drunkenness and infidelities that broke Djuna's heart. *Nightwood*, however, got revenge for heartbreak. As a conquest of Thelma's wrote to Djuna: "Your book has ruined Thelma's life, she is deadly ill & threatening suicide because of it" (165). Herring puts it best in reference to the ending with the haunted dog: "This clear message about the animality of Thelma Wood could be neither retrieved nor obscured by authorial interpretation" (168).

But whatever animality is present in the ending, it is also vectored through the invert "child" (the grown woman Robin, who clearly signals Thelma, who was nicknamed "Bird") and her noninverted lover (Barnes's likely portrait of herself in the figure of Nora). Across the novel's length, they are mother and child in the novel's figurations:

[Nora] . . . should have had a thousand children and Robin . . . should have been all of them. (101)

In Nora's heart lay the fossil of Robin, intaglio of her identity, and about it for its maintenance ran Nora's blood. (56)

"Sometimes," Nora said, "[Robin] would sit at home all day looking out of the window or playing with her toys, trains, and animals. . . . Sometimes, if she got tight by evening, I would find her standing in the middle of the room in boy's clothes, rocking from foot to foot." (147)

There goes [Nora] mother of mischief, running about, trying to get the world home. (61)

This figurative mother-child relation (Nora-mother, Robin-child) dooms these lovers, as I have said, to separate temporalities, dooms them to a time that it seems cannot arrive: the time when mother and child will inhabit the same generation or be accorded permission to wed. Generational time is the sign of their doom, which perhaps only a dog can undo. This is what the dog is doing when we see him. The dog is undoing the effects of a metaphor (women lovers as "mother" and "child") when he and Robin lie down side by side; when she herself is like a dog. That is to say, in the place of one metaphor the dog seems to offer his body for another, addressing as he does so a problem of time. The dog's time machine turns vertical impasse (the "child's" impossible reach for its "mother" as its lover) into a new horizontal relay: a lateral movement of lovers toward each other . . . if one consents for a time to *being dog*.

Given these suggestive terms, one might wonder how Deleuze and Guattari would read the dog in *Nightwood*, along with Robin's linkage (as the queer child) to becoming-animal. It is likely they would see the dog as anti-Oedipal, since he interrupts the Oedipal metaphor that keeps Robin and Nora stranded in their temporalities of mother and child. They would surely read "unnatural participation" and "alliance" between the dog and Robin in the novel's final scene, leading to an obvious state of "intensity" and to "dynamisms" of a strange sort. But would these theorists trip up on metaphor? Would they be too tempted to dismiss it as "resemblance," just as they might be tempted to dismiss the dogs in *Mrs. Dalloway* and *The Well of Loneliness* as sentimental pets? They strongly claim: "This [becoming-animal] will not involve imitating a dog, nor an analogy of relations. I must succeed in endowing the parts of my body with relations of speed and slowness that will make it become dog, in an original assemblage proceeding neither by resemblance nor by analogy" (258). One wonders whether Deleuze and Guattari would see in metaphor a crucial kind of "transport" and therefore relations of movement and rest, slowness and speed.

Commonly, metaphor and simile appear in terms of translation: a metaphor translating one thing as another (a lover as a child). But what if metaphor, I have been suggesting, were grasped not solely in terms of translation but also in terms of transport and time, a transport across a chasm of time? Two kinds of time travel would then emerge, both of which surface in *Nightwood*'s dog: (1) the time it takes a metaphor's "vehicle" literally to travel to its tenor (the time it takes to get from "dog" to the meaning it makes possible); (2) the time relations that get rearranged in a metaphor's vehicle (in our chief example: the way in which women are temporally torn asunder if they are figured as mother and child).

Nightwood offers both time travels. As to the first, we know that metaphors can offer shortcuts, making something grasped more quickly because made more familiar by comparison (Christians are sheep). And yet metaphors can take time. In Barnes they do, and generally the most estranging ones, taking no small time to construe, cause the most delay in plot advance. Indeed, though the novel seems not to move at all, or so it has seemed to many readers, it actually *moves by suspensions* largely made of metaphors.[30] Can a metaphoric suspension address a dilemma posed dramatically as a political and historical impasse? — in the case of *Nightwood*, the dilemma of two lovers ("mother" and "child") who cannot share their own historical light of day. Can the estranging metaphor of dog cause us to encounter the potential for time travel held suspended in a metaphor's vehicle? Where can the queer child in "dog" go?

As it happens, Barnes's dense opening echoes Hall's: the birth of a child "heavy with impermissible blood," who is ejected into a life that won't receive it (3). However, this is not a "queer kid" of Hall's sort (not yet, that is) but the child of a Jew. Barnes, we recall, in a much-discussed move, makes her novel's Jews and homosexuals windows onto each other's pain.[31] And it is this child—generationally burdened, to put it mildly, given that he carries four centuries of memories from Jewish history—who, when he is grown, attempts to "dazzle his own estrangement" (11).[32] Indeed, it is this child—and this very phrase, "dazzle . . . estrangement"—that links the novel's political allegory (its commentary on the queer child's estrangements) to Barnes's gorgeously wild metaphors that make these estrangements so dazzling to consider, metaphors which may be fed by revenge. In other words, in being so *inventive* in her grudge against her former lover, Barnes—wittingly?—fashions a dazzling political swipe against what blocks a lateral growth.

Importantly, the strategy of "dazzl[ing] . . . estrangement"—creatively overdoing rejection—is shared by members of the Berlin circus who enter the novel as characters connected to *Nightwood*'s Jew. The circus performers are social outcasts and share with Jews, along with homosexuals, "degradation" and "the immense disqualification of the public," though they *entertain* it. One entertaining performer in particular, known as Frau Mann (a transgendered name if ever there were one), holds a key to grasping Barnes's use of metaphors. In fact, the novel begins with suspensions, literal and figurative, that look more like limbo than they look like movement. Frau Mann's occupation, for instance, *is* suspension. She works the trapeze: "Her legs had the specialized tension common to aerial workers; something of the bar was in her wrists, the tan bark in her walk" (12). If from this description she seems to have embodied her aerial occupation—so that it is hard to distinguish metaphor from physical description ("something of the bar was in her wrists")—it is because Frau Mann *becomes* the vehicle to her tenor, metaphor turning strangely material: "She seemed to have a skin that was the pattern of her costume: a bodice of lozenges, red and yellow, low in the back and ruffled over and under the arms . . . one somehow felt they ran through her as the design runs through hard holiday candies, and the bulge in the groin where she took the bar, one foot caught in the flex of the calf, was as solid, specialized and as polished as oak. The stuff of the tights was no longer a covering, it was herself; the span of the tightly stitched crotch was so much her own flesh that she was as unsexed as a doll" (13). Candied by her costume

(costume as anatomy, anatomy still destiny), the trapeze artist whose job is suspension is sewn up in metaphor, going nowhere.

This is precisely the kind of sewing up and the kind of limbo the dog will undo, when the queer child enters into him (possesses and is possessed by him) and goes somewhere inside her suspension via the dog. But we are still a ways off from this possession. Indeed, as she is now rolled on the stage, asleep on her bed, she, the queer child, hardly seems a candidate for moving toward anything—never mind that her name is Robin, promising material or metaphoric flight. She seems enclosed, even entombed, by Barnesian metaphors, offering the kind of portrait not likely seen at the cinema or on TV: "*On a bed*, surrounded by a confusion of potted plants, exotic palms and cut flowers, faintly over-sung by the notes of unseen birds, which seemed to have been forgotten—left without the usual silencing cover, which, like cloaks on funeral urns, are cast over their cages at night by good house-wives—half flung off the support of the cushions from which, in a moment of threatened consciousness she had turned her head, *lay the young woman*, heavy and disheveled" (34) (my emphasis). This is the queer child. And this is a sentence that Woolf might have written. We notice how the sentence base is promised but suspended until the last line ("On a bed . . . lay the young woman"). The figure on the bed, surrounded by plants that are over-sung by birds who should have been covered by something "like cloaks on funeral urns," begins to hint at the queer child's peculiar inaccessibility to others or herself.

The paragraph that follows this suspension, however, demonstrates Barnes's own mad metaphorics, taking us to a remarkable portrait of the queer child's hung-up growth:

The perfume that her body exhaled was of the quality of that earth-flesh, fungi, which smells of captured dampness and yet is so dry, overcast with the odour of oil of amber, which is an inner malady of the sea, making her seem as if she had invaded a sleep incautious and entire. Her flesh was the texture of plant life, and beneath it one sensed a frame, broad, porous and sleep-worn, as if sleep were a decay fishing her beneath the visible surface. About her head there was an effulgence as of phosphorus glowing about the circumference of a body of water—as if her life lay through her in ungainly luminous deteriorations—the troubling structure of the born somnambule, who lives in two worlds—meet of child and desperado. (34–35)

This, evidently, is how you bury a grown inverted child under metaphor, making her seem dramatically submerged and held down under her culture's consciousness, even her own. Metaphor entirely covers her body ("her flesh was the texture of plant life"). And yet, though these descriptions make the figure described seem unavailable to any kind of transit, even the back-and-forth sort that comes with Frau Mann's trapeze, Robin's costume is at least alive—more vegetable than mineral, if not yet animal. Hers is more organic than Mann's polished oak; and "*life* lay through her," we are told, not designs of hard holiday candies (though this is a life, importantly so, of "ungainly luminous deteriorations"). Indeed, there may be hope for life in her decay, not to mention in her phosphoric glow. The woman/child/desperado may awake, since we learn she has "invaded" a sleep.

Whose sleep does she, the queer child, "invade"? Not hers alone. She enters into her lover's nights. Nora, in a painful vertical metaphor, dreams of their estrangement. She is standing at the top of a house, looking down "as if from a scaffold," calling out to Robin, "'Come up, this is Grandmother's room,' yet knowing it was impossible because the room was taboo" (62). "The louder she cried out the farther away went the floor below, as if Robin and she . . . were a pair of opera glasses turned to the wrong end, diminishing in their painful love," leaving Robin, as Nora sees her just before waking, "disfigured and eternalized by the hieroglyphics of sleep and pain" (62–63). Even so, her sleep suspension stands for something—indicates a waiting that is actively signaling its delay, like a car with motor running that is not yet put in motion. For Robin, figured by *Nightwood* as a child, is also the novel's sign of an invert, in this case a girlboy. Intriguingly, *Nightwood* imagines the invert as the poster child of fairy tales: "It was they ['inverts'] who were spoken of in every romance that we ever read. The girl lost, what is she but the Prince found? . . . We were impaled in our childhood upon them as they rode through our primers. . . . They go far back in our lost distance where what we never had stands waiting" (136–37). Robin-the-invert is where the future has not arrived, where something from our childhood—our love of the invert—has never grown up into culture's day. This "thin blown edge of our reverie," along which edge what is waiting may awaken, summons two feelings: "terror and joy," which are themselves "wedded somewhere back again into a formless sea where a swan (would it be ourselves, or her or him, or a mystery of all) sinks crying" (137). This is a beautifully dense image of queer-child-ghosting.

Indeed, this sinking beauty is fitting for *Nightwood*'s sleeping beauty, "where what we never had stands waiting." Nora, in fact, the metaphorical mother, can touch on her "child" only from the place of its parting (where the swan sinks crying?). No wonder the trauma of *Nightwood*'s lesbians suggests the metaphorics of amputation: "Robin's absence, as the night drew on, became a physical removal, insupportable and irreparable. As an amputated hand cannot be disowned because it is experiencing *a futurity*, of which the victim is its forebear, so Robin was an amputation that Nora could not renounce. As the wrist longs, so her heart longed, and dressing she would go out into the night that she might be 'beside herself', skirting the café in which she could catch a glimpse of Robin" (59; my emphasis). "Amputation" begins to tip the vertical mother/child metaphor on its side. Robin, according to the terms of this metaphor, no longer issues from Nora as a child but a lopped-off hand, something that has a more lateral existence post-amputation than a generational one. Amputation, then, importantly differs from abortion. It imagines not a wholesale destruction of "the child" (or "the mother," for that matter) but the kind of separation from these terms that puts one beside oneself. This, incidentally, is the brilliance of *Nightwood*. Unlike Hall's more public tale, caught up by the censors, *Nightwood*'s sense of historical impasse (and thus of prematurity) is not worn on its sleeve but on its missing limb, to be recognized by those who themselves are severed from the too-easy promise of self-propagation.

In fact, it is Robin's attempts at propagation that prove her utter incurability: marriage and childbirth do not fix the predicament of her inversion. They prove, rather, her own child's strangeness, even in the guise of his being "innocent." That is, after Robin oddly weds the child of the Jew from *Nightwood*'s opening pages, she becomes "strangely aware of some lost land in herself . . . wandering the countryside . . . alone and engrossed" (45). (She "found herself worrying about her height. Was she still growing?" 46.) At the scene of birth, we are told that "she kept crying like a child who has walked into the commencement of a horror" (48). And just after giving birth, she takes up with Nora, the figure of the mother. As for Robin's child, we learn that he is "very sensitive to animals" and "very like [Robin], except that he has . . . innocence" (117). However, being "not like other children, not cruel, or savage," his father says, "for this very reason he is called 'strange'" (115). The invert child and her innocent child are together lost children, twinning each other despite their distinctions.

Strikingly, the novel's night philosophy is tied to a theology of the lost child, who finds its own destination in a beast. This philosophy is delivered to us by the quack abortionist and homosexual Dr. O'Connor, *Nightwood's* parody of Sigmund Freud.[33]

> They [the French] think of the two [night and day] as one continually and keep it before their mind as the monks who repeat, "Lord Jesus Christ, Son of God, have mercy upon me!" . . . Bowing down from the waist, the world over they go, that they may revolve about the Great Enigma—as a relative about a cradle-. . . . [using the back of the head] when looking at the beloved in a dark place, and she is a long time coming from a great way. We swoon with the thickness of our own tongue when we say, "I love you," as in the eye of a child lost a long while will be found the contraction of that distance—a child going small in the claws of a beast, coming furiously up the furlongs of the iris. (82–83)

It is fascinating that a temporal quandary—the enigmatic coupling of night and day—gets turned by the doctor toward a stranded beloved (lesbian lover) who "is a long time coming from a great way." As if it naturally would explain such a strandedness, the figure of the child suddenly appears. More pointedly, a simple declaration of love ("I love you") takes a detour through a distance: one held in the eye of a child. According to this metaphor, the child holds in its eye an image of the distance it would have to travel in order not to be lost to its beloved—an issue as intriguingly historical and political as it is erotic. Layered onto this "contracted distance" is the image of a child (attacked? embraced? or just kept small?) in the claws of a beast. This puzzling image storms up the eye—flowers, even, in the image of the iris—as if to insist upon itself as an image that must be seen. *Nightwood* knows that if your lover-as-lost-child is approaching you her destination may well be your dog.

Here may be why. Early in the novel when Robin and Nora meet at the circus, Robin flees the gaze of a beast: the "powerful lioness . . . with its yellow eyes afire . . . [who] thrust [her paws] through the bars" (54). The animal importantly has keen links both to sorrow and suspension, since "her eyes flowed in tears that never reached the surface . . . as if a river were falling behind impassable heat." This is a poignant moving suspension, embedding subtle movement, here a flowing, inside an emotion: these hung tears. In fact, what looks like suspension-as-limbo is really a canny gloss on transport. Animals in their sorrowful engagement with our world, according to *Nightwood*, harbor secret travels—forms of time travel. At the novel's start, Dr. O'Connor mentions the cow he encountered in a cellar in the midst of a bombing raid, a cow with "tears soused all over her great black eyes" (23). "And I thought," says O'Connor, "there are directions and speeds that no one has calculated, for believe it or not that cow had gone somewhere very fast that we didn't know of, and yet was still standing there."

For these reasons, it may well be that the demon possession at the end of Hall's *The Well of Loneliness*—Stephen, the grown "homosexual," haunted by children who may "tear her to pieces"—gets revised at the end of *Nightwood* when Robin crawls on the ground with Nora's dog. In what better way, strangely enough, can *Nightwood*'s "child," who is simultaneously the grown "homosexual," get into her lover's presence, and her *present*, than to enter the spirit of her dog? The dog is someone who is not removed by generations from its mistress, who openly cries in pain and pleasure, and who past the censors can freely get into a woman's lap. Robin has taken her status as a child (the ghostly child) into her body all along, with "the face of an incurable yet to be stricken with its malady," who "yet carried the quality of the 'way back' as animals do," whose "attention . . . had already been taken by something not yet in history," who like "a figurehead in a museum, which though static . . . seemed yet to be going against the wind" "as if this girl were the converging halves of a broken fate, setting face, in sleep, toward itself in time, as an image and its reflection in a lake seem parted only by the hesitation in the hour" (41, 40, 44, 38). At the end, she shifts metaphorical schemes, and in such a way as to lateralize relations and literalize what might seem metaphorical. Robin, revising the kind of woman the novel describes "as unsexed as a doll," becomes a vehicle to her tenor, crawling back to Nora through the body of a metaphor. She becomes as sexed as a dog.

From Henry James to *Nightwood*, then, we can grasp the multiple manifestations of the queer child only by getting formal and abstract, taking on the formal dimensions of metaphor and the abstractions of queer-child time.

This might be the most surprising and challenging aspect of this chapter: some of the densest, most commingled, most experimental, most intertextual, and most telling portraits of the queer child appear in the literary fictions I consider—from the first third of the last century. And they involve dogs. The family pet swerves around the Freudian Oedipus in order to offer an interval of animal and thus a figure of sideways growth. In the guise of metaphor (one the child can actively touch), the child hangs suspended in an intensity that is a motion, an emotion, and a growth, even though from conventional angles it may look like a way of going nowhere.

One Last Vehicle: Picasso's Dog

Speaking of modernist reflections on the child, the most famous modern artist of the century is himself remembered as a big child. Yet for the simplicity this rendering implies—a prodigy Stein herself sought with relish in her self-rendering as a big baby—Picasso is mythologized as inaccessible. His genius is ungraspable. How did he know how to make us see as children when we no longer are?

In a recent photography book by David Douglas Duncan, *Picasso and Lump: A Dachshund's Odyssey*, a dog is the one who grants us access to art's child, Pablo Picasso. The dog named Lump, who arrives in style via the photographer's beautifully photographed gull-wing Mercedes ("he joined me as copilot to Picasso's door"), is something of a metaphor announcing its vehicle: the dog is almost saying, "I am here as a conveyance."[34] The dog is brought by Duncan, almost pimped by him, to show (the mythology of) Picasso's heart: his childlike joy, his (here) unguarded privacy, his vaunted spontaneity, his lust to inquire. The dog stands for access to Pablo Picasso; Picasso resembles Duncan's dog.

In vignettes titled "Lump's Eyes," "What was his magic?," "Alone with Picasso," "Private Thoughts," Lump, in Duncan's rendering, makes us green with envy—or so he's meant to do. A dog has accomplished an entrance sought by others: all those "optimistic strangers dreaming of gates swinging open for them . . . while often closed even to [Picasso's] own fragmented family" (29). And, as Duncan tells us, on Lump's first day, in 1957, he is immortalized in a piece of art: "Instantly probing [the villa's] silent rooms and mysterious garden, [Lump] saw himself in a Picasso portrait on a dedicated

5. Diego Velázquez, *Las Meninas*, 1656. Museo del Prado, Madrid.

6. Pablo Picasso (after Velázquez), *Las Meninas*, 1957.
© 2008 Estate of Pablo Picasso/Artists Rights Society (ARS), New York.

luncheon plate; later a source of wishful envy when seen by museum cura-
tors, millionaire collectors, even old friends" (12), a "ceramic souvenir" "symbolic of Picasso's lifelong spontaneous generosity." And though "there had
always been dogs around [his] studios" — often used as props in his paintings
of his children — there had not been one "in [his] arms — where Lump was
now at home" (29).

"Lump was already Picasso's shadow" (31). As such, he conveys to us
shades of the master. "Small, sensitive, and complex," "driven by curiosity,"
"never hearing the word 'no,'" Lump is a comic figure for Picasso's rampag-
ing appetites, especially when Lump eats a rabbit made for him (on the spot
from a box) by the master himself. Duncan reports with glee at capture: "My
new rapid-firing Leica recorded forever the only time in the wildly eccentric
world of modern art when someone ate art itself; fresh Picasso" (47). But
Lump is a figure for two specific postures in Picasso's repertoire: unbounded
child and frustrated child. On the one hand, Picasso, playing with his son and

daughter who are playing with Lump, is said to participate "with the equal rights of another exuberant unrestrained child" (54), being "always alert" "with . . . Lump" (57). Yet Lump himself becomes a kind of parable of teaching Picasso the limits of will, especially since Picasso is unable to mate him with a lady dachshund named Lolita—a name, we presume, a resistance to will, given new force just prior to this time.

One may ask, what does it mean that Lump ends up so visually prominent in Picasso's famous reworking of the painting *Las Meninas*, the masterpiece by Diego Velázquez (figures 5 and 6)? What does it mean that the dog, with a dwarf, is the most elemental, accessible form in the painting—offsetting, or perhaps accentuating, but surely conveying something about the complexity that is the painter himself?

Duncan doesn't say.

PART 2   Sideways Motions: Sexual Motives, Criminal Motives

CHAPTER 3 What Drives the Sexual Child?

The Mysterious Motions of Children's Motives

What does a dog have to do with pedophiles? If a dog runs to chase a car that kills a mother, how long must a pedophile wait to abduct her daughter, Dolly?

Inside this riddle are general principles, ones that connect pedophiles to animals, while conveying metaphors and motions as the signs of children's motives. This is a riddle I will explain, as we consider the twentieth century's landmark scenes of the child's sexuality. It is worth stating that our most public image of the sexual child for over half a century has not been a child—not a living child. Rather, this exceedingly well-known child, debated child, riveting child, infamous child, has been precisely a fictional child, one given form by one of the most acclaimed American novels ever written. Lolita "Dolly" Haze has become synonymous in our culture with "sexual child." A sexual child is a Lolita in our culture's idiom. So what drives this child?[1]

The interval of animal (discussed in chapter 2) makes a surprising showing in *Lolita*. Consequently, fictions of "lesbian" children—ghostly gay children with animal movements—help us read the nuanced dynamics of *Lolita*. And if *Lassie*, after being introduced in 1943, spans the remainder of the century of the child, stimulating visions of children's affections, so does *Lolita* span a half-century, stirring other visions of children's stimulations after it takes novel readers by storm in 1955.[2] Just as notably, in Nabokov's novel we have the original *To Catch a Predator* obsession on view. It takes the form of a pedophile's (Humbert Humbert's) confession, which the current show on American television always tries to wrest from the predators it catches, even though the simple satisfaction of capture is what the show promises and delivers.[3] What Nabokov renders, however, fifty years before this show's emergence, is more double-sided and sharply upsetting of TV's views. He gives a pedophile and a sly, sexual child. Quite unusually, as he depicts the abuse of this girl-child — since this pedophile is abusive — he does not underplay her animal appetites or sexual drive. Quite the contrary. At every turn, two things are true: pedophiles, like anyone, can be abusive, especially when they have more money than children (which is often so); and the abused child can be an agent with sexual motives and motions of her own.

Up to this point, I have shown that pedophilia (or, more precisely, man/boy love) and child/animal affectionate bondings inside fictions offer substitute lateral relations for engaging children's longings outside of their peers. These two foci, wildly disparate — pedophiles and animals — or, to put it differently, sexually available adults and pets, are far more similar than we might have guessed. They can offer outlets for hidden emotions. In Henry James's novella *The Pupil* (discussed in chapter 1), a boy's masochistic relations with a man allowed the boy pleasure disguised as his pain. In fictions by Virginia Woolf, Radclyffe Hall, and Djuna Barnes (in chapter 2), girls hid their pleasures and their sorrows in their dogs. Taken together, the chapters present views of the child using its delay — its presumed suspension in a world of nonadulthood — to fashion movements and sideways relations on its own behalf, often in distinction from its parents' wishes or a future predetermined by the culture of its day. Moreover, it does so often through the metaphors it finds in its domains. Children ride the "vehicles" (dogs and cars) that offer hidden access to their interests, sexual or otherwise.

The Child as Animal Is Mechanical: All Our Lolitas?

Exploring and thinking about children's vehicles, Nabokov in *Lolita* grants the child a sidetrack. In fact, he defines the sexuality of children *as* a sidetrack, requiring a new kind of reading from adults. Nabokov in this way gives us a riddle very much like one of Poe's (Monsieur Poe-Poe as Humbert

Humbert fondly calls him). It is as if Nabokov writes his own "Purloined Letter," asking himself: how can we hide the sexuality of children in plain view?[4] His answers, I think, are paradigmatic for fiction, film, and childhood studies in a broad sense. And they are indicative of my central argument. How do we see a sexual child as being something other than our own perversion? Metaphor, motion, and a curious spoiling of our visual pleasure. These are ways of seeing the often hazy motives of children's sexuality.

That is, in *Lolita* we see revisited—and also revised—the child queered by Freud.[5] This child possesses sexual wishes and aggressive urges, often in queer (mis-) alignment with fathers. Lolita, we find, is packed off to Camp Q, a clue to the reader to realize Lolita's alignment with things that are "q"ued in the novel—Quilty, for one, Humbert Humbert's "queer mirror side," who is Lolita's preferred pedophile.[6] But Lolita is queer herself. Sexually schooled by "little Lesbians," Dolly as the quintessential not-yet-straight child has her own movements with and against her two pedophiles through a set of dogs. Thus here again, in what is arguably the most famous novel ever centered on a child, the reader must contend with both dogs and pedophiles. If we would examine, question, and define the matter of children's sexual motives and therefore their consent—however much the law deems these questions out of bounds—we must theorize pedophiles and animals. And something else. We need to grasp the linguistic connections between the terms *motive* and *motion*, which share the same Latin root, *movere*, meaning "to move."[7] In fact, in *Lolita*, the animal pattern we have discovered in Woolf, Barnes, and Hall receives a new twist. In this novel, things that are animal join with things mechanical. Dogs chase cars. Indeed, Lolita Haze, in the guise of a dog after her abduction (she is Humbert's "pet," his "car pet," as he tags her), helps to drive a car that without his knowing it tails Humbert Humbert, a car he describes in his glimpses of it as a ghostly vehicle. ("[I] kept seeing that red ghost," Humbert tells us, "that glossy red beast," "swimming and shivering with lust in my mirror," 219.) "Little Haze" is thus a ghostly dog and ghostly car.

This is not the standard way of reading *Lolita*. Most of Nabokov's aficionados, including his critics, do not find meaning in the dogs emerging at points in this narrative.[8] Instead, understandably, outside of readings that solely aestheticize approaches to *Lolita*, the matter of Lolita's sexual agency, in the face of Humbert's sexual fantasies, dominates responses to this text.[9] Readers of

Lolita end up asking what drives this child to interact with pedophiles in the ways she does. Or is Lolita an only slightly unusual victim of adult lust?[10] Is she really the innocent child—the abused child—only misread as the Freudian child?

All the *Lolitas*—those of Vladimir Nabokov, Stanley Kubrick, and Adrian Lyne—one novel, two films, spanning over forty years from 1955 to 1996—seem to goad these questions. Though each, I will note, composes different answers. Their answers differ in no small part because these texts take different forms. And form—this matter could not be more important—holds the key to seeing Lolita's hidden motives, since Lolita's motives are hidden in two metaphors, those of dog and car. To crack this case, we need to discover if the films of *Lolita* engage or obscure these metaphoric answers on the cinema screen. Given that we want to probe a sexual *child* and the motives of a child, we need to ascertain if either film offers us a sexual girl, instead of a woman or sexy teen. What is distinctive about the camera's capture of a sexy child? Why does it happen to be so hard to do? These kinds of queries recall James Kincaid. He would surely ask why our culture is obsessed with these pedophilic texts, if as a culture we say we are repelled by adult/child sex.[11] That is, beyond the brilliance of Nabokov as a novelist, which I hope to show is crucial to these matters, what do these Lolitas, together or apart, end up saying about erotic innocence? The answers we discover will shave a different emphasis than Kincaid has offered.

Kubrick's film is the place to begin, at least for a moment here at the start. It presented in 1962 the shot of Lolita (figure 7) that fixed her image in the moviegoer's mind: sultry Lolita arranged on a beach towel, with her perfect figure, clad in a bikini, coyly looking up (with her sunglasses down) to meet the stare of a startled Humbert (figure 8). This was a bed on backyard grass. It was a small rectangular invitation for encountering a semiclad female form in an S-shaped curve, an invite leading into what *Vanity Fair* once called *Lolita*: "the only convincing love story of our century." All of which suggests how we love our Lolitas. We love to rehearse how we look at them with lustful eyes, lapping up their visual pleasure. Or so we love to scold ourselves. For if we are perverts who stare with lust at nubile flesh—this is a look Kubrick's shot tries to force—they (our Lolitas) are the objects of our harm. And if they are shown to be the objects of our harm, we know who they are, albeit tautologically: they are the objects of our harm. As such they cannot threaten us with something we don't know: their queer temporalities; their quantum physics motions, complete with sudden alterations in their energies; their blatant animalities; their odd linguistic wanderings; and, quite importantly, their knack of spoiling the camera's shot by fidgeting in frame or launching some other form of "eerie vulgarity." That is to say, the not-yet-straight child is not so safely solipsized in the cocoon of delay we craft for it. It moves in our suspensions and drives its bed of grass, even as we're staring directly at the child.

These are legal matters. To put it boldly, hidden in the motions of a young girl's leg—rubbery, tensile, and monkeyish, all at once—or more oddly hidden in the movements of a dog, are signs of "personhood" that the law in 1955 does not allow a twelve-year-old girl.[12] In fact, in *Lolita* the child's perversity is her path to personhood in a legal sense. The novel sees what the law in 1955 was determined not to see, what Nabokov saw in this range of locomotions: the motives of a child: motives to pursue its sexual pleasure against the law; to embrace what the law could only call its waywardness; to achieve against the law's own patriarchal leanings separation from its parents and also from the state; even the motive unlawfully to drive an adult's motor vehicle in ways we don't expect. Nabokov makes the mystery of childhood motives seen undercover in a dog or a car—and also in the literal legs of Lolita.

First, a hiatus seems to bring us up to date, though it sets the table for returning to Nabokov.

The Innocent Child Who Would Castrate You:
The Revenge of Hard Candy *(2005)*

In *Erotic Innocence*, James Kincaid's magisterial study of "the culture of child-molesting," Kincaid makes a stunning, persuasive claim. He states that Anglo-American culture, with its roots in Victorian perspectives, must be enjoying violations of innocence—or at least the thought of an innocence assaulted—given our passion for child-abuse narratives. In this paradigm, he argues elsewhere, consumers of these narratives get their titillation and their self-righteousness in the same sitting, making for a kind of "pious pornography."[13] By following such stories with an almost frightening appetite, listeners or readers can pin their outrage on a pedophile (for his "failure to be

7. Coy Lolita, iconic Lolita.
From the film *Lolita* (dir. Kubrick, 1962).

8. Startled Humbert staring (at a coy Lolita).
From the film *Lolita* (dir. Kubrick, 1962).

as loving to children as we are") while still encountering a "breached, silent child" (5). As Kincaid informs us, "the blank page" of innocence so appeals to us because it "does not interfere with our projections" (10).

So far in this book, I have been shaving the flip side of this argument, which still confirms it: perhaps we stay focused on safeguarding children because we fear them. Perhaps we are threatened by the specter of their longings that are maddeningly, palpably opaque; their leisure-time activities that often don't include us; and their robust consumer wishes that lessen our control. But if to some degree we confess these threats, we don't confess the threat of innocence itself. The cinematic feature *Hard Candy* does. In fact, this film from 2005 depicts the revenge of the innocent child: the child who isn't going to take it anymore, the child who says to abusive adults, "I am every little girl you ever watched, . . . screwed, killed," as this movie's girl announces. Here it's as if the virtual child (the made-up profile of someone fourteen) that the police use to catch predators (who troll the Internet) peeled off the screen and went to make a catch completely on her own, on behalf of all innocents. This is computer chat coming to life, hardening on both ends. The girl-as-words in an Internet chat room is going to kick the material ass of the words trying to tell her who she is (a sexy baby who is going to like him). This rather simple, elemental notion that innocence now is going to fight back necessitates, however, three different children rolled into one over the course of a feature-length film. There is first the seductive child, willingly, alluringly chatting up strangers in order to trap them; then there is the innocent child, who confronts these strangers when she has them where she wants them; finally, there is the criminal child, who conducts her own vigilante style of justice, who in her aggressions goes beyond merely identifying pedophiles. These three children who are all the same girl appear sequentially, as it were, but imply each other at every turn, as if the camera were catching three girls in synchronic condensation. The innocent child thus appears to get revenge only if supported by her Freudian bookends: her sexual and aggressive selves to the fore. Indeed, this film is rated R: a child who is the age of the child in the film (the innocent child who acts on her own) is not allowed to choose this film by herself.

Yet the film shows "clean" lines in one sense: the visual sense of its modernist chic, especially in terms of its minimal sets and sleek decor. It looks like visual pleasure has been told to go stand against the wall, to *become* at-

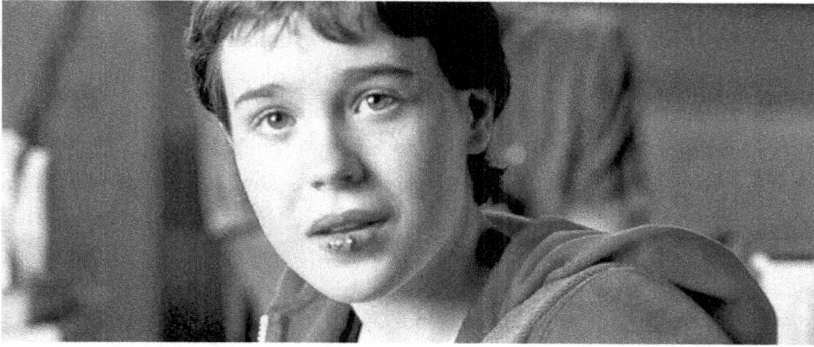

9. Hayley: just a girl who loves chocolate? From the film *Hard Candy* (2005).

tractive walls, and most of all to step away from the child. The credits of the film look drawn by Mondrian: bold red squares and strong black lines. Moreover, red walls that are horizontal rectangles, often with the characters framed against them, are intensely striking in their simplified beauty. They are screens of color for the child's play of anger.

However, our first screen is a computer. "Thonggrrl" and "Lensman" are having a chat:

[He]: "So we should finally hook up, baby?"
[She]: "Not a baby, I keep telling you."
[He]: "I'll have to see for myself. . . ."
[She]: "My big sister could drop me off at Nighthawks."
[He]: "Done. Go shower. Now."
[She]: "Get a little bossy when you're hot, do ya?"

Since we don't actually see a girl typing but only hear the motion of her quick-tapping fingers, the typist could be the police after all. But next, after a full-screen blackout, a fork plunges into a rich dessert: "Mmm, that is so good; I want more." Just as this playfully indulgent Thonggrrl (played by Ellen Page) turns in her chair to see her predator—we don't know she is trapping this man—the camera shows us her wide-eyed expression, along with the chocolate seductively but childishly clinging to her lip (figure 9). We are in the pleasure realm children excel in and that we allow them: the economy of candy.

In fact, the thirty-two-year-old (played by Patrick Wilson) who has come to meet her says to Thonggrrl: "I look at these eyes and I see a girl who reads Zadie Smith, who listens to John Mayer and Coldplay, who loves Monty Python episodes, and who desperately, madly, deeply *wants, needs, longs for*" — and here he pauses for effect — "chocolate," he concludes. This is one of the few invocations of the girl's enjoyment — she who is not played for visual pleasure of the standard female sort. She (her name is Hayley) has freckles, cropped hair (of a baby-butch sort), lips tinged with lipstick but unpierced ears (no piercings at all), a red hooded sweatshirt, and open smile. Jeff (her older counterpart) looks sophisticated, artsy, hip, and they are at a coffee shop called Nighthawks, evoking Edward Hopper, as if to underscore elemental beauty. Like (a) Lolita, Hayley talks Jeff into doing what he wants: to take her to his house. Later, retrospectively, we will regard these scenes in his car — when he seems to be making off with her — as her driving him right into her trap. She has planned to take her revenge at his house.

Once inside his stylish "crib," as she calls it, she plays along with his wish to "shoot" her: "We can see what [your camera] can bring out in me," Hayley offers. But she has perfectly timed her drug. The mickey she has slipped him (girl drugging predator) takes its effect just as she is stripping and jumping on his couch to the rhythm of a backbeat. "Come on, Jeff, shoot me," she cries, goading him with her online bravado. He scolds dizzily: "Listen . . . sit down!" When he wakes up, he's the one seated, tied to a chair. The innocent child — now not the sexy, provocative child — is scolding him: "Didn't you remember what I said about not drinking anything you didn't mix yourself? — that's good advice for anyone." When he inquires: "What the fuck are you doing?," she replies: "That's kind of been my question, Jeff — living in a house filled with pictures of half-naked teenage girls — oh, none of whom you've ever done it with." He says: "You've been stalking me." She retorts: "You've been stalking *me*." Strangely, we notice that the innocent child, with every accusation and every clever comeback, is lateralizing the very gap that she insists divides them. In her moral outrage, she sounds quite adult, dispensing adult advice to adults: "Just because a girl knows how to imitate a woman does not mean she's ready to do what a woman does — I mean you're the grownup here — if a kid is experimenting and says something flirtatious, you ignore it, you don't encourage it; if a kid says 'Hey, let's make screwdrivers,' you take the alcohol away and you don't race them to the next drink." Per-

10. Hayley with Jeff: the innocent child contemplates castration. From the film *Hard Candy* (2005).

haps stranger still, as the story pursues the question of whether Jeff has hurt any girls he has slept with, the child's rants at him become indistinguishable from those any woman would cast at her abuser. The longer they go on, the less they seem to be age-specific. The story of the man you meet at a coffee shop taking you back to his house, then raping you after he's drugged you, is far more gender- than age-determined.

And as the child's revenge gets cooking, we can't hold on to innocence. Now we find ourselves asked to analyze, on many different levels, the popular proposal that the legal system castrate "pedophiles" (almost always synonymous with "predators").[14] For after Jeff breaks free from his chair and Hayley recaptures him, almost suffocates him, Jeff emerges from this second blackout tied to a table with ice on his genitals (figure 10). Hayley has taken off Jeff's pants and plans to castrate her would-be abuser, while she shoots it on videotape (with his camera). This is the second apparatus she has captured (the computer was the first) for the sake of innocence at risk from media. Still, a castration operation is hardly a video piece for a general audience. Or perhaps it is. "Everybody will be safer if I do a little preventive maintenance," Hayley says about the castration, in a line many would probably agree with. But to see her do it, as we seem to see, produces strange effects. How *does* the viewer feel? Is this child (in)sane? She herself asks, "Was I born a . . . little vindictive bitch or did society make me that way?: I go back and forth on that," as those big bands of red intermittently cross our field of vision, as the camera pans them horizontally. When Hayley ends the operation by grinding Jeff's removed testicles in the sink disposal, we may reach our limit. (Or maybe not.)

She goes to take a shower. But the film turns again. Jeff breaks free, as we would expect, and discovers that the operation was a hoax. (The cuts were not the incisions of castration; the numbing from the ice made Jeff imagine pain; and the testicles likely belonged to an animal.) He storms the shower in a rage with a knife. But she has driven this motion, too. She has lured him right to the bathroom. Acting like the police she represents, Hayley repeatedly attacks him with a stun gun. She then calls Jeff's one love, a woman his age, and poses as a member of the LAPD, asking this woman to come to the house. Next she rigs a noose and hauls him into it while he's passed out yet again. Now he has a choice dictated by her: he can either kill himself (and then she'll dump all evidence against him) or she will kill him and write his confession (like a Lolita who has commandeered a pen). In any event, Jeff's one love is on her way, summoned by Hayley posing as a detective.

Yet to make sure that viewers don't tip too strongly toward the pedophile, away from the child, losing their grip on revenge-of-the-innocents, the movie has Jeff now confess to Hayley about a missing girl they've discussed throughout: "I didn't kill her. I just watched." He offers to give up the name of the killer. But there's no need. Hayley has already caught and killed him. (The other guy, too, claims only to have watched.) In gray silhouette, Jeff jumps to his death. Hayley walks away in her red (riding) hood, wolfish and just. Innocence never has looked so strange.

Prelude to Legs: Before There Was Lolita

Before there was Lolita and her strange revenge, there was a portrait of child romance — a fairy-tale version of child sexuality, perfectly lateral, free of abuse. This was Humbert's first great love, at age thirteen, drenched in allusions to Edgar Allan Poe, one of Anglo-American literature's canonical authors to practice child-love outside of literature. So before Lolita there was Annabel Leigh: a girl of Humbert's age and class, with many of his interests ("the softness and fragility of baby animals caused us the same intense pain," 12).

Each as sexually inexperienced as the other, "all at once" they were "madly, clumsily, shamelessly, agonizingly in love with each other," but—and here comes the sudden slash of race—"unable," says Humbert, "even to mate as slum children would have so easily found an opportunity to do" (12)—"slum children" some kind of (racist) oxymoron in this presentation. Caught in the delay of a white wealthy childhood, Humbert and Annabel prove once again how sexual sexual delay can be: "a few feet away from our elders" on the beach, "we would sprawl all morning, in a petrified paroxysm of desire"; "her hand, half-hidden in the sand, would creep toward me"; "then, her opalescent knee would start on a long cautious journey" and they might "graze each other's salty lips" (12). In other words, "these incomplete contacts drove our healthy and inexperienced young bodies to such a state of exasperation that not even the cold blue water, under which we still clawed at each other, could bring relief" (12).

Two "unsuccessful" "trysts" from Humbert's viewpoint round out his profile of his early sexuality, his ironic case of arrested development. Famously, the sexuality scholar John Money, among other scholars, has deemed *interference* with juvenile sex play a cause of pedophilia. According to this theory, the child gets stuck in a juvenile phase he does not grow out of as he ages, and thus he seeks to repeat this phase in spite of his age.[15] In *Lolita*, "my 'Annabel' phase" (14), as Humbert names it, comprises forms of interference strung together. For example, at their first tryst, Annabel and Humbert manage for a moment "to deceive the vicious vigilance of . . . family" and meet each other for a brief encounter "in a nervous and slender-leaved mimosa grove at the back of [her] villa" (14). Here Annabel does get pleasured in a way never described for Lolita: "Her legs, her lovely live legs, were not too close together, and when my hand located what it sought, a dreamy and eerie expression, half-pleasure, half-pain, came over those childish features" (14). (Humbert continues with "her solitary ecstasy" at some length, making the later absence of such descriptions striking.) But when it comes to Humbert's turn—"I gave her to hold in her awkward fist the scepter of my passion" (15)—his sexual "overflowing" is cut off by a cat: "and as we drew away from each other, and with aching veins attended to what was probably a prowling cat, there came from the house her mother's voice calling her, with a rising frantic note" (15). Their second (final) tryst, this one on a beach "in a violet shadow of some red rocks," is likewise interrupted, doubly so by Humbert's use of metaphor and narrative closure: for "I was on my knees, and on the point of possessing my darling, when two bearded bathers, the old man of the sea and his brother, came out of the sea with exclamations of ribald encouragement, and four months later she died of typhus in Corfu" (13), leaving him "haunted . . . ever since" (15).

This is a sexual fairy tale of obstacle. Almost in reverse of the John Money thesis (though it still amounts to a pedophile's arrest), Humbert grows past his dead love object, who is now stopped in time at thirteen, destining him to be an older lover (to have a generational split on his hands) if he would be faithful to this love. Indeed, a nymphet, in Humbert's view, occupies an "island of entranced time," offering to Humbert "a certain distance that the inner eye thrills to surmount" (17). Humbert is thus a distance junkie, attracted now to *interval* in a way that differs from, but also touches on, Mrs. Dalloway's worship of a singular moment in time. And, weirdly, it will happen that Humbert himself will be chased by an interval that overtakes him.

But not before Annabel's legs ride again (to mix the novel's metaphors).

Prelude to Legs, Dogs, and Cars: "Motive" and "Motion" in Child Sexuality

There is much to grasp about these literal legs, especially in the novel's most famous scene, in which Lolita moves her legs in Humbert's lap, thereby causing the pedophile to climax when he makes rhythmic use of her movements. It is not surprising, I will suggest, that Nabokov plays with Lolita's motions as signs of her hidden and hazy intents. Even linguistically there is a point to connecting the terms "motion" and "motive," as if they were some kind of Siamese twins joined at the leg. Both, I have said, share the Latin root, *movere*, for "to move."[16] "Motion" is not just "the action or process of chang[ing] position"; it is also "a prompting from within; an impulse or inclination," says the dictionary. "Motive" is almost indistinguishable: by definition, "an impulse acting as incitement to action"—though this impulse (and, therefore, motive) is variously rendered as an emotion, a desire, or a need (of a physical sort). A motive, then, which we may commonly think of as explanatory in a legal context—what was the motive for that murder?—is more hieroglyphic than we might expect: a mysterious impulse to act, to move.

In fact, in *Lolita*, in dynamics we are going to dissect in chapter 4, sexual desire and criminal motive sit beside each other. To understand Humbert

Humbert's motives for the crime of pedophilia is to explore the cave of his desire: "Why does the way she walks—a child, mind you, a mere child, excite me so abominably? Analyze it. A faint suggestion of turned in toes. A kind of wiggly looseness below the knee prolonged to the end of each foot-fall"; "a bit of adhesive tape across her big toe"; "monkeyish feet!" "I dared stroke her bare leg along the gooseberry fuzz of her shin . . . I laughed and addressed myself to Haze [Lolita's mother] across Lo's legs" (41, 51, 45–46). Since he self-confesses for the length of the book, it would seem as if Lolita can only appear inside his mouth, strapped to his motives, literally broken down on the tip of his tongue: "My sin, my soul. Lo-lee-ta: the tip of the tongue taking a trip of three steps down the palate to tap, at three, on the teeth. Lo. Lee. Ta" (9). But fortunately Nabokov is not satisfied with this. He starts to hide Lolita—and her own competing motives—inside the legs that Humbert loves and the motions he describes but cannot comprehend. Legs and locomotions launch from Humbert's words that rhapsodize Lolita. A leg and a dog on his tongue make her seen—seen, that is, as a moving suspension, an interval of animal, inside his solipsism.

Quite instructively, recent work in the fields of pedagogy and education history has made motion a central concern. Bernadette M. Baker's treatise *In Perpetual Motion* signals this trend.[17] Taking the writings of John Locke, Jean-Jacques Rousseau, Johann Herbart, and G. Stanley Hall as her specific focus (as one might expect for a pedagogy expert), Baker nonetheless finds it crucial to consider thoughts about motion going back to Plato, if we would understand modern views of children. In fact, she asserts that Locke wrote the first modern theory of the child in part by adapting the new mechanical theories forged by Isaac Newton, Locke's close friend. One wants to know for education history, in Baker's estimation, the forerunners to Newton in conceptualizing power. They are, unsurprisingly, Plato, Aristotle, and Aristotelians of various stripes.

The depths of these views are not crucial for *Lolita*, as one might imagine. But the terms put into play—"becoming," "cause," "change," "self-mover," "particle," and "force"—as well as the general movement of this history toward mechanical philosophies are most germane. One begins to realize how subtly but centrally something like motive is implied by diverse philosophies of motion (though Baker doesn't say so) and how the visibility of motion can mark invisible change—issues *Lolita* is bound up with in depicting its child. For example, in Plato's *Timaeus*, movement, though visible and sensory, is only a symbol of something real, pointing to something real and invisible that is behind it. Still, distinctions among different movements stand for crucial differences between and among plants, animals, children, and adults. The ability to self-move is one distinction among these living objects; balance in movement is another. Plants do not self-move, of course, but animals do. Human adults can move themselves and *display* invisible reason by harmonious motions. As Plato puts it (and Baker quotes him): The "best" motion "is that motion which is produced in oneself by oneself, since it is most akin to the movement of thought and of the universe; motion produced by another is inferior; and worst of all is that, whereby, while the body lies inert, its several parts are moved by foreign agents" (86). Plato sees the child as in some ways like the animal, in its often imbalanced movements, its energetic wildness, and its lack of reason — all of which education must address.

As for Aristotle, in his *Physics* he famously makes motion the internal principle of nature and presumes that movement and rest must have a cause. In other words, the evidence of being natural (not being art) is movement and change. Or, as Baker quotes him: "Each of them [natural things] has within itself a principle of motion and of stationariness (in respect of place, or of growth and decrease, or way of alteration)" (88). In fact, Baker states: "For Aristotle, motion mattered time. Without motion, one would not know time had passed" (92). And, importantly, the child with its "potential to become fully human in an adult form" over time is seen as "possessing an internal power or capacity to move or grow" (97). Moreover, Aristotle most directly creates a potential link between motion and motive by implying that where you see motion there is "cause." What moves the mover? he asks intently, requiring finally his well-known notion of a prime mover that starts a chain of movements — so tricky for legal concepts of motive (which we pursue in chapter 4). Nonetheless, in a line so pertinent for *Lolita*, Baker states that "Aristotle's theory of causes could be applied equally to beings as different [from each other] as humans and cats" (94).

The large corpus of work we know as Aristotelianism does not, in Baker's view, change the critical focus on motion she traces to Locke. Though thinkers such as Thomas Aquinas "reworked" "every element of [Aristotle's] *Physics*," "the specificity of such interpretations did not undermine the necessity of concepts of motion and power" (98–99), making this necessity the "one continuity between Plato's, Aristotle's, and Aristotelianism's lines of argument" (100). And though mechanical philosophies of all sorts blossomed in the seventeenth century while Newton was writing his *Principia*, according to Baker, "what they had in common was a view of the universe as foundationally a particle-force relationship" (100). With his four key concepts — inertia, mass, force, and gravity — Newton posits that observable events are composed of "systems of material objects," which are themselves composed of "elementary particles" (101). "Man," for example, is one kind of particle and the child is "one of the smallest particles" (111), yet particles of any kind can be in relations of force with each other. For "all visible, physical things could be subject to the same laws of motion" (102).

Change, once again, was something read in relation to motion. Change in an object could not be seen if it simply maintained its present course, without moving itself through space. Or, as Baker summarizes: "If something moved or stopped moving, one was now looking at a change in state. . . . One was now asking what outside combination of forces had produced the change" (106). And this change was "relational": an object's movement could only be marked in relation to other objects' positions. These "leveling effect[s]," as Baker calls them, which I might call horizontalizing or lateralizing effects, were crucial to Locke's view of human relations in a general sense and to his view of the child specifically. For the child, too, in Locke's conception, possesses "an active, resistive, and mobilizing capacity to apply its own force against other human particles that could also generate force" (121), especially in that "bounded arena" of the family, which makes "so visible how particles could influence each other" (121).

Visible motions indicate otherwise unseen change. All these philosophers, from Plato to Locke, make some version of this assertion. In addition, they variously add reason, time, and cause to the list of the invisibilities motion matters forth. All of which suggests that something we call "motive" — "an impulse acting as incitement to action" — might be read back from the sight of certain motions. But we should not forget emotion, which after all is an attribute of motive. Motion may make it so our emotions are seen as hidden. But what kind of motions, and whose, indeed?

Charles Darwin, in his study *The Expression of the Emotions in Man and Animals*, must deal expressly with this hiddenness in human beings.[18] The focus of his treatise is to grasp how certain facial and bodily movements ever became, over time, the repetitive, almost rote ways that specific emotions (for example, guilt or joy) are expressed by people or a range of animals. Habit turns out to be the answer, he believes: "the movements of [certain] organs" for certain emotions in human beings and animals "have become firmly associated together through long-continued habit" (7). But most intriguingly, in forging this link between people and animals, Darwin must admit that it's hard to see what people feel. In a casual exercise, he gives a series of photographic plates, showing an old man making a range of facial expressions, to a group of people—in fact, "without a word of explanation, to above twenty educated persons of various ages and both sexes, asking them, in each case, by what emotion or feeling the old man was supposed to be agitated" (14). Darwin then reports: "Several of the expressions were instantly recognized by almost everyone, though described not exactly in the same terms. . . . On the other hand, the most widely different judgments were pronounced in regard to some of them" (14). And, indeed, he admits, "If I had examined them without any explanation, no doubt I should have been as much perplexed, in some cases, as other persons have been" (14). In a survey he circulates in 1867, in order to see if emotional expression is fairly uniform across "the races," Darwin asks such questions as, "When a man is indignant or defiant does he frown, hold his body and head erect, square his shoulders and clench his fists?" and "Can guilty, or sly . . . expressions be recognized? though I know not how these can be defined" (16). From thirty-six answers collected by "missionaries or protectors of the aborigines," Darwin concludes that "the same state of mind is expressed throughout the world with remarkable uniformity" (17).

Still, he confesses, "Man himself cannot express love and humility by external signs, so plainly as does a dog, when with drooping ears, hanging lips, flexuous body, and wagging tail, he meets his beloved master" (11). The problem with human beings, then, is threefold: the "movements" of human expression are "often extremely slight, and of a fleeting nature"; our "sympathy" with a "deep emotion" we witness may distract our "close observation"; and "our imagination is [a] . . . still more serious source of error," "for if from the nature of the circumstances we expect to see any expression, we readily imagine its presence" (13). By contrast, Darwin states, "In observing animals, we are not so likely to be biased by our imagination; and we may feel safe that their expressions are not conventional" (17).

Not surprisingly, Darwin himself could not imagine that a dog beside a girl might express the feelings of the girl by its side, as we observed in *The Well of Loneliness*. Nor could he foresee what *Lolita* demonstrates: that certain locomotions—of people on legs or in their cars—might indicate specific emotions, not to mention motives.

Legs over Lap: Girl on the Move

The premier scene of Dolly's active legs is the only sex scene the novel describes—excised, as it happens, from both Kubrick's and Lyne's *Lolitas*.[19] The scene's conceit is Humbert's attempt to climax through Lolita by means of her movements in his lap, all while she remains blissfully unaware, or so he imagines, of his bliss. As he tells it, the visual pleasure of Lolita ("[her] skirt, tight in the bodice, short-sleeved, pink" [57]) gives way quickly to her "monkeyish nimbleness" as they playfully wrestle for control of a certain magazine. She grabs at it, while he whisks it out of reach; she twists, and Humbert notes for us their knot. "Pity," Humbert writes, "no film had recorded the curious pattern, the monogrammic linkage of our simultaneous or overlapping moves" (58). And yet Professor Humbert is a simpleminded reader of this important overlap. He can only break it out on two separate planes: the movement of his motives and what he presumes are her motiveless movements as she moves those curious legs on Humbert's lap:

> She was all over me. Caught her by her thin knobby wrist. . . . She twisted herself free, recoiled, and lay back. . . . Then . . . the impudent child extended her legs across my lap. By this time I was in a state of excitement bordering on insanity. . . . Sitting there, on the sofa, I managed to attune, by a series of stealthy movements, my masked lust to her guileless limbs. . . . and all the while keeping a maniac's inner eye on my distant golden goal, I cautiously increased the magic friction that was doing away . . . [with the] psychologically very friable texture of the material divide (pajamas and robe) between the weight of two sunburnt legs . . . and the hidden tumor of an unspeakable passion. . . . and every movement she made, every shuffle and ripple, helped me to conceal and to improve the secret

system of tactile correspondence between beast and beauty: between my gagged, bursting beast and the beauty of her dimpled body in its innocent cotton frock. (58–59)

To preserve her innocence, he aims "to divert the little maiden's attention," as he puts it. Straining toward the twitching of Lolita's impish legs, lost in the magic friction they provide, Humbert recites "something nicely mechanical": "the words of a foolish song that was then popular — O my Carmen, my little Carmen, something, something . . . the cars, and the bars, and the barmen; I kept repeating this automatic stuff and holding her under its special spell" (59). It seems to him to work. "Lolita had been safely solipsized" (60). Lolita is not perverted but diverted. She is presumably sidetracked by Humbert. Yet precisely in her diversions is a clue to her link to things mechanical, which suggests the presence of a motor force within her. She takes a swerve, as it were, in this scene, overtaking Humbert at the level of her legs but also subtly at the level of his words: "her voice stole and corrected the tune I had been mutilating" (59). As "the corpuscles of Krause were entering the phase of frenzy," Humbert writes, as he approached climax "suspended on the brink of that voluptuous abyss," "I kept repeating chance words after her — barmen, alarmin,' my charmin,' my carmen, ahmen, ahahamen" (60). Humbert, while coming, falls behind Lolita in a prefigurement of his predicament. He, in Plato's disparaging terms, can't self-move (in the usual sense) and his "parts are moved by foreign agents" — the legs of Lolita. In fact, what we come to understand only later is that in this moment, with his Dolly in his lap, Humbert loses her. In her diversions by linguistic wandering, her advance on Humbert at the level of his letters due to her legs, Nabokov has planted his first detective clue to the mystery of Lolita's childhood sexuality and its motive forces — all while allowing them to keep to themselves.

Motion is what we are reading in this scene: motion remembered by a recollecting Humbert who describes it as he "read" it. And so we get her motion in the form of his reading. But what motive is implied by her movements? Humbert thinks her innocence hinges on this reading. At a minimum, do her motions that are themselves relational (marked in relation to his positions) indicate any change in their relation? Dramatically, they do. (Un)knowingly, she has sexually pleasured him, which changes everything. She, in Baker's summary of Newton, is "a force [that] . . . causally affect[s] another in a bounded network of impulse interactions" (110). But Humbert aims to read her as "innocent shanks," "young weight," a "dimpled body in its innocent . . . frock" (60, 59). To him she is an innocence he rubs himself against. As for her motions, he reads them as mindless: "her legs twitched a little"; "there she lolled . . . almost asprawl . . . losing her slipper, rubbing the heel of her slipperless foot in its sloppy anklet" (59). Indeed, especially since they come from a child, they would seem imbalanced and wild in Plato's view. What moves the mover, in Aristotle's sense? We don't at all know if Lolita has a motive (a desire, emotion, or physical need) in a singular sense at this time, but if she has a motive (of any sort at all) it is an active invisibility in this scene. The scene proves Darwin's point: it's hard to know what people feel. If Humbert weren't narrating his temporal progress toward his "distant golden goal," could we reliably read it from his face or his adjustments in posture or position? A dog reaching climax could not be so deceptive in being so demure. Could a young girl?

The Dog and Car Trap: How the Girl Drives You

There are cunning clues—involving dogs and cars—to a girl's motives as we move from Humbert's lap. En route to these clues, Nabokov, I have said, amps up both Lolita's harm and agency at the same time, so that, as Humbert's brutality increases, Lolita's motions become more visible. This dynamic is loudly hinted at by the end of the lap scene. Just before the climax, Nabokov has Humbert running his hand up Lolita's leg to pause at "a yellowish-violet bruise on her lovely . . . thigh"—before "I crushed out against her left buttock the last throb of the longest ecstasy man or monster had ever known" (60–61). It seems as if Lolita, abused against her knowledge, as some might say, has been made to cause effects in which she has no share: "Blessed be the Lord," Humbert narrates, "she had noticed nothing!" (61). Are there clues suggesting otherwise? "'Oh, it's nothing at all,' she cried with a sudden shrill note in her voice," as Humbert's thumb presses past the bruise to the "hollow of her groin," "and she wiggled, and squirmed, and threw her head back, and her teeth rested on her glistening underlip as she half-turned away" (61). Actually, the clues themselves surround the bruise in the form of motions—squirming, wiggling, even half-turning—we struggle to read.

Memorably, her agency emerges invisibly in the second sex scene — the scene withheld from the reader's view, which Humbert simply says took place between 6 and 6:15 a.m.[20] At the Enchanted Hunters Hotel, where enraptured Humbert has decided to drug her (again, to keep her innocent) before he rapes her, Lolita defies this plan in store for her. Not only does she suddenly awaken; she suggests an act that she whispers in his ear. Though she's suggesting the movements of "sex," it clearly appears, her motives are unclear by Humbert's report. In fact, he seems almost oddly incurious about why she moves him toward his wish. He only notes Lolita's disconnection from adults, which he flatly describes as mechanical, in one sense, and animal, in another: "She saw the stark act merely as part of a youngster's furtive world, unknown to adults. What adults did for purposes of procreation was no business of hers. My life was handled by little Lo . . . as if it were an insensate gadget unconnected with me. . . . But really these are irrelevant matters; I am not concerned with so-called 'sex' at all. Anybody can imagine those elements of animality" (133–34). Even in Humbert's telling, however, the tables are turned in two important ways: "it was she who seduced me" (132) and "I was not even her first lover" (135). Now we learn of Lolita's "sapphic diversions" with girls and her presumed coaching in kissing by "a little Lesbian" one year before her intercourse with Charlie at Camp Q — coitus possibly motivated by her camaraderie with Barbara, a fellow camper whose name she is calling out in her sleep the night Humbert drugs her.

Yet the dialectic of harm and agency presses on. Part One ends on the note of her harm. Driving away from the fateful hotel, preparing to tell nubile Lolita her mother is dead, Humbert feels "as if I were sitting with the small ghost of somebody I had just killed" (140); and as she "said I had torn something inside her . . . we almost ran over some little animal or other that was crossing the road with tail erect" (141). Sobbing after hearing of her mother's demise, Lolita "[makes] it up very gently" with Humbert: "You see," he writes in a finalizing line, "she had absolutely nowhere else to go" (142). So begins the presentation of Lolita as a battered (childish) wife.[21] At the very least, the abuse images Humbert offers cross over into codes that define domestic violence. At one point he holds Lolita hard, hurts her badly, and fears her wrist might snap; at another, he reports, "I ripped her shirt off, I unzipped the rest of her. I tore off her sandals. Wildly, I pursued the shadow of her infidelity" (215); at yet another, "Without a word I delivered a tremendous backhand cut that caught her smack on her hot hard little cheekbone" (227); he even metaphorizes her as a "sweat-stained distracted cringing trained animal" with himself as "tamer" (169). Directly suggesting her training in wifeliness, Humbert later offers Lolita a "trousseau" as restitution for all that he's done to her (278). And readers may recall the end of the lap scene where Humbert decides to finish the ditty he's been garbling to Lolita: "O my Carmen, my little Carmen / . . . . And, O my charmin,' our dreadful fights / And the something town where so gaily, arm in / Arm, we went, and our final row, / And the gun I killed you with, O my Carmen, / The gun I am holding now. (Drew his .32 automatic, I guess, and put a bullet through his moll's eye.)" (61–62). In other words, after Humbert's climax, a woman dies, though she does not come.

In monetary terms, Lolita is both the fifties wife and consumer child wrapped up together. In fact, when Humbert is plying Lolita with presents he hopes will lure her into tenderness, the girl could just as easily be a wife before his bounty. And as dreamily as Humbert watches the motions of the girl toward the trap he sets for her, so does Lolita fall under its spell: "Oh, what a dreamy pet! She walked up to the open suitcase as if stalking it from afar, at a kind of slow-motion walk . . . (. . . were we both plunged in the same enchanted mist?) She stepped up to it, lifting her rather high-heeled feet rather high, and bending her beautiful boy-knees while she walked through dilating space with the lentor of one walking under water or in a flight dream. Then she raised by the armlets a copper-colored, charming and quite expensive vest" (120). This moneyed lure is bad news for Humbert, nonetheless. If it marks her ceding of control on one level, it also marks her independence on another. She is not in thrall to her enchanted hunter. She is under the spell of money and in thrall to advertisements (as I suggested in my introduction): "She believed, with a kind of celestial trust, any advertisement or advice that appeared in *Movie Love* or *Screen Land* — Starasil Starves Pimples, or 'You better watch out if you're wearing your shirttails outside your jeans, gals, because Jill says you shouldn't.' . . . She it was to whom ads were dedicated: the ideal consumer, the subject and object of every foul poster" (148). Here the foulness that Humbert often claims for himself finds a far more efficient force in a source outside him. And it's worth remembering that Quilty is a figure that Dolly knows in part from cigarette ads. Moreover, Lolita stays with her abuser for the reason many wives do: she can't afford to leave. Money in this way represents Humbert's extreme vulnerability, in his abuse, to the one he abuses: "she might accumulate sufficient cash to run away" (185). Humbert must increasingly bribe his child-wife if he would get sex without use of force: "I might fondly demand an additional kiss, or even a whole collection of assorted caresses, when I knew she coveted very badly some item of juvenile amusement. . . . O Reader! Laugh not, as you imagine me, on the very rack of joy noisily emitting dimes and quarters . . . like some sonorous, jingly and wholly demented machine vomiting riches" (184). (Once again, Dolly is forcing Humbert's lust down mechanical paths, against his will.)

Germane to issues of juvenile justice, which we explored at the start of this book, Humbert's only power over willful Lolita, which he must continually impress upon her, is the threat of public welfare, ironically enough. Actually, Humbert describes this irony in almost the exact terms used by Anthony M. Platt fourteen years later in his benchmark study *The Child Savers: The Invention of Delinquency.* Humbert says: "So I go to jail. Okay. . . . But what happens to you, my orphan? . . . You become the ward of the Department of Public Welfare. . . . I don't know if you have ever heard of the laws relating to dependent, neglected, incorrigible and delinquent children. . . . [You] will be given a choice of various dwelling places, all more or less the same, the correctional school, the reformatory, the juvenile detention home, or one of those admirable girls' protectories. . . . You will be analyzed and institutionalized, my pet. . . . This is the situation, this is the choice. Don't you think that . . . Dolores Haze had better stick to her old man?" (151). No wonder Lolita needs hidden motions around this "choice"—the kind of lack of choice that *Hard Candy*'s Hayley is getting revenge for when she is giving Jeff his bad options.

Returning now to Lolita's hidden motives, we find our second clue among dogs (her legs were a clue as much as a question). If we read for dogs, bundles of motion each time we see them—we will find clues to Lolita's intents. We know that the dog is a clue to her motives because Humbert tells us in an aside: "Every once in a while I have to remind the reader of my appearance much as a professional novelist, who has given a character of his some mannerism or a dog, has to go on producing that dog or that mannerism every time the character crops up in . . . the book" (104). The dog is a sign that Quilty is lurking about Lolita and that she makes secret diversions toward him, moving as a dolly through the metaphor of dog. In the Enchanted Hunters' Hotel, Lolita, we read, "sank down on her haunches to caress a pale-faced, blue-freckled, black-eared cocker spaniel swooning on the floral carpet under her hand" — "as who would not, my heart," Humbert adds (117). With projective sympathy, Humbert can read the spaniel's swoon as twinning his own. The movement of the dog is how he feels. What he can't see is how doglike Lolita is here caressing a figure for her motion, since she will swoon (is already swooning?) for Clare Quilty, who is at this hotel.[22] A dog has already figured her diversions from Humbert's machinations, for when Humbert called Camp Q to tell Lolita he was marrying her mother, a dog was distracting her: "I had to repeat it twice because something was preventing her from giving me her attention. . . . 'When is the wedding? Hold on a sec, the pup — That pup here has got hold of my sock. Listen-' . . . and I realized as I hung up that a couple of hours at that camp had been sufficient to blot out with new impressions that image of handsome Humbert Humbert from little Lolita's mind" (72). Specifically, a dog is sufficient for this blotting.

Later, on their car trip west, Humbert panics that Lolita has escaped, only to find her cavorting with a dog, who in retrospect appears to be Quilty's: "Oh Lolita! There she was playing with a damned dog, not me. . . . but suddenly something in the pattern of her motions, as she dashed this way and that . . . struck me . . . there was an ecstasy, a madness about her frolics that was too much of a glad thing." We can't help but notice how Nabokov makes the "madness" of Dolly's "motions," her frolics with the dog, precisely the sign of her sexual motives, as he makes the sight of Quilty's covered penis reminiscent of a beast (as in the lap scene he had made Humbert's). For next, a bather "half-concealed" by tree shade catches Humbert's eyes with "his tight wet black bathing trunks bloated and bursting with vigor where his great fat bullybag was pulled up and back like a padded shield over his reversed beasthood. . . . And I . . . knew that the child . . . knew he was looking, enjoyed the lechery of his look and was putting on a show of gambol and glee [with Quilty's dog]" (237). Indeed, Humbert figures Lolita's disobedience to his own wishes in doglike terms, giving her resistive force (in Newtonian and Lockean understandings) a visible (e)motion he conveys to readers. Not only is she "my reluctant pet" but "she would be, figuratively speaking, wagging her tiny tail, her whole behind in fact as little bitches do—while some grinning stranger accosted us and began a . . . conversation" (164).

For all of Humbert's obvious animus against Lolita's canine connections ("I loathe dogs," Humbert says in passing), we must recall that a neighborhood dog enters the story as Humbert's ally. The dog is like Lolita's vibrant legs in Humbert's lap. The dog brings about what Humbert clearly plots but can't bring himself to put into motion: the murder of Charlotte. ("I just couldn't make myself do it!" 87.) It is the dog who chases the car that swerves and kills Lolita's mother. The dog is the prime mover, in this case, the one who "had finally run to earth" (98) one of the cars he loved to chase; though it is the car and the driver of the car that seem a nearer cause. Hence the driver makes a diagram relating several causes, "with all kinds of impressive arrows and dotted lines in varicolored inks" (102): "Mrs. H. H.'s trajectory was illustrated at several points by a series of those little outline figures— doll-like wee career girl or WAC—used in statistics as visual aids. Very clearly and conclusively, this route came into contact with a boldly traced sinuous line representing two consecutive swerves—one which the Beale car made to avoid the Junk dog (dog not shown), and the second, a kind of exaggerated continuation of the first, meant to avert the tragedy. A very black cross indicated the spot where the trim little outline figure had at last come to rest on the sidewalk" (102). Here is the poor man's Lockean analysis, minus David Hume's familiar billiard balls that he used to illustrate associated causes. In *Lolita*'s case, these motions add up to a detailed diagram of Humbert's wish: his wish to kill his wife, which a dog and car now stand for in his mind (and his readers' too), along with the visibly hidden clue "(dog not shown)."

What these events now directly enable is Humbert's abduction, also by car, of his Lolita, his pet, from Camp Q. Yet though the dog seems to offer fulfillment of Humbert's desire, bringing fake father and daughter together, the dog is like Lolita on her legs, in a car, or just on a sex drive: a body with its own intents that may remain obscure. Why do dogs—but do only some dogs—run down cars? The answer to the question that is chasing Humbert's tale—what drives Lolita, and who is chasing Humbert in the car that drives behind him?—is not so much Quilty as it is something hazier. The answer to the detective mystery is the *mystery* of childhood sexuality, with its visible but hieroglyphic motions. A perceptible hieroglyph is what the dog and car figure forth. They mark the motions of a motive that's obscure but is *seen* as opaque. They are the "vehicles" allowing the child to ride as she chooses by means of a sidetrack. For the dog and car moving Humbert toward his wish are captured by Lolita, Humbert's "car pet," just as she earlier in the lap scene overtook Humbert's "mechanical" use of the Carmen ditty, with its pun on cars. She is not a carpet (speaking of puns) he can walk (or drive) all over.

Nabokov, to be sure, plays with the car throughout his novel as a kind of closet for tabooed relations. It is not merely the handy vehicle of Humbert's abduction. The car is a "bounded arena" for particle-force relations between a man and a wayward girl—and an arena for their relations with outside forces. The novel imagines legal relations, for example, largely in the form of transportation violations. Every traffic infraction provides Lolita with the chance to frighten Humbert with the thought that she might talk to the cops. Hence her wonderful quips in the car that undermine Humbert's attempts at control: "Green light, you dope"; "You got a flat, mister"; "Drive on." At many moments, all the transgressive energy of incest and the pedophilic urge is transferred to the car: "'Easy!' cried Lo, lurching forward, as an accursed truck in front of us, its backside carbuncles pulsating, stopped at a crossing. If we did not get to the hotel soon . . . I felt I would lose all control over the Haze jalopy with its ineffectual wipers and whimsical brakes" (116). The car is its own eerie suspension of legal relations as long as it keeps suspension in motion, allowing for Humbert's "internal combustion."[23] His pedophilia is autoerotic to the point of excluding the child and her diversions—until her diversions come back to haunt him, showing Humbert forgetting the arc of his own plot: dogs chase cars.

Indeed, when he first thinks a car might be tailing them, he begins to worry a detective is behind them, chasing them slowly in hazy pursuit. (He doesn't know that Quilty and Lolita are conspiring to move him to places they are choosing.) Thus his paranoia *is* a sign of Haze. Each of Humbert's paranoid feelings marks the girl-child's sexuality, as it is discernibly felt as a motion creeping up behind him. (A detective plot is truly chasing his confessional.) And more than being chased by a genre, Humbert is being chased by an interval, as if "the distance" (between a man's age and a girl's age) he "thrills to surmount"—that he himself defines *as* pedophilia—is taking revenge and menacing him: "But next day, like pain in a fatal disease . . . there it was again behind us, that glossy red beast. . . . as if there were some spell cast on that interspace, a zone of evil mirth and magic, a zone whose very precision and stability had a glass-like virtue that was almost artistic. . . . and no matter how and where we drove, the enchanted interspace slid on intact, mathematical. . . . And all the time I was aware of a private blaze on my right: her joyful eye, her flaming cheek" (219).

Humbert, in fact, may drive Lolita all over the country, but, as the novel in a thousand ways indicates, Dolly is now driving Humbert from behind — as she sits beside him. Communicating constantly with Quilty who follows their every move a few lengths back, she is wrapped up in Quilty and the car that's chasing Humbert. For it's the great joke of the plot to have Humbert's pet be in league with Mr. Quilty, her preferred pedophile, who with Lolita's knowledge and help steers sad Humbert to a predetermined terminus in the state of Utah, where both Dolly and her Quilty disappear. The queer child's agency in *Lolita* is, by definition, a detective fiction that defeats the motives of a self-accusing narrative. This way of answering a mystery with a mystery — children's motives appear in the hieroglyphics of their motions — makes the more compelling twin of Humbert Humbert not Clare Quilty but the law itself. Like Nabokov's pedophile, who is himself shockingly incurious about Lolita's wishes, American legal constructions of the child in 1955 rob children of their motives. To the motives of the child and the wish of children to move in certain ways, even sexual ways, justice has been blind. And yet there is a world to see inside a leg — or perhaps a dog.

Spoiled Pleasure, or How to See a Girl

Standard in cinema, there is the leg of visual pleasure, a woman's sexy shapely leg — even when liquid in its allurement, generally still. More often than not, it is bordered by cloth, which can seductively set off its bareness.

At a key point in film-theory history, Laura Mulvey told us we are perverts at the movies. We sit in darkness like Peeping Toms, peering in the window of the cinema screen, watching while beautiful women are stilled in states of undress.[24] What classic Hollywood cinema offers us in such a moment, Mulvey informs us, is visual pleasure that matches society's preexisting fascination with the female form. So compelling is this pleasure that, when it's on the screen, it tends to stop the progress of narrative itself, freezing the action for this important moment of erotic contemplation. Outside these moments, the male protagonist, who inhabits three-dimensional space, moves the story forward.

Mulvey's theory (1975) is so old now, and so exploded, rightly so, from so many angles, especially from the angles of race and queerness, which present serious dilemmas for her views. Yet, as if it's been given new life, Mulvey's theory reveals the quandary of the sexual girl on the cinema screen. To grasp how Mulvey reveals this quandary, we must investigate the heart of her views: cinema's offering of a visual enthrallment that attaches to an optic arrest. That is to say, in order for the viewer to attach to the *screen*, absent of objects, "he" must be given a worthy lure. An arresting image is the key to this allurement. And, says Mulvey, it tends to be a woman in beautiful arrest—or in graceful motion (walking, dancing, fluidly gesturing) meant to add to her allure.[25] This supposition offered by Mulvey, we should recall, was a striking transformation of film theory's focus on filmic fetish as put forward by Christian Metz in his seminal essay "The Imaginary Signifier."[26] What Mulvey did was to gender this fetish—she is famous for this move— but also to make it a matter of motion, or really nonmotion, I would suggest. Implied by her theory is the assumption that a woman offers visual pleasure by being a form of motion stilled—something at odds with the body of a child, as we've seen in *Lolita*.

It is worth recalling what Mulvey surely borrows from theorists like Metz. To boil it down: she builds upon his notions of fantasy, perversion, and, of course, fetishism. Metz, to begin, strongly reminds us that the cinema's signifier is itself "imaginary" in a bold sense. True, it takes a material form— in its visual and auditory images—but these *images* are closer to "fantasy" (Metz's word) than, for example, the signifiers of the theatrical stage that are real objects in "real . . . space" (409). Moreover, this fantasy, as Metz calls it, involves its viewer in "perceptual passions" (420). "I am in the film by my look's caress" (417), as he puts it, and I am caressing unconsenting objects that are prey to my fixation (423). As Metz proceeds to say, "cinematic scopophilia," "with its inevitable keyhole effect," "which is 'non-authorized' in the sense I have just pointed out, is authorized however by the mere fact of its institutionalization" (425). In other words, moviegoing is socially sanctioned perversion on a mass scale, enhanced by the "cinemas of big cities, with their highly anonymous clientele entering or leaving furtively, in the dark, in the middle of the action" (425). Or as Metz expresses it: "The cinema is based on the legalization and generalization of the prohibited practice": "going to the cinema is one licit activity among others with its place in the admissible pastimes of the day or the week, and yet that place is a 'hole' in the social cloth, a *loophole* opening on to something slightly more crazy, slightly less approved than what one does the rest of the time" (425). What is the "fetish" at the heart of this perversion? Something less sexy than all of this might sound: it is the "prowess" of the camera itself: "the technical equipment of the cinema": "the machinery that is carrying them away": the "exploit" of an image the camera produces that "arrests" the "fetishist" caressing the screen (431).

Mulvey found a lot to work with here. In my estimation, the story of her gendering the fetish of the image should be more specific. Mulvey, I would say, ties a movie's mechanical prowess to its production of a woman's-body-*not*-in-motion. It is film's capacity to arrest a woman—in the form of arresting beauty—that makes its fetish particularly powerful. Mulvey says as much when she reminds us that film's visual fascination is based on "pre-existing patterns" of allure, which are set in the social cement of a "formal beauty" and "erotic pleasure" that are tethered to "the image of a woman" (483–85). Hence, Mulvey's well-known assertions: "In a world ordered by sexual imbalance, pleasure in looking has been split between active/male and passive/female. . . . In their traditional exhibitionist role women are simultaneously looked at and displayed. . . . from pin-ups to strip-tease, from Ziegfeld to Busby Berkeley. . . . Her visual presence tends to . . . freeze the flow of action in moments of erotic contemplation. . . . 'What counts is what the heroine provokes . . . in . . . mak[ing] [the hero] act the way he does'" (487–88). In herself, she is image, "to-be-looked-at-ness," an "icon," "an illu-sion cut to the measure of desire" (493). The woman is balanced and grace-ful movement, if she is indeed movement at all, for motion, it would seem, compromises beauty.

Here, then, is the quandary for anyone depicting a sexual girl on the cinema screen. Mulvey's theory makes us ask: how can the girl offer visual pleasure without looking like the figure of a woman and therefore ceasing to be seen as a child? What devolves from how the body of a child (a female child) is captured by the camera and put on-screen? Can we ever *see* a sexual girl? This was the dilemma for Stanley Kubrick and Adrian Lyne who, thirty years apart, each filmed *Lolita*. Kubrick in 1962 used an actress shy of sixteen (this was Sue Lyon), while in 1996 Lyne took up this challenge with Dominique Swain, age fourteen, to depict Lolita, who is twelve in the novel. In neither case, of course, could a twelve-year-old play the fictional youngster from the late forties. Despite this common obstacle, Kubrick and Lyne part ways, nonetheless, precisely on this matter of a sexual girl. Each man's take on this issue, moreover, can be perceived from how he films a female's motions.[27]

Telling in Kubrick, the camera offers the usual look as it looks at Lolita. She is standard visual pleasure as we gaze through Humbert's eyes that stare at her on her bed of grass or catch her on the dance floor making patterned motions. Dolly runs like a Hitchcock actress—Grace Kelly–like—all skirt, no legs, with lilt and sway. (Needless to say, never is Kubrick's Dolly compared to dogs or cars.) Even her intriguing seduction of Humbert with an egg over easy (the only such scene I have seen in the movies) looks more sultry than energetic or vulgar. These looks normalize Lolita and Humbert. Lolita's offering of a visual pleasure, especially the sexualized sort Mulvey claims, is the film's *obedience* to required morals. Lolita's sexiness guarantees that there is no pedophilia to see. Even if the film had given us the lap scene or the novel's explicit reference to sex at the hotel, which of course it doesn't, it wouldn't really matter.[28] Our eyes are telling us that she is not a child: she is a sexy cinematic still. In a hotel scene, we see Lolita, perfectly arranged in a tidy dress and high-heeled shoes, legs crossed in equipoise, lying on a bed (figure 11). Moreover, since we get our visual pleasure just how we expect it, Humbert looks as though he consumes her body normally, just as we do. We are all just the usual perverts who go to the movies for our pleasure. There is nothing special about Humbert Humbert. In fact, there is a curious effect on the movie when Lolita is the obvious image of erotic arrest. Given that the narrative due to her sexiness can't go anywhere near pedophilia, the queerness endemic to this topic is pumped out into the eddied pools of Quilty: into those long campy riffs by Peter Sellers in which he flirts homosexually with Humbert or even with desk clerks. In a rambling scene, Quilty says to Humbert: "I'm not really with someone, I'm with you. . . . I noticed your face and I said to myself 'there's a guy with the most normal-looking face' . . . because I'm a normal guy. It would be great for two normal-looking guys like us to get together and talk about world events—you know, in a normal

11. Lolita for the camera: optic arrest. From the film *Lolita* (dir. Kubrick, 1962).

sort of way. . . . I don't have any children, or boys, or little tall girls or—I'm not even . . . are you married? . . . maybe I was thinking you want to get away from your wife for awhile . . . I get so carried away being so normal and everything." Closeted gayness works overtime to mark the space of another perversion the film won't let us hear or see.

Lyne, by contrast, gives us a pedophile and a child. Not incidentally, he shows fidelity to dogs and cars, whatever he or his viewers make of them. As Professor Humbert arrives by car to meet Lolita at the Haze home, a yapping little dog runs out to chase the vehicle, causing the car to swerve dramatically, knocking Humbert noticeably off balance. The dog makes other important appearances, including as the cause of Charlotte's fatal accident and as Quilty's pet on-leash at the hotel, where we see Lolita get down on her "haunches," as the novel describes, to caress this cocker spaniel (figure 12).[29] The car, for its part, and the cryptogrammic game between cars, are beautifully rendered along lonely roads, where Humbert glimpses ghostliness and an eerie threat in his rearview mirror. The retro bodies of the cars themselves, especially Quilty's car with its gleam and bulk, suggestively lend the visual pleasure we look for in women, thus telling us to attend to their seductions. But, as I say, it's unclear what specific links between Lolita and

12. Lolita greeting a figure for herself. From the film *Lolita* (dir. Lyne, 1996).

these motions Lyne or his viewers finally make. Lyne's fidelities don't guarantee that a girl appears as a girl on the screen.[30]

Lyne rather uses one clever way to make a girl apparent. The way to show a girl is carefully to spoil our visual pleasure—literally to give it for a certain interval, then take it away (figures 13, 14, and 15). Take it away by showing a retainer in the onset of a smile; filming Lolita fishing her skirt out of her bottom as she enters a hotel; or depicting Lolita in motion—the frenetic kind of motion we cannot associate with beautiful women. (Lyne uses all these strategies repeatedly.) This development in reverse—making a girl by spoiling a woman, rolling back a woman in forward frames—makes the girl (the sexual girl) the spoiling of our pleasure in our own perversion. One could put it this way: Adrian Lyne, feminist nemesis, makes us Mulvey's perverts for a moment, makes us feel the comfort of our usual perversion, our Playboy-channel gaze as it extends to the beauty of a girl, before he rips the rug of our perversion out from under us, so that he may offer a sexual child.[31] Lolita can be sexual on her own terms only if, definitively, and also finally, we can't accuse ourselves of perversion. In this case, we can't—or at least it would be hard. Humbert is the pervert of whom we ask: how can you find yourself attracted to that, since we cannot? Robbed in this way of our well-rehearsed shame, which is to say of our usual pleasure, we are left to

13. Wet Lolita.
From the film *Lolita* (dir. Lyne, 1996).

14. Lolita with retainer: spoiling a smile, revealing a girl.
From the film *Lolita* (dir. Lyne, 1996).

15. Lolita and her bottom: vulgar Lolita, being a girl. From the film *Lolita* (dir. Lyne, 1996).

contemplate how the child appears in the queerness of time. She appears to us as a moving suspension in an interval of animal and as a kind of temporal rollback, spoiling our sense of how we cause harm. No wonder Lyne's *Lolita* was nearly banned from theaters. The spoiling of our pleasure in our self-accusations, a spoiling that takes place at the hands of a child, a child who is queered as a metaphoric animal, making a leg lie down with a dog, is the kind of hotbed we're still afraid to see.

CHAPTER 4 Feeling Like Killing?

Murderous Motives of the Queer Child

The matter of children's motives is especially pressing and confounding for the law. Beyond whether children can be said to have motives in a sexual sense, there is the matter of criminal motives. If a child murders, can s/he have intended it, according to the law? The question of these motives even takes us into dreams. What after all does a murder fulfill—or perhaps spoil—in terms of a wish?

Lolita, already in 1955, was sounding the depths of the sexual child by making the mystery of her motives seen precisely as the mystery of her motions. Lolita's locomotions—apparent as hidden, or at least folded into the movements of legs, dogs, and cars—are the novel's signs that *Lolita* has a sidetrack. A sexual girl grows alongside but strikingly apart from the arc of her (fake) father's future for her. For Humbert cannot see, until it is too late, the child's threat growing to the side of his own. How to read a sidetrack is one of the lessons Nabokov's novel teaches, as do the works we have now examined by James, Woolf, Barnes, and Hall. Each in its way shows how to read a sidetrack and respect a little haze: man/boy masochism or girls' access to themselves through their dogs.

In the case of murder, this haze does not subside. Can a child be threatening? Or ever feel like killing? Truman Capote and Peter Jackson, in their depictions of well-known murders, scrutinize these questions. In fact, they are two sophisticated

CHARGED WITH THE DRAINAGE OF DREAMS, THE POLICE CATCH THEM IN THEIR FILTERS.
—JEAN GENET, *QUERELLE*

thinkers on children's motives and the problem of motive in a general legal sense. They show why the "homosexual" child and the normative child (that is, the queerly innocent child) can symbolize motive's conceptual binds — how it's a thorn in the law's own side.

(E)motions, or Feeling beside Oneself

Both of the girls hit their victim with a brick until her skull was badly broken. Using a purse to hide the brick, the girls then swung it by means of a stocking. The other killers, a pair of men with a different set of victims, had cut one throat with a hunting knife, then shot the other victims, one through a pillow, at point-blank range.

Swinging a brick; holding a knife against human skin; pulling a trigger against a head knowing you can't reverse that pull. Who, if anyone, feels like killing? What, if anything, is this feeling? And what kind of feeling is a motive for murder? A set of densities thickening motive — also thickening the queerness of children — surrounds these two different scenes of slaughter, both from the fifties, and their portrayals in two famous texts: Truman Capote's *In Cold Blood* (1965) and Peter Jackson's *Heavenly Creatures* (1994). Motive is the mystery behind these murders, the clotted matter clinging to them — intriguingly so since motive, in each case, was shared by two killers working in tandem. How, it was asked, could two individuals, in the same moment, reach the same rage?

With Capote's *In Cold Blood*, the people of Kansas had good reason to feel almost cheated on the question of motive, to turn their suspicions back on themselves, locking their doors against each other. Capote, quoting a detective about the murder of the Clutters in 1959 (four family members, one whose throat was gruesomely slit), notes that it "was a psychological accident, virtually an impersonal act; the victims might as well have been killed by lightning."[1] The detective is referring to the fact that the Clutters were killed by two men who had never met them, who drove hundreds of miles to kill them with no apparent payoff in the form of robbery, though, as it later came to be known, the men mistakenly believed they would find a buried safe on the family farm. This circumstance "failed," says Capote, "to satisfy [the FBI's] sense of . . . design," which, according to the details of the murders, seemed to hinge on rage or revenge (245). That is to say, the bureau's agents could not discover a form for the feelings that they at last uncovered.

Jackson's *Heavenly Creatures* mines a murder five years prior to the murder of the Clutters. This was the killing in New Zealand of a mother, committed by her daughter and the daughter's "special" friend, who desperately sought to live together. Cannily, Jackson's film makes the meaning of motive rotate among the definitions the dictionary offers: "an emotion," "a desire," "a physical need."[2] On the latter count, there is even motion, as the film displays the two girls' almost inexplicable, inexhaustible movements on the screen. The word *motive*, as we've seen, comes from the Latin word *movere* meaning "to move." If a motive is a motion propelling an action, what kind of motion, exactly, is it? How far back in the chain of explanation must we go to capture motive? How many other motives (or simple drives toward motions) lie beneath motives? Motive is the mystery inside the explanation, especially since the lawyers defending the girls made a plea for "joint insanity"—the girls moved to madness at the same time.

Another factor makes motive dense and the question of pairs of killers fraught. Each of these artists, Capote and Jackson, gives us a portrait of a queer child—a seemingly protohomosexual child (Perry in one text, Pauline in the other), paired with a seemingly normative partner (Dick, Juliet). And both artists, Capote and Jackson, through the queer child, end up displaying unforeseen motives that don't sound like feeling-like-killing at all: for Jackson, the two girls' wish to run through a manicured garden, or down a long dock, or up a staircase to flop on a bed in a beautiful room; for Capote, the wish, felt or faked by two different men, to sing on a stage or drive down to Mexico dreaming of gold. Here, in fact, is the heart of my claim: it's the *specificities* of queer children (children who include the normative child) that make them emblematic of a general problem: the problem of motive as a form of explanation when it is more often a living, growing, cubist form of dramatically mismatched feelings and movements from different temporalities and multilayered sideways inclinations. If motive is a feeling, then the urge to kill is often made from feelings that bear no resemblance to the feelings of the killing itself when performed. The feeling of running through a garden or digging for gold is not the feeling of smashing a head with a swinging brick. One set of feelings may motivate the killing that then leads to the other set of feelings—a pack of completely different feelings that the killer had perhaps never sought, and that perhaps spoil the motivating feelings. Hence, a motive, many-layered as it is, may not seem like any of its elements at the point of murder, because of their spoiling.[3]

Children symbolize motive's layerings for a striking reason: for better or worse, in the figure of the child, in the context of murder, we tend to take motives back to unspoiled, childlike feelings, and thus we undo murderous motives altogether, even as we seek their origins in childhood. For as we know, children are those peculiar legal creatures (especially in the Anglo-American fifties) who are generally deemed by the law not to have a motive to harm, or, most especially, any rational intent to kill. Other motor forces and other banks of feeling quite aside from blood lust may animate their actions, we seem to believe, but these feelings and motives *in themselves* can't add up to a feeling-like-killing.[4] In this way, our sentimental view of the child makes our model of motive *more* complex, makes for a model of surreptitious sideways growth (for motive and the child) that, as a culture, we otherwise deny.

The protohomosexual child symbolizes another significant feature of motive. Both have the features of a backward birth. Legally, there cannot be a motive to murder until there is a killing—or an attempt, or a conspiracy, to kill. A motive to murder is technically, legally, born backward from the point of (attempted) death. Yet by the time it is born *at* death, the motive to kill has itself expired. No one exemplifies this problematic better than the protohomosexual child. As I laid out at the start of this book: such a child, with no established forms to hold itself, or explain itself, in the public, legal field, is like an explanation unavailable to itself in the present tense. Just like a motive, the protogay child can only publicly appear retrospectively, after a death. Only after one's straight life has died can the tag "homosexual child" be applied. This is a purely retrospective application, or so I have claimed, because all children are first presumed straight and are only allowed to come out as gay, or queer, or homosexual when it is thought they could know their sexuality—in their late teens or after, presumptively. For this reason, the phrase "gay child" acts as a gravestone marking a death: the point at which one's future as a straight adult expired, along with parental plans for one's future. From this death, at this point of death, the gay child is born, even if one is eighteen or forty-five. This kind of backward birthing mechanism makes investigations into motives for queerness a retrospective search for layered forms of feelings, desires, and needs that led to this death of one's straight life. Yet by the time the gravestone is placed ("I was a gay child"), the "child," by the legal way we define it, has expired.

These intriguing aspects of the seemingly normative, queerly innocent child, on the one hand, and the "homosexual" child, on the other, emblematize the features of motive: its way of making one feel unlike or beside oneself and its way of only ever being birthed backward. Even more powerfully, in the hands of Jackson and Capote, these aspects of these children prove to be an incarnation — a kind of bent embodiment — of both Freudian *and* legal issues surrounding motive, especially its temporal, sideways slides. In fact, these issues may even raise the question of whether some murders are the kind of reproductions that Freud called dreams.

Freud's Queer Children: Dreaming, Deferring, and Turning on Their Sides

Dreaming aside for just a moment, and legal issues to come still later, one can now clearly perceive an assertion that is central to this book: the protohomosexual child literalizes a concept that Derrida said had "govern[ed] the whole of Freud's thought": *Nachträglichkeit*.[5] Rendered by critics as "afterwardness," "retro-causality," "deferred effect," and "belated understanding," this conception so favored by Freud marks a certain way that the past gets grasped: namely, as read through its future consequences.[6] Sometimes deemed "the ghost in the nursery," this essential Freudian view claims that childhood traumas may only be felt as traumas — only consciously received as traumatic — much later in life through the action of "belated understanding."[7] At this point of "deferred effect," the trauma is retroactively caused, so that a person finds past and present elements of her ego-structures sitting beside each other in time, in a horizontalizing, cubist arrangement. In this respect, the protohomosexual child shows the pattern of a ghost in the nursery, when it finds itself retrospectively caused by "deferred effect" — even though this child may have consciously known it was being deferred all along.[8]

Despite this difference on the score of consciousness, which I have made an important difference at points in this book, the theorist who directly builds a model of motive, one including the child in queer ways, is, of course, Freud. He speaks squarely of "the motive for dreaming" and often links this motive to the child inside the dreamer.[9] According to Freud, in many cases the dream is a "peculiar" "reproduction" of particular "impressions" from childhood, "so that, to our surprise, *we find the child and the child's impulses still living on in the dream*" — and "experiences from childhood also play a part in dreams whose content would never have led one to suppose it" (221–22, 224, 223). That is to say, the dream itself is a backward birth, a "peculiar" "reproduction" of childhood motives that cause the dream. And, quite importantly, as we have seen with murder, these motives manifest in an act — the dream — that may not resemble the motives at all. Why? Because, as Freud famously claims, the dream "fulfills" a "wish," a "motive," in both "distorted" and "unconscious" fashion (343). The motive and its manifestation "are presented to us," he explains, "like two versions of the same subject-matter in two different languages," making the dream's content seem "nonsensical" as "a transcript" of the motive (311–13). Yet both "languages" of the dream *are* the dream, splitting the dream into its motive (its "dream-thoughts" or "wishes") and its act (its "manifestation" or "manifest content"). These "two versions," as Freud deems them, may explain why we commonly speak of wishes as dreams, as if dreams have yet to manifest ("or come true," as is often said). Moreover, the dream is at once a backward and sideways emotion: a way in which we are both behind and beside ourselves through condensation and displacement. Or as Freud ends up asking: "Are all the dream-thoughts [comprising 'the motive'] present alongside one another? or do they occur in sequence? or do a number of trains of thoughts start out simultaneously from different centres and afterwards unite?" (315). Once again, the difference between Freud's model and the issues for my book may be one of consciousness. For murder, like a dream, may be a distorted, disguised fulfillment of unconscious wishes, but it may also be a spoiling of certain conscious feelings — certain "emotionally cathected ideas," in Freud's words.[10] Murder may be a manifest content for a set of wishes it does not resemble and does not fulfill. Murder may manifest as a failed dream.

In fascinating ways, something of these dynamics appears in judicial issues from the 1950s to the 1990s, especially as legal scholars seek to separate, conceptually and linguistically, the matter of "motive" from "criminal intent."

Motive and Intent in Criminal Law:
Concepts Not at Home with Themselves or Each Other

In Anglo-American law, "intent" is a grounding legal concept that ends up looking definitionally ill at ease. As readers may know, in criminal law, "intent" is something distinct from "motive." Intent refers to the mental state of mind (*mens rea*) of a person legally accused of committing a crime. The prosecution, in its criminal case against this person, "must prove that the defendant intended to commit the illegal act."[11] It "need not prove the defendant's motive" (130), which, as something distinct from intent, explains why this person acted in the manner that she or he did. As a legal encyclopedia informs us: "In determining the guilt of a criminal defendant, courts are generally not concerned with *why* the defendant committed the alleged crime, but *whether* the defendant committed the crime," though "a defendant's motive is important in other stages of a criminal case, such as police investigation and sentencing" (130).

One can see immediately that the law simplifies matters for itself. Instead of getting caught in the complications (temporal and otherwise) I spelled out for motive, which are often the psychologically thickest and most narratively interesting aspects of a case, especially if one takes a long view of motive that extends back to childhood, the law stays focused on something that sounds both immediate and narrow: intent to kill at the time of the act. But even here entanglement enters. So much so that a British treatise, *The Mental Element in Crime* (a set of lectures from the 1950s), opens with a striking complaint: "A layman might find it painfully ridiculous that, after a thousand years of legal development, lawyers should still be arguing about the expressions used to denote the basic ideas of our legal system."[12] For "it would be simple to start by postulating that, as a minimum, *mens rea* means an intention to do the forbidden act—were it not for the fact that there is no judicial agreement upon the meaning of intention" (10).

The author Glanville Williams has an axe to grind. He feels that English judges lag behind academic legal commentators from New Zealand, England, and America on this score, all of whom show very "little disagreement" on the issues he presents.[13] But we soon discover why this difference doesn't matter; why his distinctions between English judges and a host of Anglo-American academics fail to signify on this count. For no matter what academic elements he draws upon, Williams himself cannot un-kink the serious contortions endemic to "intention," even when he offers his ideal definition. Fundamentally, Williams wants an understanding of intent that does not involve "a legal fiction—that is to say, such a violent twist of meaning as to make the legal language misleading," "to cheat with words" and thereby cause a "murder of the English language" by "tortur[ing] the word 'intention'" (26, 29, 30). And so he attempts to state succinctly that "among [the] synonyms [for 'intent'], perhaps the most helpful for purposes of definition is the word 'desire.' A consequence is intended when it is desired to follow as the result of the actor's conduct. This meaning runs through all the relevant definitions of intention given in the Oxford English Dictionary" (10). But within two pages Williams must admit that of course there are crimes that are desired, in one sense, while also not desired at all. Thus we might say, though Williams does not, that intent-as-desire splits from itself along the very axis that defines it. Williams, for his part, puts it this way: "The actor can be taken to intend not only the consequences that he positively desires [for example, gaining money through a robbery], but also other consequences [for example, having to kill someone in the midst of a robbery] known to be inseparable from the consequence he desires, even though they are not themselves desired" (12, 13). Or, as Williams next explains, in a different case:

> The consequence need not be desired as an end in itself; it may be desired as a means to another end. . . . There may be a series of ends, each a link in a chain of purpose. Every link in the chain, when it happens, is an intended consequence of the original act. Suppose that a burglar is arrested when breaking into premises. It would obviously be no defense for him to say that his sole intention was to provide a nurse for his sick daughter, and for that purpose to take money from the premises, but that he had no desire or intention to deprive anyone of anything. Such an argument would be fatuous. He intended (1) to steal money (2) in order to help his daughter. These are two intentions, and the one does not displace the other. English lawyers call the first an "intent" and the second a "motive"; this is because the first (the intent to steal) enters into the definition of burglary and is legally relevant, while the second (the motive of helping the daughter) is legally irrelevant, except perhaps in relation to sentence.

Although the verbal distinction between "intention" and "motive" is convenient, it must be realized that the remoter intention called motive is still an intention.

The arguments of Williams reveal three things. First, intention splits from itself in certain moments insofar as one may not, in any way at all, desire an act one legally intends and so, by legal definition, desires; intention is also a many-layered thing, since motive itself "is still an intention" and may involve "a series of ends." Second, in this respect, and quite strikingly, motive can show the nondesire for a criminal act inside the very intention to commit it, where intention is defined as desire. Third, this situation makes for a peculiar set of "inseparables" in some crimes, queerly yoking widely different sets of feelings and clearly mismatched inclinations, not to mention distinctive bodily actions undertaken at different points of time — for example, a man's committing burglary to help his sick daughter. All these points will return in telling ways in the crimes depicted by Capote and Jackson — and all the more complexly in the acts of paired killers.

Tellingly, too, these issues all return over the years in legal theory. For example, in 1990 another book appears that returns to these problems, indicating that they are still quite alive and unresolved. R. A. Duff, in *Intention, Agency, and Criminal Liability: Philosophy of Action and the Criminal Law*, revisits the ground gone over by Williams and raises further problems for the question of intent. Indeed, as if he were echoing Williams, Duff confesses: "One might be puzzled by the fact that controversy persists over the meaning of intention: if the concept plays such a crucial role in the determination of criminal liability, it should surely by now have a clear and agreed upon meaning."[14]

Duff says that it does not. But, most intriguingly, since this issue strikes at the heart of the backward birthing mechanism I have suggested for motive and the protogay child, Duff appears to detect a temporal problem with intent, though his wording stops short of giving it the shape I gave it earlier. Duff inquires: "What is it to have a bare intention to bring about some result in the future? We cannot say that it is to act as I do because I believe that my action might have that result (for I am not yet acting)" (68). "Bare intentions become intentions with which I act when I put them into action; a reason for action becomes the reason for which I act when I act on it." Duff concludes — in a statement that sounds as if it could explain the linguistic bind of the protogay child — that all of this, unhelpfully, "does not distinguish cases in which I *now* intend to act in the future, from those in which I have as yet formed no intention but *will* form an intention in the future" (68).

Notice that these problems emerge for these critics of British legal discourse (one from the fifties, the other from the nineties) as they tangle with the central, defining terms of criminal responsibility — as Capote and Jackson also do. That is to say, if *In Cold Blood* and *Heavenly Creatures* seem to call up models of motive that sound as if they wed the thoughts of Jacques Derrida, Judith Butler, and Sigmund Freud, that is because, in strictly legal terms, intention potentially differs from itself and from the expandable "series of ends" that the law calls motive. This chain of ends joins to intent, layers intent, by virtue of a criminal act that, as one looks back *from* the act, will be seen as caused by these many ends that are not the act but "inseparable" from it. And so for those acquainted with theory, *différance* (the inseparable motions of differing and deferring that attend meaning) seems implied by the law's own efforts to stabilize intent.[15] Butler might add that in order for a motive to exist over time, before it is enacted, it would need to be repeated — "to be instituted again and again," as she puts it, "which is to say that it runs the risk of becoming *de*-instituted [non self-identical] at every interval."[16] Even Freud's concept of *Nachträglichkeit* would seem germane to legal definition, since motive, in its complicated series of ends, which can seem to reach ever further back in time (even into childhood) in an extensive temporal chain, is an example, supremely, of a deferred action — it *is* deferral until it is an action and then not itself — which then causes, from the point of action, attributions of meaning to past events that are being read through (what have become) their future consequences. Motive, therefore, stretches out sideways, as it is a gathering — a synchronic spread — of backward views. And this backward and sideways temporality is the heart of motive's mysterious motions.

Capote's Boy Adventurers: In Cold Blood

Although the FBI may not have seen a meaning — a "design," wrote Capote — behind the Clutter murders, before or after the killers were caught, this would not be so for Capote. As a reporter for *The New Yorker* who, in converting this story for his novel, came to have strong (even sexual) feelings for one of the killers, Capote himself had a design. He aimed, it appears, to smuggle a story into our heads and arrange around it an effulgence of sympathy. He proposed, that is, to investigate why certain motives for murder do not look like themselves, especially the motives of a queer child. To do so, he would have to unspoil motive (back to its undoing), separate one man's motive from intent (while also not denying intent), and birth a queer child backward from the killing, taking the form of sentimental sympathies (his and his readers') for a queer and disturbing ride.

Capote was exactly the person for the job. As a friend of Capote's once said of him, one of his "most distinguishing qualities as a writer was that he could interpret the inside of the brain of a child."[17] This is precisely what the Clutter murder case allowed him to do. And this is why we are pulled inside, taken for what Capote himself calls "the long ride" (*In Cold Blood*, 202). We ride in the closet of a car with a man (Dick Hickock, murderer number one) and a figurative child (Perry Smith, murderer number two and the object of our sympathy): "Little Perry," "such a kid," says Dick with disgust, "wetting his bed," "sucking his thumb," "spooky as hell" (108), played in the 1967 movie by Robert Blake. This is the grown, queer man-child with his impossible childhood trailing—crazy, unaccountable dreams still attached; the gifted child who is born out of temporal joint with himself. This is the child Capote loves because Capote, at least in his mind, *is* him. Capote made for himself, says a friend, "the special persona of a child prodigy"; "Truman," says another, "remained a child, I think, all his life" (*TC*, 35, 27). And so he describes Perry Smith as himself: "no taller," we read, "than a twelve-year-old-child" (15), "a chunky . . . child-man" (224), whose "tiny feet . . . would have neatly fitted into a delicate lady's dancing slippers" (15), and who, toward his end, before execution, sleeping all day, says of himself: "I pretend I'm a tiny little baby" (321). ("I used to think he looked almost fetal," one acquaintance said about Capote: "his funny, mincing little walk, the baby voice, the infantile gestures" [*TC*, 42].)

Capote, who may have been in love with Smith (and become his lover in his visits to the prison) (*TC*, 188), structures the novel to birth this child, but not to flag Capote's own motivated interests—of sympathy wed to his own star-search for money and fame through a best-selling story.[18] And so he runs the novel, for much of its length, on parallel tracks which perfectly serve his temporal aims. Along track one, we are always in Kansas, case unsolved, watching the detectives try to figure out who would want to harm the Clutters. Along track two, in seesawing chapters, we are on the road with Perry and Dick, with feelings, desires, and physical needs from many different time frames driving two completely different people to the killings (and after, away from them) that, in other chapters, along track one, have already taken place and so birthed the motive to murder from the start. The effect of such a structure—motive reaching backward to miss itself as, in another form, it is driving forward—coupled with Capote's absence from his narrative, and his constant use of free indirect discourse, is rather cleverly to closet a motive: namely, his own. For, through this structure, Capote can hide his own set of feelings while explaining those of the two different killers. What these explanations allow is the chance, in a neutral voice, or often in the voices of others, to give Perry Smith the dramatically sympathetic trial he never had, to show the nondesire of Perry's motive (a sandwich of layered childish dreams, effeminate, elaborate Las Vegas hopes, and adventures pitched to boys) inside his legally confessed intent. Such a generous rendering, furthermore, also helps Capote soothe his own guilt over not doing more to assist the appeals delaying the deaths of Perry and Dick. In any event, through his own layered motives, Capote explores, at every turn, the sensitive boy's defeat within his family, and thus how the queer boy is formed by feelings in search of feeling-forms.

Capote's prose starts to hold these feelings. Indeed, before we know it, the killing of the Clutters, in Capote's hands, is the result of Perry's *missing* the chance for a possible homosexual connection with a friend, as I show in a moment. But first, we need to understand the frames Capote builds for holding the cubist motive-in-motion that moves Perry Smith. One frame, of course, involves the Clutters. Capote needs a sympathetic view of Perry's targets in part to better sympathize with Perry himself. For not only does a tender portrait of the Clutters help Capote to hide his own moves, but it lets him subtly twin the victims with their killer on two different scores: temporal strangeness and poignant significance. Seated in the narrative as people also out of temporal joint, who do not know that motive in a car is headed toward them and so they are dead—both at the time of the actual telling and then in the future unfolding of the narrative—the Clutter family members are saturated signifiers. Everything about them is potentially poignant, no matter how ordinary in another context. Ordinariness thus starts to seem eerie and newly peculiar in Capote's hands, in part because it *was* estranging to Capote in ways he found enticing: "the village of Holcomb stands on the high wheat plains of western Kansas, a lonesome area that other Kansans call 'out there'" (3); "horses, herds of cattle, a white cluster of grain elevators rising as gracefully as Greek temples are visible long before a traveler reaches them" (3); "drama, in the shape of exceptional happenings, had never stopped there" (5). Yet one senses that the Clutters—especially the father and the daughter—fit the oxymoron of exceptionally normal. That is to say, they're too normal to be usual, living in "almost the exact middle of the continental United States" (33). Indeed, they are deemed "of all the people in the world" (one wonders: really? of all the people?) "the least likely to be murdered" (85); or, as one person puts it: "Feeling wouldn't run half so high if this had happened to anyone *except* the Clutters. Anyone *less* admired. Prosperous. Secure. . . . That such a thing could happen to them—well, it's like being told there is no God" (88). But this loss of meaning is precisely what makes every detail of their persons, in Capote's telling, so drenched in significance, as if the gods of meaning were rising up before us. Every instant of their nondeath ticks with foreboding as we read it through their end.

In a weirdly similar way, what we learn about Perry's background seems—by virtue of its simply being background, selected by Capote *as* this killer's background—as if it must explain his future lethal actions, though here we may feel more on the hunt for those specific saturated signifiers that tell the story of why he pulled the trigger at a later point in time. Intriguingly, the ones we likely pull out are the ones we're trained to see: alcoholic mother; roaming, gypsy childhood; first arrest at eight; detention-home life; and (because he is half Cherokee?) a sense of being his white father's "nigger." But this is right where Capote pulls a fast one. A child's "rotten life" as a motive for murder (later, in adulthood) is painfully familiar. (Here the "neglected child" and the "delinquent" match up in the manner of the juvenile courts.)[19] But murder by reason of childish, sunny pamphlets and narrative genres that act as forms to hold a child's feelings is less well known. According to Capote, it is due in part to films that Perry saw (especially *The Treasure of the Sierra Madre*, which he saw eight times and clung to as a kind of template for his dreams) that he hooked up with Dick. Indeed, before we know it, the case of small-town neighborly breakdown—starting people locking their doors against each other—is the result of a boy's adventure story, a certain fantasy of bodily movement (performed with other boys) that revolves more around digging for treasure and riding in cars than it does around a family's buried safe.

In fact, Perry's motive, his secret reason, for returning to Kansas is not to meet Dick but to meet a "best friend," the "faggot" Willie-Jay, who is being paroled. (Throughout the novel are sprinkled signifiers that could suggest— are meant to suggest?—Perry's own faggotry: his endless mirror-gazing; his "girlish hands"; his "mannered," swishy writing; his "lispy, whispery voice"; his "sweaty studies of weight-lifting" athletes; the buffing of his nails to "a silky pink sheen"; and his persistent "theatrical fantasy" of being a performer, "Perry O'Parsons," in a Las Vegas club, "where, wearing a white top hat and white tuxedo, he strutted about, . . . sang 'You Are My Sunshine,' and tap-danced up a short flight of gold-painted . . . steps," while singing to "a strange audience, mostly men and mostly Negroes," 15, 119, 176, 178, 254, 319.) That Perry, in rather Shakespearean fashion, misses meeting his friend's bus is fateful for the Clutters. For Willie-Jay, who divined in Perry a poet, something "rare" and savable, brought to him the kind of "high-carat appre-ciation that [was] . . . more alluring than buried gold" (45). Capote makes it sound like the giving of a ring. In fact, Willie-Jay, the clear homosexual, is the only force that competes with Perry's dreams, his elaborate longing for a boy's adventures. For in place of touching bodies, Perry touches maps: one map, in fact, "was ragged, so thumbed that it had grown as supple as a piece of chamois" (14). The point of the maps is always the same: find the road to buried gold, to Acapulco, Cozumel, or Sierra Madre. Then, embrace that fantasy law, finders keepers: the fantasy of robbery that is fully free of charge: legal and maybe nobody hurt. Here is Capote in Perry's head: "Since childhood, for more than half his thirty-one years, [Perry] had been sending off for literature ('FORTUNES IN DIVING! Train at Home in Your Spare Time . . .' 'SUNKEN TREASURE! . . . Amazing Offer . . .') that stoked a longing to realize an adventure his imagination swiftly and over and over enabled him to experience: the dream of drifting downward through strange waters, of plunging toward a green sea-dusk, sliding past the scaly, savage-eyed protectors of a ship's hulk that loomed ahead, a Spanish galleon—a drowned cargo of diamonds and pearls, heaping caskets of gold. A car horn honked. At last—Dick" (16–17). Before Capote has practical Dick put an end to this dream, honking his horn (and even his name) in staccato prose, we see the logic of Capote's narration: we start off with language close to the source—Perry's booklets forming his dreams; but as soon as it's time to render Perry's more liquid sense of reverie, Truman Capote is in his place, lending the child whatever refinement his dreams might require: alliteration ("dream of drifting downward"), Old English kenning (in the form of "sea-dusk"), metaphor ("savage-eyed protectors"), topped with the jewels (diamonds and pearls) a queer might seek, along with gold.

As for Dick, a self-professed "normal" (although he admits to pedophilia with girls, which he considers normal), Capote's trick is to absent Dick, who is never a child, from this specific temporality. This Dick, bad Dick, evacuates his childhood, has no memories of life before ten, before he was an "outstanding athlete," "star player," and "pretty good student." Normal envy, normal resentment, normal pedophilia, Capote implies, form the adventures of Dick who dreams of a family safe, though who confesses that his main desire for the "score" at the Clutters is to rape the Clutters' daughter. This is a Dick who, even so, can't act on his own. His desire—his intent—needs, it seems, another man's motives (so different from Dick's), and so he must lasso a man-child's differential, queer temporality that has been shown not to be Dick's own. Specifically, Dick must find a way to capture the queer child's fantasy of boyhood adventures with boys who seek gold. "Dick became convinced that Perry was that rarity, 'a natural killer' . . . [and] that such a gift could . . . be profitably exploited. . . . He had proceeded to woo Perry . . . pretend . . . that he believed all the buried-treasure stuff and shared his beachcomber yearnings . . . none of which appealed to Dick, who wanted 'a regular life' [and] . . . 'plenty of blond chicken'" (55). Assuming we should find him distasteful enough, Capote still stacks the deck against Dick: Dick has a pattern of running down dogs. Apparently feeling like killing them, he even swerves to hit them. From these depictions emerges a sense of Dick as the driving desire behind the killings, with Perry's motives and background ensuring that he will be the motion at the critical moment, making him pull the fateful trigger four separate times (and cut one throat). In this doomed way, Perry Smith's inseparables—his four acts of murder, his life as a child, his "twisted tenderness," his possible protohomosexual longings, his failure to meet up with a homosexual, his attraction to Dick's athletic swagger, and his love of the boy's adventure story, joining Jane Austen to Joseph Conrad—are legally wedded to each other.

Hence the thoughts of the FBI detective Alvin Dewey at the end of the novel: "[Dick's] execution had not disturbed him.... But Smith['s]... aroused another response, for Perry possessed a quality, the aura of an exiled animal, a creature walking wounded, that the detective could not disregard. He remembered his first meeting with Perry ... the dwarfish boy-man seated in the metal chair, his small booted feet not quite brushing the floor. And when Dewey now opened his eyes, [at Perry's hanging], that is what he saw: the same childish feet, tilted, dangling" (340–41). That these are Capote's words about Perry, put in Dewey's mind so they can come to us through an FBI agent, is not in doubt. There are no quotations in this passage—only Capote's poetic feet, one might say—leaving Capote's regressive adventure, his queer temporality of the queer child, to hang, as emotive, in readers' minds.

Jackson's Killer Starlets: Heavenly Creatures

Jackson, like Capote, births motive backward by starting with a killing; then, like Capote, unspoils motive, to the point of complication, by spinning it backward in temporal terms while he is birthing a protohomosexual child on the screen. In fact, more dramatically than does Capote, Jackson reads motives back to their sources in childlike wishes for physical motions. This sort of rendering is anything but simple or sentimental and results in Jackson's artistic rendition of motive as a cubist form of feelings, desires, and needs (many starkly physical) feeding off each other at differential rates and involving temporal backbends—all of which is spoiled in the flash of a brick when the action of criminal intent spoils the motive that seemingly moved it.

Heavenly Creatures does not represent the subsequent trial, a media sensation that, even so, lasted all of six days. The defense argued for the killers' innocence by reason of something they called "joint insanity"—two girls suffering from madness simultaneously, making their presumptive homosexuality merely a symptom of their diseased minds.[20] The prosecution countered that the killers, Pauline and Juliet, were "intelligent" and "perfectly sane," even if "precocious and dirty-minded girls"—with a motive to kill

16. Pauline and Juliet: girls spending energy, running with wealth.
From the film *Heavenly Creatures* (1994).

Pauline's mother so as to be together (Glazumina and Laurie, 84). Jackson, in his film, crucially transforms two legal questions central to these criminal proceedings. First, he complicates the question of insanity by temporally turning the two girls' adolescent status back toward their status as children of parents who cannot seem to grasp their ambitions, fantasies, and longings to move with each other as a pair in the world. Second, he complicates the question of their queerness, their so-called homosexual relationship, by giving it the status of a class attraction that unfolds differently for each girl but at the same time. Both of these girls, in Jackson's depiction, are quite seriously in love with a family—Juliet's family, a wealthy family—for the sake of the physical motions that wealth and luxury can provide them. They seem to know, as if they have read or intuited claims from Georges Bataille's essay "The Notion of Expenditure," that wealth is foremost the power to spend oneself and one's belongings to the point of extremity.[21]

Indeed, fantasies, along with the girls' wonderfully campy travels into their own Fourth Dimension, are launched from the garden at Juliet's beautiful upper-class home (and on vacation), where Jackson frees their limbs back to childhood (figure 16). Here they move with obvious abandon, as if movement—physical motion and emotional exhaustion—were the point of wealth; as if feeling, together as a pair, at the same time, were the motive force of life (something Jackson would return to cinematically with his hobbits).[22] On the film's evidence, the pair's ability to pull the camera into their feelings and their frenzied motion depends upon a wish to spend one's time always to the point of physical exhaustion, the temporal point at which (e)motions run out. Running in and out of emotional states, the girls rarely cease in their physical movements until they are spent—but on their own terms and in their own time.

Given that the girls, in Jackson's understanding, want to be some kind of sibling-lovers who have the same parents, who will foster their in-loveness, they are bound to be defeated. Pauline (who is also called "Paul," "Charles," and "Gina, the gypsy") is destined to be read as a "wayward child," with "unhealthy," "unwholesome" feelings for her friend—as Juliet's father tells Pauline's parents—since she is in love with a family not her own. For her plan to succeed, she would have to divorce her lower-class parents in order to wed a wealthier pair. There is no form—and no legal method—for that queer wish. Never mind the fact that Juliet's own normative wish for her parents' love is dashed by their constant neglect of her. In Jackson's account, both of these girls are in love with a family that neither of them actually possesses. Being bereft of the family they choose could explain, in the film's terms, why they are obsessed with birthing between them a royal family, a ruling family, calling themselves Charles and Deborah (the royals in question) who have a son who wreaks his havoc (at the age of ten) on any of their obstacles. Sexually, then, and for compelling reasons, these two girls bond around a set of heterosexual parents (figures for themselves), which they mold in clay and which they animate, worship, and rule, entering into their parents' temporality, at least in their own minds, while they exploit the prerogatives of childhood's imaginary powers.

On this point of imaginary powers there is quite a lot to say. Jackson makes these powers almost synonymous with moviegoing and moviemaking. In his formal choices for how he renders the girls' joint motives, it is as if he's filming their making of a movie, starring themselves (their favorite film to see). In a scene on a beach, the two girls kneel next to a castle they have made in the sand (a mini stage-set): as they narrate fervently ("Charles clutches his wounded shoulder as he gallops into the courtyard; Deborah awaits his return in their . . . boudoir . . . she smells his scent from fifty paces and urges his steed onward"), the camera makes us rapidly swoop inside the castle, up its tiny steps, and burst into the bedroom ("he flings open the door and launches himself at the bed, ravishing her; oh, God, yes!"). This is how the viewer of *Heavenly Creatures* seems to be captive to the girls' camera, as if Jackson's own filmmaking is taking their direction. But how does he extend this moviemaking parable, making the killers seem less insane than cinematic in their fantasies?

First, he makes the girls into quintessential emblems of the moviegoer. In fact, in the film, they are seen attending films — one in particular, starring Orson Welles (himself a symbol of the actor/movie maker), who, they imagine, chases them back to Juliet's house and scares them into pleasuring each other, so that they each, in alternating moments, wear his face (or the face of their son) while making love. In this weird way, the moviegoer of Jackson's film may grasp that the girls, at the height of their fantasies, show us one face of our own film-viewing: namely, according to claims we might tease from the theories of Christian Metz and Laura Mulvey, how the viewer is positioned as a child with scopophilia; as a kind of pervert with erotic wishes, often tinged with violence; as a fetishist who is giving nonsexual objects — for example, the celluloid image — sexual resonance; and as a fantasy-ridden lunatic lost in the fourth dimension of film, as it were, and constantly confusing movie fantasy with reality in our obsessions.[23] Thus we should grasp, from years of moviegoing, the appealing position of perverted-child-who-is-taken-up-with-fantasies.

Jackson's second ploy is to split our fetishism, as viewers of his film, along the very lines that Pauline splits hers: along the lines of class. That is to say, *Heavenly Creatures* makes us find our visual pleasure, or at least one form of it, in the film's location of upper-class "objects." With the camera's long, objectifying gaze, the film caresses Juliet's body (Kate Winslet's upright posture, feminine gestures, and perfect complexion); her mother's more beautiful, stilled erotic form; and, most important, Juliet's house, with its formal elegance and inviting gardens. Even in several campy scenes where the camera seems snatched by the person of Pauline, the camera catches Juliet stilled in its lens, dressed as a princess on a bridge by a fountain or sweeping down a staircase in an elegant gown. And she is doubled by her stunning mother, who stands, in our first vision of her, in a three-quarter turn, coyly for the camera. Jackson is making it patently clear that Pauline sees this family (Juliet sees it in Pauline's gaze) as a fetishistic lure. In this case, the girl (a rather unusual bearer of the gaze) fetishizes class, in a way that Mulvey never taught us to expect. Precisely, however Jackson might term it, he makes

Juliet, her mother, and their home the objects of our "fetishistic scopophilia," while training our "sadistic voyeurism" (both of these are Mulvey's terms, 490, 492)—as if they come together (mother and child) as victims of the camera. One recalls that Mulvey's sense of these terms is that they split visual enthrallment and visual punishment between them. "Fetishistic scopophilia" defines the way the camera "builds up the physical beauty of the object, transforming it into something satisfying in itself" (490). "Sadistic voyeurism," on the other hand, is the camera's way of "asserting control, and subjecting the guilty person through punishment or forgiveness" (490). That Jackson splits these propensities between Pauline and Juliet, making the gypsy child (Pauline) and also her mother the objects of our sadistic gaze (they are dowdy, overweight, and caught in a range of awkward poses), may well add to the viewer's tender sense of their raw class bind—the different sorrows for mother and child when the child would like to cleave to the family that enthralls her, not her own.

Jackson's third technique is most engaging. As if he were defying the Hollywood tendency to equate feminine beauty with stasis (even though in other ways he relies upon it, as I have just shown), he makes the *motion* of the female body compatible with and defining of a new visual pleasure—one that, in moments, either displaces the fetishistic gaze on the female form or outright spoils it, making a girl-child a form of spoiled pleasure that might capture the interest of the camera.[24] This dynamic emerges from the start. Playing off the genre of the fifties travelogue and its thematization of motion, Jackson overlays old documentary footage of Christchurch (which shows an airplane aloft above the city, buses in the bustling downtown district, bicycles, and cars) with the frenzied running of two girls' legs: first, legs dirty and bloody in the trees; then, legs tidy and joyful on a boat. The camera seems to struggle to match their pace as it follows the girls, largely focused on their legs. These are not legs of visual pleasure, not those of years of Hollywood gazing; these are legs with a mind of their own, fleeing from murder (in the one image-track) and running toward a mother (in an image from the other), as if these legs are of two different minds. Scenes that follow also focus on motions—even in a stripping scene, in which the girls undress themselves as they are running, laughing, and singing to a bold soundtrack by Mario Lanza, the operatic tenor. The clay-figure scenes—in which clay modeling never looked so active—especially make it seem as if the girls are

17. Pauline: a starlet in her film-fantasy. From the film *Heavenly Creatures* (1994).

starlets in an animated feature they have written and directed. As the only people (the only regular celluloid images) in a world of clay (figure 17), they dance, they twirl, but they also witness royals-made-of-clay slicing up inferiors and peasants copulating with each other with abandon.

Jackson, nonetheless, shows one set of images as different from the rest. In sepia tones, he depicts the central, most cherished fantasy held by the girls—as if it were a tasteful, cinematic short. In these rolling images, the two girls imagine they are running on the deck of a large cruise ship. They are calling out "Mummy" and "Daddy" to Juliet's parents, who turn to the girls with embraces and smiles (figure 18); the two girls kiss on the lips before the parents, almost as if they are wedding in front of them. This short "film" is their ideal image of themselves as sister-lovers—their misrecognition, as Jacques Lacan would put it, as a *pair* of children in the family mirror.[25] This is the most coherent and least ambiguous scene of visual pleasure in the film, and Jackson dignifies it with a gravity their many other fantasies lack. The parents look dashing, not mismatched as they do in other scenes (figure 19); the two girls' running looks measured and appropriate to their joy; the boat is in keeping with the class they wish to share; and the sepia look of the scene makes it seem like a photographic still of a moment that took place, though it never has.

These are the motions and crisscrossing motives, according to Jackson, that lead two girls to kill the symbol of their obstacles: the lower-class mother. Yet this killing severely spoils the feelings that set it into motion—as

18. The cruise-ship fantasy of being sister-lovers.
From the film *Heavenly Creatures* (1994).

19. Parents looking dashing to the eyes that love them.
From the film *Heavenly Creatures* (1994).

20. Fantasy spoiled by the murder it moved. From the film *Heavenly Creatures* (1994).

the film's last scene, the murder of the mother, makes sadly clear. Notably bloody and cruel, this killing not only spoils the spectator's visual pleasure but also immediately cuts the cord between the girls, as is conveyed by the sepia scenes that cross-cut the murder. Their fantasy image—and, therefore, their motive—is sharply spoiled: between the cracking motions of the brick are sepia-tinted clips: Pauline is stranded on the dock while the ocean liner pulls out of port, with Juliet and her parents aboard (figure 20), and the two girls are crying inconsolably. The legal punishment for these girls—for their queer lineup of legal inseparables—is lifetime separation from each other. Sent to separate prisons, they are, ironically, by legal decree, said to be "Detained at her Majesty's Pleasure"—detained by a royal, and for the intent that was not their wish.

This is Jackson's own hung time for the queer child, his way of answering, through a set of layered, fantastic inclinations, what kind of feeling is a motive for murder. It is a feeling so different from the killing that will birth a dream that is likely to be drained.

Elephant: *Motive Goes to School*

How have these issues evolved in recent years? Do they persist? How have they stretched to include the violence so prevalent in schools? One recent film makes a canny reply. *Elephant*'s experiment is boldly elemental, especially in contrast to the pretzel logics under display by Jackson and Capote.

But if *Elephant* (dir. Gus Van Sant, 2003) is not as rich in its logical twists, it is forceful in its spareness, before its devastation. As if it refuses the "why?" that has emerged from the high school slayings along the lines of Columbine, *Elephant* strips down to students-in-motion. Animal-like, without our knowledge of what propels them, students cross surprisingly vast tracks of space in their high school setting, as if crossing space on the fields, in the halls, through gyms and cafeterias were what they were born for. Yet, as director Gus Van Sant follows student bodies as a violent day unfolds in their midst, there is his experiment. He moves temporally and diachronically *through* synchronic spread, giving the day as a synchrony. The camera, that is, is constantly backing up from its linear chain to offer a scene that was taking place simultaneously with the one before it, so that our progress "up to" the killings is often turning sideways for stretches of time. From these perspectives, we perceive a chessboard of bodies all in motion, with varying motives, passing each other and crossing one another as they pursue a "series of ends," which they may in part be unaware of. "Why did the chicken cross the road?" is the joke that comes to mind. This kind of question, impossible to answer, is what the camera of *Elephant* captures.

Again, we have the tease of saturated signifiers. We meet a boy with a bull on his shirt. Does the bull mean target—as in "bull's-eye"—or does it mean aggression? Or neither?, we wonder. Then we meet a beautiful jock with "Lifeguard" on his sweatshirt. Is this shirt ironic? Is this boy the killer? (Neither boy is.) But soon enough our questions are displaced by motions. A four-minute shot, uncut and on the move, captures the "lifeguard" crossing a field, climbing stairs, turning corners, and walking long hallways. Even the visual pleasure of his beauty bows to the camera's attention to his motion. (It is that unusual, by dint of length and angles.) And though all the signs of Columbine are here—two boy killers who are disaffected, bullied, or unpopular, with a rage against jocks in particular, and with erotic connections to each other—they are not linked in a causal chain. One does not know which signs are contributing, combining, building, or receding, since the film refuses to order them or even weight them differentially. In fact, the question of causality is thematized, but also pulverized, in a scene with the Gay/Straight Alliance at the school, in which we hear overlapping snippets of: ". . . a Trojan on it, OK? . . . so we were talking about walking down the street being gay . . . how can you tell? or can you tell? . . . see, that's the

21. Dog in motion, announcing the killers.
From the film *Elephant* (2003).

22. Before the killings, killers getting close.
From the film *Elephant* (2003).

thing, I don't think you can . . . well, if you have tons of symbols and stuff . . . but I don't think . . . did you guys see the cover story on *The Oregonian* about the gay rams? . . . apparently, the farmers can't tell if the rams are gay or not."

On the heels of this ranging discussion, we see the boy with the bull on his shirt playing with a dog that is leaping for a ball in a slow-motion shot: this is the image (the motion of the dog) that precedes our view of the killers each (initial) time we see them (figure 21). And here, like Capote, Van Sant puts a queer child into the mix. One of the killers seems surprisingly "sensitive": from his soft eyes and gentle bearing to his love of drawing and playing Beethoven on the piano. (The "Moonlight" Sonata and "Für Elise" suffuse the film's soundtrack, as if he were providing it.) This same boy also clearly likes guns, Nazi documentaries and, in some way, the other boy killer (who is lacking sensitivities), since they passionately kiss in the shower as a prelude to their killings (figure 22). Do they feel like killing? It appears that they do. Do they "have fun," as one instructs the other? Perhaps they do, though it is hard to tell. What we see is something of what we saw before in the film's other scenes: two students crossing voluminous space, in long attentive shots, though this time with guns. The sensitive boy has a look of concern (at moments, fear), a brief slight smile, confusion, worry ("fuck!"), fatigue, and then surprisingly little reaction to his own (?) point-blank killing of his partner-in-arms. We end in a meat locker where he has cornered the "lifeguard" and his beautiful girlfriend (visual pleasure made simply into meat).

Here, in *Elephant*, we have seen intent in the criminal sense. There is no doubt about it. But have we seen motive — perhaps the elephant in the room, as the saying goes? We cannot say. What we do know is that we have been forced to share the camera's interests: its punning play on the camera's "development" of a set of students. What is forced is something rare. A deep curiosity. For we are made to watch, less for the purpose of "understanding" than inhabiting, the pleasure, elation, boredom, disappointment, and mysterious repetition of a set of student motions: a moving set of signs, still emerging into meaning.

PART 3   Sideways Futures: Color and Money

CHAPTER 5 Oedipus Raced, or the Child Queered by Color

Birthing "Your" Parents via Intrusions

Murder is a matter of connection and intrusion, as we've just seen. In texts by Peter Jackson and Truman Capote, members of families are killed by "children" who are in some way connected to them or intrude upon them before they kill them. *Heavenly Creatures* could have been called *Guess Who's Coming to Dinner* if the title hadn't been taken by a famous racial comedy from 1967. The families of the heavenly creatures in question, Pauline and Juliet, never guessed that killers were at the dinner table — never mind girls whose motive for murder would be so domestic compared to the slaughter that would kill their own connection.[1]

In Cold Blood, with its own queer child, is itself an instance of a family's visitation by killers in their home. It is an instance, one could even say, of "six degrees of separation": a phrase that is a comment on lateral connections between human beings, as opposed to kinship structures, and a phrase that was the title of a film about race in 1993. Proposed as a theory in 1929, in a story called "Chains" by Frigyes Karinthy, a writer from Hungary, "six degrees of separation" is a concept that claims that all people on the planet are connected to each other by no more than five intermediary people in a chain of acquaintance. Indeed, through a chain of acquaintance and events, the Clutters were killed by strangers who "knew" them — who knew them

"WHAT ARE THE CHARGES?"
"HE CAME INTO OUR HOUSE."
"HE COOKED US DINNER. . . ."
"HE SAID HE WAS THE SON OF SIDNEY POITIER."
—FROM *SIX DEGREES OF SEPARATION*

through someone who had worked the family's farm, who himself went to prison where he got to know these strangers who later killed the Clutters based on something he had said.[2]

Connection, one could say, is a form of intrusion. It's a human door to someone's guarded hearth. Intrusion, moreover, can force new connections. Putting "the family" in a different kind of light, this chiasmus—connection is intrusion, intrusion is connection—connects three intrusions, all involving children. Children, in these remarkable cases, birth their parents, as if parents, in a crazy kind of lateral, are newly made when their children turn against them, as we see in the films *Blood Diamond*, *Guess Who's Coming to Dinner*, and *Six Degrees of Separation*. Each of these intrusions—one involving a biological son, another a son-in-law, and yet another a gay hustler—also concern what Americans call "children of color." These are peculiar children, I have said, since at the level of their representation they make "experience"—scenes of suffering, knowledge, or strength, tinged with the variable hues of courage, oppression, despair, or even excitement—intrude upon "innocence," as we have seen with William Blake's poem "The Little Black Boy" (in my introduction).[3] In fact, this chapter braids together the strands of the child queered by color, the child queered by innocence, the ghostly gay child, the grown homosexual, and the Freudian child who is Oedipalized in several directions all at once. Crafting these strands that become so entwined, these films manifest, and indeed require, intricate forms: triangulated plotlines tied to jolting visual grafts (in *Blood Diamond*); visually striking architectural setups of their film sets (in *Guess* and *Six*); and the tautological character logic of "being who you are" (in all three films). For these reasons, these films make Oedipalization—an often dead and deadening issue in theory circles—both inevitable and lively again, by making it surface in contexts as diverse as child soldiering, "mixed marriage," and queer hustling of one's "father" (not to mention fathers' acts of sleeping with their "sons"). They also make the spatialization of so-called mirror relations (I am that image over there in the mirror) a temporal matter (I must *become* who I say I've been), inserting a time gap inside tautology, so that I don't yet match my views of what I see or who I "am." These are views that aggressively confront the people who hold them, aggressions via intrusions by children. Moreover, each film's featured intrusion raises the specter of children's futures—futures that threaten to be suspended dreams. Yet these suspensions critique the very liberals who, with some compassion, call attention to them, revealing the limits of who these liberals say they have been and continue to be.

Sons and Lovers in Blood Diamond (2006): The Future That Was Africa[4]

Intrusions of the most intimate sort, and of a visually aggressive sort, are the infrastructure of this film about family — and about children who become brutal killers through no motive of their own. Part of the film's visual aggression is its use of visual grafts, attaching violent shots of children to the stock images we have encountered in endless pictures. In this way, in the film, standard shots of agile men (sweatily hoisting monster guns so as to coolly blow someone away) are routinely affixed with more jolting shots of children capping adults in the chest from a few feet away.[5] Furthermore, all of this visual truculence serves to celebrate African fatherhood, though in a most unusual way: by grimly rendering one man's attempts, a father's attempts, to recapture his son who was forced to become a "child soldier," the actual fate of some 200,000 children on the African continent, as the film tells us.[6] Formally, importantly, the narrative stretches from a boy's abduction to his retrieval by his father (Djimon Hounsou), making the father, through this ordeal, become his son's father all over again. Here is another instance of grafting, this time attaching Hollywood action — gritty, fine-grained shots of pursuit — and conspicuous Hollywood abs to an African father (as the signs, presumably, of fine fatherhood).[7]

But this is only the film's beating heart. *Blood* additionally attaches to this story the massive context of the civil war in Sierra Leone, fought in 1999 and financed by diamonds mined in that country and sold for guns. Since the United States, according to the film, is "responsible for two thirds of all diamond purchases," U.S. consumers are brought inside this story as complicit participants in these events. For this reason, the narrative encompasses and visually features two white protagonists: a diamond smuggler from Zimbabwe (Leonardo DiCaprio) and a liberal journalist from America (Jennifer Connelly), who just happen to lust for each other, in the typical Hollywood style. In a deft way, this specific pairing encourages viewers (largely white ones) to ride their usual, self-absorbed focus on love and action involving white people into the territory of black families suffering historically specific traumas — and perhaps to find there the "innocent child" who, *through abuse,* confirms "Western" notions of child protections. There are very queer circuits to all of this. As the smuggler himself articulates, he is part of a threesome of people using each other: he makes use of the African father to find a huge diamond the father discovered; the journalist uses the smuggler in order to crack the story of these diamonds and their networks; and the father uses the idealistic journalist in order to locate his lost family.[8] In other words, this triangular structure has a love story forming one side (the smuggler and the journalist), an action story forming yet another (the smuggler and the father), and a political exposé forming the third (the smuggler, the journalist, and the father all together). Only through this structure can the film bind together three bold issues that touch on each other: the role of "Western" liberal intentions (or lack thereof) in easing the suffering of African families; the journey of certain African fathers back to themselves after their child's becoming a killer; and the overarching future of "Africa" as an ongoing, present unfolding of its persistent colonial past, so that its future seems always what it was to "Western" eyes. One more formal device props this structure. The image of a striking, hovering, beautifully violent sun punctuates the movie at several points throughout, giving the feel of something suspended and hanging in the balance while the violence rages.

The film begins with a small burst of light: the father strikes a match in the dark.[9] Though we don't know it, here begins the narrative of an unusual Oedipal struggle: your son will want to kill you, and very well might, but from no real motive at all. He will have no impulse to sleep with your wife or rob you of your power; he will want to kill you—and kill anybody—just to survive, until he starts to feel like killing because the boy next to him gives him that feeling. Indeed, the scene of the lighted match, followed by the first presentation of the sun ball, next gives way to the father and son discussing how Freetown, Sierra Leone, was a utopia at its inception:[10] "Someday, when the war is over, our world will be a paradise," the son tells his father, mapping this future. Then the sound of American rap punctures this talking, announcing advancing trucks with young African males, some of them children, brandishing rifles, machine guns, and boomboxes.[11] "Papa!" is the last clear word we hear, since chaos ensues, with families fleeing from children and teens who gun them down at point-blank range. (Some of the younger children struggle to wield the machine guns they are firing.) The father is caught while his family flees. And the rebel leader, a black African named Captain Poison, the man in charge of the young male brood, informs his captives: "The government wants you to vote—'the future is in your hands'—we now de future—no more hands, no more voting," and thus he proceeds to chop off hands as the sign of this future. This specific action, however, reels backward to reference slavery, since Belgium's King Leopold in the 1890s, as the film reminds us, established this practice in order to keep black slaves in line. The father is spared and sent to the mines to help find the diamonds that fund Captain Poison.[12]

We grasp by this point this Oedipal nightmare, even for the father himself: this African father *is* a slave, veritably ringed by disastrous fathers: Captain Poison; the faceless government; and the history of "Western" intrusions that have nakedly raped the land. Or, as *Blood* has a character tell us at the Conference on Diamonds in Antwerp, Belgium (run by the G8), "Throughout the history of Africa, whenever a substance of value is found the locals die, in great number and in misery"; "this was true of ivory, rubber, gold, and oil—it is now true of diamonds." In other words, the "history" of the "misery" of "Africa" only gets wider over time, as its future is eyed by "the West." And, to be sure, what the father doesn't know, even after he finds and secretly hides a diamond the size of a bird's egg, is that his son has been taken by the rebels (led by Captain Poison) and is being turned by them into a "soldier." We the viewers know this fact, because we are shown the son's transformation in a set of brutal scenes. (And here the representational strategies, in their brutality, hark back to those of *Bastard out of Carolina*.)

The first of these depictions starts with a shot that could be from a slave ship: bare black torsos, captured in low light, lying side by side (figure 23). The black rebels enter, yelling into darkness: "Your mothers and fathers are dead; your brothers and sisters are dead; we are your family now!" They shout out these words as they whip the boys, who respond by crying. These boys' suffering now turns *out* from them just as it most fully takes hold of them. For, without delay or intervening image, the next shot shows these children with machine guns shooting black dummies that look like a family (a father, mother, and small child). A rebel teen instructs them: "Your parents are weak—they're the farmers, they're the fishermen. . . . but you are the heroes who will save the nation; you are not children anymore, you are men. . . . Repeat after me: 'Shed their blood!'" They weakly repeat, "Shed their blood." Now we see the father's son with a weapon and a blindfold on his eyes being made to shoot a man (a person not a dummy) without either seeing or willing this murder (figure 24). After the killing, the son (about ten?) bears a numbed look of shocked realization. The captain tells him, for once with a tenderness, as he touches the cheek of the boy, making him some kind of peer *and* son: "I know, I know, it's hard. . . . but you are a soldier of the revolution now. . . . Whatever you need — guns, CDs, food — come to me — I will take care of you." Later, this care encompasses plying the children with heroin or watching them shoot each other with drugs, while other children look into the camera and boldly declare: "I am Baby Killer"; "I am the Master of Disaster"; "I am See Me No More." These kinds of shots are the apotheosis of "Western" fears in this Hollywood picture: children as drugged-up killing machines, left to raise each other and spur each other on. One could not forge a more riveting example for "Western" eyes of the neglected-or-abused child, who is conceived as the innocent child, turning so rapidly into the murderous child "we" fear. The climax to this threat is what one would guess: when the father, with the smuggler, at last finds his son, his son screams "Traitor!" "I do not know you!" and turns his father over to the others. But when the boy holds a gun on his father and seems about to kill him, the father's interpellation of the child as his son — "Look at me. . . . You are a good boy. . . . You love soccer and school. . . . I know they made you do bad things. . . . I am your father who loves you and you are going home with me to be my son again" — is enough to pull the boy away from the feeling-like-killing children by his side.[13]

One can see why this film crafts these sentiments. Presumably, viewers need to think these children can go back to the future they were once fore-seeing, despite their experience, even though many (most?) of these children never find their families again. So the film's formula for our emotions follows brutal, realistic shots with tender uplift that would subdue them. Or, at times, it reverses this formula, in its treatment of liberal intentions to intervene in "Africa." That is to say, the film embraces these intents while swiftly undercutting their naiveté. To do so, the movie puts them into dialogue — into would-be intercourse — with the smuggler the journalist pursues. The two protagonists, when they first meet, heighten this intercourse, as well as their attraction, through their pacing, syntax, and word choice, as if their lines were pricking each other, sexually, linguistically: "The world is falling apart and all we hear about are blowjobs," she begins, referring to the

23. Vulnerable "soldiers," figurative slaves.
From the film *Blood Diamond* (2006).

24. Murder without motive: the father's son in training.
From the film *Blood Diamond* (2006).

Clinton-Lewinsky scandal. "When was the last time the world wasn't falling apart?" the smuggler answers, starting the see-saw.

> "Oh, a cynic—why don't you sit down and make me miserable?"
> "American?"
> "Guilty."
> "Americans usually are."
> "Says the white South African?"
> "I'm from Rhodesia."
> "We say Zimbabwe now, don't we?"
> "Do we? So don't tell me, you're here to make a difference, are you?"

The smuggler voices "Africa" as the definitive icon of a future suspended: "Peace Corps types only stay around long enough to realize they're not really helping anyone; the government only wants to stay in power until they've stolen enough to go into exile somewhere else; and the rebels [aren't] sure they want to take over—otherwise they'd have to govern this mess . . . TIA. This is Africa."

As we learn in later scenes, the smuggler has earned his cynical views, or so he implies. When he was nine, his mother was raped and shot by rebels, while his father was decapitated. ("Boo hoo, right?" he says sarcastically, just a few minutes before he does cry.) He, as a consequence, was sent to South Africa where he himself became a young soldier under a white South African commander—a commander selling weapons to the very same rebels the commander is suppressing on behalf of the government. "So what are you—nihilist, opportunist?" the journalist asks the smuggler. "Maybe I wasn't breast-fed as a child." "Think I haven't met people like you before?" she asks, standing her ground. "I think you get off on people like me." She doesn't disagree and later embraces the smuggler's critique of her, only to turn her confession of hopelessness back on him *through* their shared sexual energy. She explodes: "Do you think I'm exploiting [the father's] grief? You're right, it's shit—like one of those infomercials with little black babies with swollen bellies and flies in their eyes. . . . It might be enough to make some people cry for a minute, even write a check, but it's not going to be enough to make it stop. . . . I need facts, I need names. . . . So if . . . you're not really going to help me, and we're not really going to screw, then why don't you get the fuck out of my face and let me do my work?"

The action picture embedded in this film, and promised on the cover of the DVD, is about to begin.[14] As if to clear the ground for it, the smuggler arranges to have the journalist sent to safety, making for a *coitus interruptus* in the viewers' wish to see these two have sex. (The viewer must sacrifice too, after all.)[15] Now the smuggler and father head off to find the diamond and the son, respectively, making an evident metaphorical link between the future jewel and the child.[16] As most viewers probably foresee, the smuggler dies in his cynical efforts to abscond with the stone, after the child has been secured. Seeing he is mortally wounded, he gives the diamond to the father, sealing their bond, and sharpshoots the father and son to their safety. ("Take your boy home, huh?") Calling the journalist on satellite phone, the smuggler, here at his personal end, seems to acknowledge the red globe of the sun that gorgeously lights his death: "I'm looking at an incredible view . . . and I wish you were here. . . . It's a real story now . . . write the hell out of it." Of course, she does. The third side of the narrative's triangle can be completed. She and the father now use the diamond to cut a deal for the rest of the father's family to be found (his wife and other children)—and, in the process, she is able to trap key members of the "Western" network who are funding war.[17] Liberal intentions wed to the smuggler's cynical actions—the intercourse we *do* see—triumph at this climax, alongside the father's becoming a father all over again.

More than that, through this structure, it can appear that one diamond and one child pursued by a father, a smuggler, and a journalist lead to forty nations jointly signing onto "the Kimberley Process" in January 2003: "an effort to stem the flow of conflict diamonds."[18] Yet as this film comes to its close, the future flattens all over again, in the words left for the viewer to contemplate: "But illegal diamonds are still finding their way to market. It is up to the consumer to insist that a diamond is conflict-free. Sierra Leone is at peace. There are still 200,000 child soldiers in Africa."[19]

The Future in America: Children as Intruders in an Oedipus Raced

The children—intruders—we next consider are not at all killers, though they are a "threat." And they are not in Africa. The children in this case are family intruders *because* they are children who are queered by their color— queered, more precisely, in American contexts, first in the sixties, then in the nineties. They are the children who have entered white families through acts of "mixed marriage," reproduction, or friendship. And they are the children who, like "gay" children, were clearly unforeseen by the families they appear in. As such, these children are themselves a kind of ghost. They are "strangers in the family"—to borrow the tag often used of "gay" children in recent years—who would like to be acknowledged by the families they "invade."[20] They are also tied to a backward birth. In this case, not their own. As if in reverse, these children birth parents. They create the context in which the parents prove to be their best or worst selves. That is, the child-intruder, the child queered by color, makes parents reflect upon their ethics of inclusion ("guess who's coming to dinner?") and reflect upon their image as liberal intellectuals. By mirroring liberals back to themselves, the child queered by color reveals their attempts—births their attempts—to become who they say they have been all along, in a growth the child is supplying from the side.

This is the dynamic in two telling films on American race. *Guess Who's Coming to Dinner* won Oscars in 1968 for depicting liberal parents (Spencer Tracy, Katharine Hepburn) coming to terms with their white daughter's marriage to a "Negro" doctor, played by the famous "Negro" actor Sidney Poitier. *Six Degrees of Separation*, in 1993, based on John Guare's play of this name from 1990, directly reflects on the issues of *Guess*. It shows a black homosexual's intrusion into a wealthy white liberal family by posing as their children's schoolmate from boarding school, and, more invitingly, as the son of Sidney Poitier. The ultimate goal of this boy is embrace (later, adoption) by white wealthy parents.

In distinct ways, these two films, from two different times, are haunted by the specter of the "gay" child. *Six Degrees of Separation* makes this haunting obvious when we learn that "Poitier's son" is actually a streetwalker who "does" men. By contrast, it is probably retrospectively that any viewers of *Guess* find a prescient, spectral presence of homosexuality in a film that never mentions it.[21] Yet in *Guess*, taking place in San Francisco just before Stonewall, resistance to "interracial" marriage has the signs of gay struggles to come: people's shock at seeing a black-white passionate kiss in public view (which startles a taxi driver in the first scene); the expectation of acceptance from liberals; the sad realization that even liberal parents need time to adjust to the less-than-happy sight of their newest relation; parents' confession that they "never thought that such a thing could happen" in their family; and, most intriguingly, the "problem" of children, since children of "mixed marriages" will be "mixed" themselves, thus guaranteeing more children queered by color. Since *Six* injects a gay protagonist into its playful engagement with *Guess*, the earlier film looks even more as though it harbors phantom meanings alongside its focus on race relations. Both films, moreover, call out their liberal characters for what they don't (fore)see. Responding to the children they didn't see growing (either in their families or in the larger culture) is a retrospective task for the parents who accept it. No wonder they are birthed at this critical juncture, becoming themselves all over again as they become the parents of children they've just met.

Several theories speak to this birth. As one might guess, Freud's theory of the Oedipus complex (the boy must break his attachment to his mother and submit to his father) gets revised when children birth their parents in reverse. It also sharply gets revised in the face of African American history and depictions of "Negro" families. In her fully pathbreaking essay from the 1980s, "Mama's Baby, Papa's Maybe: An American Grammar Book," Hortense Spillers teaches us to puncture two different myths about black families: that in 1960s America blacks *could* obey white family symbolics but perversely did not; and that black "matriarchal structure," which supposedly explained this perversity, existed in the place of more normal patriarchy. These are myths, says Spillers, and they appear in official form in the 1965 "Moynihan Report" on the Negro Family (appearing, we should note, two years before *Guess*), where it is asserted, as Spillers reminds us: "In essence, the Negro community has been forced into a matriarchal structure which, because it is so far out of line with the *rest of American society*, seriously retards the progress of the group as a whole, and imposes a crushing burden on the Negro male and, in consequence, on a great many Negro women as well."[22]

What Spillers wants to show, by contrast, are "confounded identities, a meeting ground of investments and privations in the national treasury of rhetorical wealth" (65). That is to say, she wants to show how the game is rigged, a game that makes it seem as if Negro mothers, in some simple sense, by the 1960s have made a power grab and displaced their men; as if a black mother ever *could* stake this place in a national symbolic that at that time was so beholden to "white fathers," such as the liberal Daniel Patrick Moynihan, the New York senator. Spillers thus states: "According to. . . . Moynihan's celebrated 'Report' . . . the 'Negro Family' has no Father to speak of—his Name, his Law, his Symbolic function mark the impressive missing agencies in the essential life of the black community, the 'Report' maintains, and it is, surprisingly, the fault of the Daughter, or the female line. This stunning reversal of the castration thematic, displacing the Name and the Law of the Father to the territory of the Mother and Daughter, becomes an aspect of the African-American female's misnaming" (66). She is misnamed as a father-displacer, the *cause* of "father-lacking" in the "Negro Family," making this family the sad mirror opposite of the "white family" (whose father is in charge), so that, says the report, "it is clearly a disadvantage for a minority group to be operating under one principle, while the great majority of the population . . . is operating on another" (65–66). So strongly does the report believe its claims, Spillers says, that they become the frozen, mythological rendering of black families for all time. "Apparently spontaneous," she continues, "these 'actants' are *wholly* generated, with neither past nor future, as tribal currents moving out of time. Moynihan's 'Families' are pure present and always tense. 'Ethnicity' in this case freezes in meaning, takes on constancy, assumes the look and the affects of the Eternal" (66). TIAA: This is Africa-America, Moynihan seems to be saying.

It is not surprising that Spillers, from here, leaps back from the sixties to the time of slavery in order to demonstrate several points. First, she explains, in powerful terms, that the Middle Passage that brought "the slaves" to American soil "culturally 'unmade'" them: "Those African persons in 'Middle Passage' were literally suspended in the 'oceanic,' if we think of the latter in its Freudian orientation as an analogy for undifferentiated identity, removed from the indigenous land and culture, and not-yet 'American' either" (72). Beyond that, these people, "unmade" as persons—more than metaphorically counted as animals (or as property)—were largely ungendered. For, as Spillers puts it, "under these conditions, one is neither female, nor male, as both subjects are taken into 'account' as *quantities*" (72). As proof of her claim, Spillers cites the fact that "the owner of 'The Brookes' [an English slave ship]. . . . had recommended that 'five females be reckoned as four males, and three boys or girls as equal to two grown persons'" (72).

Perhaps more importantly, Spillers analyzes the way in which "blood relations" were obviously and dramatically "throw[n] into crisis" by the fact of slavery. "Kinship" ceases to hold its meaning, Spillers points out, when "*it*

can be invaded at any given and arbitrary moment by . . . property relations" (74).
"In effect," she says, getting at the root of confounded identities, "under the
conditions of captivity, the offspring of the female does not 'belong' to the
Mother, nor is s/he [the offspring] 'related' to the 'owner,' though the latter
'possesses' it, and in the African-American instance, often fathered it, *and*,
as often, without whatever benefit of patrimony" (74). The effective result
is offspring "unrelated both to their begetters and to their owners," Spillers
contends, citing Claude Meillassoux.[23] Even more striking for my purposes,
Spillers proceeds to state that what were off-limits to slaves were the "vertical" relations (her term) of patronymics and the transfer of titles, entitle-
ments, and real estate from *"fathers to sons"* (74). Rather, "captive persons
were *forced* into patterns of *dispersal*, beginning with the Trade itself, into the
horizontal relatedness of language groups, discourse formations, bloodlines,
names, and properties by the legal arrangements of enslavement" (75).

What does all this history have to do with the Moynihan Report and the
1960s? Exactly this, in Spillers' words: "The dominant culture, in a fatal mis-
understanding, assigns a matriarchist value where it does not belong. . . .
Such naming is false because the female could not, in fact, claim her child,
and false, once again, because 'motherhood' is not perceived in the prevail-
ing social climate as a legitimate procedure of cultural inheritance" (80). And
though she does not say it, Spillers, it seems, is everywhere implying that
black men and women, at the time of Moynihan, are greatly damaged, more
than anything else, by their enforced, complicated, and misnamed relations
to white men positioned as their fathers, in the sense of white men being the
judges of "Negro Families" (judged "pathological") and the legal gatekeep-
ers of miscegenation. Remarkably, the U.S. Supreme Court struck down
American antimiscegenation laws only in 1967, two years after the Moynihan
Report had been issued (and six months before *Guess Who's Coming to Dinner*
was released).

For all these reasons, it should interest us that in *Guess* and *Six*, two liberal films, the black male protagonist seeks the approval of a white father—
seeks to be his son—through different sets of knotted and strange delibera-
tions. However, both films feature striking disappointment in the blindness
of fathers toward their new sons. And in each film, it is mothers who adapt,
accept, and adopt in ways the fathers are late to come to, if at all. Even so, in
each film, the child-intruder (a child queered by color) yearns to be Oedipal-

ized to a white man—and to his house, the father's appendage. The black son's wish for this father's embrace does something else, too, especially in *Guess*. It reveals an Oedipus raced. In this paradigm, the child queered by color (the Negro doctor, named John Prentice, who wants to be apprenticed to his white family) is like the Freudian girl in two respects: he, like she, must change his love-object and change his relation to his own body. In Freud's way of thinking, the girl, as she is Oedipalized to her father, must shift her love-object from her mother to her father and shift her body-focus away from her clitoris (the source of her pleasure) to her vagina.[24] Whatever one thinks of these claims aside—certainly Freud on the clitoris is comical—*Guess* shows the doctor making key shifts in his objects of love. In a crucial way, he shifts from a black metaphorical "mother" (his *two* black parents) to a white metaphorical "father" (his new white parents, their daughter, their maid, and their big white house). He also redirects his bodily focus—away from his own black skin to ideas of no color at all, as if he is a "black boy" freed from his color "cloud" and now embraced as a colorless "lamb" (in the striking idioms used by William Blake).[25]

Yet, as I have said, the black child-intruder, for all his submission, and against some of Freud's explicit expectations, is birthing a family in these two films, conceiving of parents embracing black children they (the parents) did not think they had. He does so by mirroring them to themselves in ways that engage their political views, sexual feelings, dreams, and even the views from their homes. Ironically, the black child-intruder reveals that liberal parents in one respect occupy the structural position of the "gay" child: they are reaching themselves on delay. Protogay children, as we have explored, cannot be seen by the public to be "gay" until they are no longer children. They become themselves (who they say they've been) when they are no longer who they say they were. The paradigm for liberal parents (implied by *Six* and *Guess*) goes something like this: they (liberal parents) cannot be "liberal" in the eyes of others until for a time they are actually not. They cannot be confirmed as who they say they are—liberal, accepting, loving parents—until a situation puts a stop to their acceptance—at least for a time, whether momentarily or for a longer stretch. After this lag (this delay in acceptance), they can then confirm they are who they have *been*; the only problem being: they haven't really been who they are until now. Subtle though it seems, the uniqueness of these parents' position (their difference from the "gay" child) is the temporal gap between who they say they have been (all along) and who they say they continue to be. Since they are *almost* self-continuous, in their estimation of themselves, they may imagine that they have never differed from themselves at all — only perhaps been suspended in thought. This particular model of duration that depends upon hiatus is another version of *Nachträglichkeit*, or "deferred effect." But, once again, this is a false latency, in key respects. The parents, as I say, are truly becoming who they have *not* been, since, until now, no one has helped them *be* their words. Theirs is thus an analogue, in temporal terms, to Lacanian (mis)recognition in the mirror: what sits between them and themselves is time, rendered by a queer child who gets inside their image.[26]

As regards this mirroring, one more theory pertains to these films. It concerns the role of space. Beatriz Colomina, in the field of architecture, using film theory, has shaped perspectives on "domestic voyeurism": how the space of a house directs the occupants' gaze.[27] It does so, first, toward those who enter. (The house directs us to see who comes to dinner.) But for those inside the house, interior space may also lead the gaze toward the view that the house, almost acting like a camera, with its picture windows, captures for its owners. The house, in this way, can be a picture-taking mechanism. In fact, though Colomina never tells us so, the house is something between a fetish in the film theory sense — a beautiful, arresting, optical lure — and a camera that could take such an image, as if a stunning female body on the movie screen (elegant, serene, inviting, well-arranged) could take its own picture while it's on display. Like a woman's body, in a fetishistic sense, the house is a reflection of a man's position: it's a place he penetrates and thus it is his body — also his views, literally so — in an extended sense.[28]

Colomina, as I say, doesn't tread this path. Instead, she presents two different kinds of houses: those of the famous architects Adolf Loos and Le Corbusier. Quoting Walter Benjamin that "to live is to leave traces," Colomina asks how occupants of houses are positioned to leave their traces on interiors, especially as their houses structure how they gaze. For example, in a Loos house, with a large sofa placed against a window, occupants face back into their rooms, "theatre-box" style, monitoring movements in the interior and making the thresholds of these spaces tense, "so that an intruder could be easily seen" (figures 25 and 26). By contrast, houses by Le Corbusier "throw the subject towards the periphery of the house," since "these houses

25. Adolph Loos interior: the stage is clearly set.
© 2008 Artists Rights Society (ARS), New York / VBK, Vienna.

26. Adolph Loos interior: the couch controls the gaze.
© 2008 Artists Rights Society (ARS), New York / VBK, Vienna.

[are] frames for a view," allowing a person a view of the world (figures 27 and 28). The house is "between the eye and the view," much as a camera mediates a view when we hold it to our eye as we contemplate a picture. The house is in the structural position of the camera.

I will confirm but invert this latter claim. I will suggest that the view looks back. The view becomes a mirror that provides a reflection and a bodily ego for the one who "owns" this view. One finds that one's views (one's outlook on the world) come back to oneself in aggressive form, even in the form of children-intruders. In the separate cases of *Guess* and *Six*, the implied architecture of each film's house tells us all we need to know about the family's sense of self. It also tells us what intrusion would look like from the family's viewpoint, since an intruder would have to find a way, physically, to enter the space of the family. What do intrusion and mirroring look like in each film?

The Force of Inclusion in Guess Who's Coming to Dinner

The arc of *Guess*, given that it is a comedy, starts from intrusion and moves toward the gesture (and message) of inclusion. We likely suspect that the interracial lovers will eventually be accepted, because the white family the doctor seeks to join (especially the father, Matthew Drayton) is known across the city to have progressive views. The father is a "lifelong fighting liberal." So as to make a drama out of this foregone liberal conclusion, the film makes the timing of acceptance its issue. The doctor and fiancée, a woman named Joey, have only one night to get their families' blessings, since they are leaving for his work overseas. (With his credentials from Yale and Johns Hopkins, he will be working on world health in Africa.) It is this wish for their parents' immediate confirmation of their couplehood that sets the stage for conflict. The tight time frame also, conveniently, sets the limits for what the film addresses: there is no time, in this single evening, to see if the couple will in fact face hatred, or struggle with each other, or have their own children (who add to their threat)—all of which lies beyond the bounds of comedy.

As for intrusion, John and Joey arrive at her house ahead of her parents and go inside without yet knowing if they are welcome, though Joey just assumes so. Met at the door by the family's black maid—a belligerent Tillie (Isabel Sanford), who is not a fan of interracial marriage and accuses the

27. Le Corbusier picture-taking windows.

28. Le Corbusier terrace owning views.

29. Tension at the threshold: Tillie unhappily meets the "intruder."
From the film *Guess Who's Coming to Dinner* (1967).

well-mannered Poitier character, John, of "black power" — Dr. Prentice feels a palpable tension at the threshold (figure 29). In fact, his fiancée has literally pulled him into the foyer, yanking his arm with cheerful bravado, and soothed Tillie's ire by striking the pose of the maid's little favorite from earlier years. (Joey is "Little Joey" to Tillie and later to her father.) This is the first of this couple's regressions back to the status of supplicating children. Now inside the home, Dr. John Prentice softly cat-paws through the house, as if he *is* intruding, or leaving marks. (The whiteness of the rug almost begs to show his footprints.) The camera, in collusion with his need to scope the scene, patiently pans the rooms of the spacious, clearly artistic, quasi-modernist, white-walled house, with large picture windows looking onto a terrace that overlooks the city and the Golden Gate Bridge. Here's a room with a view. Intimate and removed from the city, since it's high on a hill, the house is looking onto the world, positioned in a way that occupants can think that the world is looking back. (The world is looking to see what they do.) But there is also a couch against the window, making its sitters look back into the room and thus providing a theater-box space for "domestic melodramas" of intrusion and control. In fact, it's as if the film set of *Guess* has made a spacious Le Corbusier terrace share a central wall with a Loos-type space.

The first real look between John and a parent (who sits on this couch) comes when he provides an optical shock to Joey's mother (Katharine Hepburn), who clearly didn't know that the doctor would be black. She looks as though she'll faint. Joey to her mother: "He thinks you're going to faint because he is a Negro": the mother to them both, regaining something of regal composure: "I don't suppose you'd mind if I said 'My goodness'?" Her concerned surprise is mild compared to that of Joey's father (Spencer Tracy). When he learns that the doctor before him—acceptable as his daughter's friend (in fact, fully admirable)—may become his son-in-law, Matt Drayton balks. He can't give his blessing—certainly not yet. He needs some time to think and reflect; which he does on his terrace, which offers him views, though for most of the film his back is literally turned to his views (figures 30, 31, and 32). Matt, however, thinks he needs to meditate on his job as father (and on the threatening death of his dreams?), to protect his daughter—to protect both of them, son and daughter—from the harm headed their way as a couple. He thinks they're irresponsible not to be fearful and to press him for acceptance, especially in such a compressed time frame. Only briefly does he mention the delicate subject (the most racist subject the film must engage) of the interracial children the couple might produce, thus multiplying the original problem of their pairing. "Doctor," says Matt, "there's one thing we haven't talked about: have you given any thought to the problems your children are going to have?" John answers him: "Yes . . . and we'll have children; otherwise I don't know what you'd call it, but you couldn't call it a marriage." Therefore, children are not a side concern. Though they remain an unseen threat in this film suspended in the span of an evening, they hover at the edges. Indeed, in John's reply to Matt, the sacredness of marriage, according to his logic, only proves to be itself at a later point in time, through an action—reproduction—that is strictly supplemental to the state of marriage. No wonder John and Joey are surrounded by children in the film's first scene, as they ride an escalator at the airport, making this visual a future retroaction of Matt's deepest worries. This is the kind of picture haunting Matt, which his more beautiful views must dislodge. In a subtler way, the film's seemingly unrelated but rather insistent focus on art—a taste-

30. Awkward Matt and the elegant doctor.
From the film *Guess Who's Coming to Dinner* (1967).

31. They are windows on the world.
From the film *Guess Who's Coming to Dinner* (1967).

32. Matt amidst his thoughts, his back to his views.
From the film *Guess Who's Coming to Dinner* (1967).

less sculpture in a gallery at the start, Joey's mother's creative idea to put art "originals" in hotel rooms instead of otherwise "bad reproductions," and the tasteful pieces that grace the family home — are ways of doing two things at once: defining racism as bad taste (heaven forbid) and raising the troubling specter of reproduction itself (what makes a good one?).[29] As Matt wonders out loud at one point: "How do you suppose a colored mailman [John's father] produced a son with all those qualities?"

Suffice it to say, Matt Drayton starts to think that, on temporal grounds, he can't condone the marriage: the world in 1967, he believes, is not yet ready for it. He is soon joined in this view by John's father, who with John's mother has flown up for "dinner." The fathers are against the interracial marriage. The mothers (and the Drayton family friend, a Catholic priest) are almost immediately for the pairing, since they are "not thinking," as the fathers tell them. The film thus settles into thinking mode, becoming a reflection on people reflecting on a new kind of marriage (and perhaps reproduction). The old word for what John and Joey seek to do, which haunts the film but is never spoken, is "miscegenation": "the interbreeding of what are presumed to be distinct human races, especially marriage between white and nonwhite persons," says the dictionary.[30] Probably, the word would itself be inflammatory, because it would evoke white racist objections to, among other things, the integration of public schools, where black and white children might socially (even sexually) mix.[31] Matt is not a racist, he would urgently protest. He is just protecting the children in front of him, who might be hated for having children. In an aside, John's father's own objections ("You're way out of line, boy") are voiced and responded to. In fact, the calm, elegant doctor, played so deferentially by Poitier, who literally bows or backs his way into every room, explodes at his father: "I owe you nothing; you brought me into the world. . . . yet you don't own me. . . . not until your whole generation has lain down and died will the dead weight of you be off our backs! You must get off my back!" This astonishing reply would be better aimed at Matt, the film's white patriarch. But here the implication is that *blacks* are lagging, dragging, resisting (one thinks of the maid), not enough "with it," in the lingo of the times, to see new relations in a new light.[32] Or as John ends his speech in a kinder, gentler mode, noticeably not in accord with black power: "Dad, you think of yourself as a colored man. I think of myself as a man." Even so, the father remains unconvinced, even through the end of the film.

But that doesn't matter. What matters is what Matt thinks and where his reflections are now leading him. In some remarkable scenes of looking—out windows, off the terrace, at the mirror—which bounce the image of Matt back to him (and to the viewer positioned *as* Matt?), Matt reflects on his liberal reputation and his potential break with it. The priest says he is "thrown"; "you're not yourself, laddie."[33] In fact, he is in danger of losing his wife—at least her admiration for him. So what can turn Matt? What turns out to swing him is the memory of his feelings, his sensations long ago for his wife. However, these feelings are called up in him by the black mother, who speaks fresh from her feeling of seeing her black son's love. It is as if she carries it *for* John *to* Matt, then holds it up to Matt as a kind of mirror, so that she assists in John's birthing Matt and lets the film avoid a black man/white man confrontation out of keeping with its taste. *She* confronts Matt: "You and my husband might as well be blind men . . . I believe that men grow old and when sexual things no longer matter to them, they forget it all, forget what true passion is. If you ever felt what my son feels for your daughter, you've forgotten everything about it."

Matt takes these thoughts and reflects on them. We see him reflect—for a long time. With the camera tracking him in patient lengthy shots, we see him stand on the terrace of his house, thinking, staring out at his view. As if his view looks back at him, and whispers in his ear, he says "I'll be a son of a bitch!" He now has his answer and is going to pronounce it — in a remarkable patriarchal fashion. He gathers everyone into the living room. (Here they sit between Matt and his view.) He tells his daughter she must "shut up." He narrates the day and tells John directly that his crucial mistake was putting so much stock in what Matt and his wife thought — though, of course, for the sake of the film (and its majority-white audience) this is all that's crucial. So what does Matt think? He thinks the mirror opposite of what John's mother said he thinks (which was said for John, as she reproduced his views). Or as Matt puts it: "Strange as it seems, that's the first statement said to me all day with which I'm prepared to take issue. Because you're wrong. You're as wrong as you can be. . . . I know exactly how [John] feels. . . . There is absolutely nothing that your son feels for my daughter that I didn't feel for Christina. . . . The memories are still there — clear, intact, indestructible; and they'll be there if I live to be one hundred."

With this pronouncement, the movie can end. Matt has been given the chance to match his views, from his house to his head. Through John Prentice, through John's mother, Matt has become who he says he is. And who he is is who he's been (according to him), albeit excepting the critical interval when, according to others watching him (the priest and Matt's wife), he was "not himself." He is birthed back to what he has (and has not ever) been before: the father of a daughter and the man she plans to love. All will sit down to the family supper table. Even an Irish Catholic priest, the closest friend of this Protestant family, gets to come to dinner. The family's maid, however, who has been the one most upset by the events, can't sit down with the family at the end, since she must serve the dinner and the families gathered there.

This particular crack in inclusion shares some dilemmas with William Blake's "The Little Black Boy." In that poem, the little black boy, by the poem's end, still seems to be serving the white boy in Heaven, even after both have been freed from their colors. Here, in *Guess*, the Negro who "has been a member of this family for twenty-two years," as Matt describes the maid, is included — as a servant. Since she is the only black person so far to be a Drayton family "member," she is a sign of fault lines in the family's image. Alignment of black and white in the end still looks premature, held in suspense, as if suffering a temporal gap.

Gay and Black Child, Mother and Father, Side by Side in Six Degrees of Separation

Twenty-five years later, *Six* exploits this gap, as if it has only grown with time. Now the black child who intrudes upon the family is a streetwise kid who is guilty in the end only of cooking the parents a dinner. This makes the doctor character from *Guess* into the Drayton family maid—John becomes Tillie who is now called Paul (played by Will Smith)—raising the question of whether an "underclass" black, not to mention a black homosexual, can be a son to a white wealthy father.

Aggressively, the black child's entrance in this film, and into this family, is due to the fact that he is wounded in the side and bleeding at their door. (Paul steps in through a hole in his body, as if he carries a doorway in his side.) Children and art are his topics, in succession, as he steps across the threshold, nearly dripping blood. Mentioning their children—"I'm so sorry to bother you, but I've been hurt and I've lost everything and I didn't know where to go. Your children—I'm a friend of—," Paul, with the doorman still in tow, enters into the parents' apartment (figure 33). It has red walls, soft light, good art, and plentiful horizontal windows that capture views of Manhattan—but, at night, reflect the room back onto itself, mixing the outside views with all the interior ones, making the occupants, through the camera's work, look as if they're walking in the sky above the street, as if they are safely ensconced in the views they are literally above. This is a theater box floating in the air, ready for performances the parents can control (figure 34).[34] Paul, as it happens, was mugged in Central Park, his money and briefcase stolen from him, or so he says. Now he uses a phrase from the title of Walter Benjamin's famous essay "The Work of Art in the Age of Mechanical Reproduction," as he tells them: "In this age of mechanical reproduction they managed to get the only copy of my thesis." Again, the theme of art hints at reproductive matters and the question of tasteful or degraded copies.

But this entrance, intrusive as it is, is not the film's start. The film begins

33. Wound-as-door: Paul gets past the threshold.
From the film *Six Degrees of Separation* (1993).

34. The Kittredges' living room as a theater box floating in the air.
From the film *Six Degrees of Separation* (1993).

in chaos with the phrases "I am shaking." "Is anything gone?" "We could have been killed." "Slashed—our throats slashed." A double-sided Kandinsky painting, with contrasting styles, "chaos" and "control," on its two different sides, has not been taken. Soon we're at a wedding with a husband and wife, Flan (Donald Sutherland) and Ouisa Kittredge (Stockard Channing), telling the story behind these phrases to a group of wealthy white New Yorkers like themselves. They were having an evening with a friend, they both explain— an extremely wealthy white South African ("King Midas rich. Literally. Gold mines.")—from whom they were hoping to leverage money in order to buy, then sell, a Cézanne. ("Mid-period. . . . One of his first uses of a pale color being forced to carry the weight of the picture. The experiment that would pay off with the apples. A burst of color asked to carry so much.") With the burst of color just about to arrive—an apple that would like to fall from their tree—Flan and Ouisa were as yet unaware of "the weight" they or he would be "forced to carry" in a relation pregnant with their parenthood. As they tell their listeners, using their distinctive verbal patter, mixing references to African rebellions with Broadway show tunes, constantly syntactically echoing both themselves and each other via word copies: "We weren't auditioning but I kept thinking Two million dollars two million dollars." Flan follows: "It's like when people say 'Don't think about the elephants' and all you can think about is elephants elephants."

Into this audition, held in the air, enters Paul Poitier (as he calls himself), passing and glassing, one could say, since his distinctive, mirroring way of getting in (besides his wound) is to tell these parents things about themselves by referencing their children: "Your children said you were kind. All the kids were sitting around the dorm one night dishing the shit out of their parents. But your kids were silent and said, 'No, not our parents. Not Flan and Ouisa. Not the Kittredges. The Kittredges are kind.'" ("Can you believe what the kids said?" Ouisa asks Flan in disbelief.) From here Paul provides the group with an experience: he tells them of Poitier ("barrier breaker of the fifties and sixties," star of *Guess Who's Coming to Dinner*); of Poitier's aim to make a film of *Cats* (of all the bad reproductions); and of his stolen thesis on *Catcher in the Rye*: "The book is primarily about paralysis. The boy can't function. At the end, before he can run away and start a new life, it starts to rain and he folds." As in Blake's "The Little Black Boy," here experience comes to sheltered whites through a black body seeking connection. It is as

35. Optical shock: boys in your bed. From the film *Six Degrees of Separation* (1993).

if blackness, as we saw in Blake, is thought to be older, experientially, and more absorbing of life, than whiteness, and thus a bridge to, a door opening onto, color and imaginative force (the qualities Flan finds in Cézanne). The proof of Paul's value in these terms, and his link to the unfolding theme of good or bad reproductions (or even art originals), is the fact that Flan gets the money for the painting from their rich, South African friend. (Flan and Ouisa, in typical fashion: "He's in." "He's in?" "He's in for two million." "Two million!" Paul inserts himself inside their echo: "Two million dollars? . . . I'm glad I helped.")

The experience the Kittredges didn't count on, as they next narrate, was that of finding Paul, who they believed was Poitier's son, having sex with a hustler in their own daughter's bed, after Paul had stayed the night. Now the optical shock of the interracial kiss in *Guess* is clearly updated (figure 35). Ouisa, like the surrogate parent she's becoming, explodes at this intrusion: "You went out after we went to sleep and picked up this thing?" Flan: "You brought this thing into our house! Thing! Thing! Get out of my house!" Paul pleads: "Please. Don't tell my father. I don't want him to know. I haven't told him. . . . I couldn't be alone. You had so much." "And that's that," Ouisa tells her listeners in a perfect doubled phrase.

The story continues, however, as it now elicits copies of these stories (or similar stories) among their friends, as if Paul has spread his "experience" across the chain of their connections. "Do we have a story to tell you!" "Do we have a story to tell *you!*" The cops are unimpressed: "What are the charges?" "He came into our house." "He cooked us dinner." "He told us the story of *Catcher in the Rye*." "He said he was the son of Sidney Poitier." In fact, when they tell the story to their children, with a kind of attraction in their voices ("he has this wild quality—yet a real elegance and a real concern and a real consideration"), one of their children openly whines: "You should have divorced all your children and just let this dreamboat stay." The children are obviously the bad reproductions both films are concerned about: *Guess* rather earnestly, *Six* more ironically, since the bad copies are clearly the white kids, who, if anything, don't remove the parents enough from themselves. Selfish, petulant, privileged, and increasingly histrionic ("Mom said sleeping with you was like sleeping with a salad made of bad dressing. Why you had to bring me into the world!")—qualities underscored by the bad acting that depicts them—the children are the kind of mirrors one couldn't wish upon oneself.[35] They are the counterpart to the red room that throws the views of Ouisa and Flan back on themselves in unthinking reflection. "Even" the image of a black homosexual con, queered and colored, is a better way to have one's image birthed backward in an opportunity for liberal confirmation of "we have hearts." And Paul at least brings plotting to their lives: "intruders," "thieves," and (imaginary) "black crack addicts," whom they enjoy discussing.

It is through their kids, nonetheless, that the story behind Paul, the person behind Paul, named Trent Conway, starts to emerge. He is a white homosexual classmate of Flan's and Ouisa's daughter from prep school. Paul is the creation of a ghostly gay child. For Trent is a kind of gay-child Pygmalion, who, in shaping Paul, teaching Paul to be mannered, would like to have *himself* seen through this figure of the cultured black straight son of Sidney Poitier: an acceptable and visible civil rights icon. Or, as this wealthy gay boy tells Paul—Paul who is a hustler, found "in a doorway" and willing to trade single pieces of his clothing for facts about these rich white parents—"Then I'll come into one of these homes one day," says the white boy, "and you'll be there and I'll be presented to you. And I'll pretend to meet you for the first time and our friendship will be witnessed by my friends, our parents' friends. If it all happens under their noses, they can't judge me. They can't disparage you. I'll make you a guest in their houses" (figure 36). In this theater-box version of home life, where intrusion is converted into only one degree of separation, Paul and this queer boy will be hospitable transports for each

36. Gay boy and black boy playing at Pygmalion.
From the film *Six Degrees of Separation* (1993).

other to the eyes (and houses) of white friends and family. And so this gay boy makes a black boy in his image: "This is the way you must speak. Hear my accent. Hear my voice. Never say you're going horse-back riding. You say you're going riding. And don't say couch. Say sofa. And you say *bodd*-ill. It's bottle. Say bottle of beer." Is Paul "gay"? Should he, does he, learn to say that about Paul Poitier? He never does take that word to himself — or shun it, for that matter. We only know that he hustles men (at least that we see); and then he is having sex with a man (a hustler) when Ouisa walks in on him — as if Paul-the-hustler *is* Trent Conway with a street kid in his bed.

There is a last intriguing twist of the knife for Flan and Ouisa in relation to Paul, posing as a straight child sent by a queer child, sent in order to give these parents a chance to confirm themselves as liberal in relation to a black. How will they respond to a "Poitier" now that he is not the wealthy actor's son they had supposed? News of Paul resurfaces when he starts to pose — for their doorman, most of all, keeping the theme of doorway entries firmly in view — as Flan's "secret son" from a former relationship, "the Negro son you deny," as the doorman accuses Flan after spitting at him. Befriending a boyfriend and girlfriend from Utah — these two kids are the quintessential markers for a white innocence, as Blake conceives of it — Paul moves in with them based on his lie (told to the kids, Rick and Elizabeth) that he is "the child of Flan's hippie days," "his radical days" of freedom marching to register black voters in the South. Once again, Paul is (dangerously) viewed as a fount of experience. With a bunch of money he has borrowed from the kids, Paul takes Rick to the Rainbow Room, where they dance a tango ("nothing like this ever happened in Utah"), followed by sex in Central Park. Rick explains: "He asked if he could fuck me and I had never done anything like that and he did and it was fantastic. . . . I wanted experience. I am here to have experience. But . . . I didn't come here to be *this*. My father said I was a fool and I can't have him be right." Rick kills himself.

In a last phone call to Ouisa, Paul, about to be arrested for bilking the Utah couple of their money, makes his most passionate plea to be her child. Flan disengages, but does so in a way that reminds us he could easily be a father to a con: "Oh please. I am not a bullshitter but never bullshit a bullshitter." Ouisa, on the other hand, after scolding Paul with a script written for gay-youth-at-risk ("You were lunatic! And picking that dreck off the street. Are you suicidal? Do you have AIDS? Are you infected?"), can't help but be charmed by Paul's self-report of his new love of art: "I went to a museum! I liked Toulouse-Lautrec!" "As well you should," she says. Together, they drift in and out of dreaming their impossible relationship, ending with Ouisa's (unconscious?) reference to a film title and cliché, as she tells Paul: "We'll have a wonderful life." Paul is arrested, nevertheless, and since Ouisa never has known Paul's identity, his real name, she can't find any record of him with the police. Like the ghost he is, Paul just dissolves.[36] Ouisa tells Flan and a group of listeners at a fancy luncheon, using the dinner theme from the earlier *Guess* once more: "And we turn him into an anecdote to dine out on. Or dine in on. But it was an experience. I will not turn him into an anecdote. . . . How do we *keep* the experience?" Seeing Flan's obvious lack of interest, Ouisa insists: "He did more for us in a few hours than our children ever did. He wanted to be your child. . . . You were attracted to him — ." Flan shoots back, refusing to be conceived (of) as a parent in the language of attraction: "Cut me out of that pathology!"

The child queered by color, by the end of *Six*, has birthed a single parent: not the black mother of Blake's imagination in "The Little Black Boy." And not the poor mother of the standard American imagination of a black street kid. This is a Katharine Hepburn for a black boy going to prison, seemingly for seducing a white boy out of money freely given: "And when you come [to prison to visit]," Paul queries Ouisa in that last call, "you'll wear your best clothes and knock 'em dead?" "I'll knock 'em dead," she mirrors in her answer. Whatever Paul will become from here—however he will grow in the suspension he is left in—he has done what Poitier never did. He has made the split in the echoing selves of liberal intellectual and liberal intellectual fully apparent, against all odds. Ouisa ends by saying of her husband, his "father": "We're a terrible match."

This is an Oedipus newly raced.

When "Your" Father Beds You

The layers to these issues are even more fraught than one might guess. For in *Guess Who* (2005) we get a farce—now not a comedy or comedy-drama—out of *Guess Who's Coming to Dinner*.[37] This film's conceit involves a black daughter's bringing a white boy (Ashton Kutcher) home to *her* father (Bernie Mac). This time the black man is clearly in charge, though, of course, only farcically so. And even though now the terms are flipped—the fairly wealthy family with liberal views and a ruling patriarch is a black family—a certain tricky logic, snaking through *Guess* and *Six* before it, becomes full-blown in this obvious romp, when it happens that the father makes the "son"—his daughter's boyfriend—now sleep with him (figures 37 and 38). Indeed, one wonders, when watching *Guess Who*, what in the earlier, serious comedies could give rise to the junior high yuck-it-up scenes in which the father spoons his future son-in-law and mumbles to him "that's my girl" while he's asleep. Perhaps there is nothing that links these scenes to the earlier films. Or maybe there is something that, even faintly, grounds these actions.

Implicit in both of the earlier films is the father's admiration for, and nearly stated attraction to, his would-be son. ("You were attracted to him," says Ouisa to Flan, who blushes before he denies it.) And maybe because they pose no threats and offer no barriers, mothers and daughters, despite their vaunted visual pleasure (especially in *Guess*), are beside the point—even when they are not—as Spillers might force us to see in these films. (In *Blood Diamond*, this is blatantly true: finding his son is the father's sole focus in terms of the drama; his missing wife and daughter are barely even characters.) Hence, the more primal wedding, the matrimonial more truly sought, with the frisson this seeking implies, is son to father and father to son. There must be a mutual intellectual and bodily sizing up between them that the camera both catches and deflects, so as to keep it shy of erotics,

37. "Son" in bed with "father."
From the film *Guess Who* (2005).

38. The "son" and "father" can't stay apart.
From the film *Guess Who* (2005).

while conveying subtle suggestions of this flavor. In *Guess Who's Coming to Dinner*, John's accomplishments—absurdly enumerated by the filmmakers so as to make his race his only "problem"—truly rival and trump Matt's own. More than that, Poitier's fully transfixing presence—his posture and clothes and the way he moves across physical space—easily outdoes frumpy Matt, whose collar is made to awkwardly poke up around his neck in the film's first half. Viewers thus can't help but feel, since we are truly set up to feel, that anyone this elegant, talented, and honorable *must* win over the heart (and maybe the eyes) of this father, which is the only seduction that matters or hangs in the balance throughout the film. Heart and eyes and head are metonyms for each other in this film's visual register, both at the climax to the story and throughout. These two men have talks on the terrace, where we can see Matt's beautiful views looking over his shoulder, as the appealing doctor, cosmopolitan and beautifully presented, matches them in front of "his" father. Flan, on the other hand, revises his attractions precisely when he finds Paul with (another) man—"You brought this thing into our house?"—which Flan never does get over as the sign of Paul's betrayal.[38] Up to this point, Flan, every bit as much as Ouisa, has been charmed beyond all reckoning, which Donald Sutherland plays to a T. Flan is the one to bandage Paul's wound (and thus touch him bodily on the abdomen) and Flan commences his and his wife's being "star fuckers," however he denies it, in relation to Paul's being Poitier's son.[39] Flan, in fact, more than anyone else, is caught being earnest in the face of Paul's thesis on *Catcher in the Rye*: "I hope your muggers read *every* word," he emotionally asserts, prompting Ouisa to laugh out loud at his enthrallment. Paul, of course, repays Flan's investment by later claiming to be Flan's son, Paul Poitier-Kittredge, as he calls himself, and seeks out Flanders more than Ouisa so as to learn the business that his "father" runs.

So perhaps it's not so strange—though it seems so at first—that *Guess Who* is riddled with (homophobic?) humor of that mixed anxious-juvenile-flirtatious sort so common to straight comedy in our current climate. The ostensible reason that the father beds the son is to keep him from sleeping prematurely with his daughter—"I don't want to hear you talking about sleeping with my daughter; you sleeping with me now"; this reason doubly pertains to the father's catching these "children" in a compromising pose, complete with lingerie that makes his future son-in-law look like a transvestite. ("Just for the record," the boyfriend offers, "I'm not a cross-dresser.") These, however, are plot contortions that sit to the side of a central element that brings together all these films, including *Blood Diamond*: namely, money. Money is what drives all these plots, along with race—including the plot of the Moynihan Report. "Negro Families" are largely "pathological," one imagines Moynihan thinking, because their incomes indicate lesser possibilities for lucrative futures. *Guess* approves of John in the end, and Matt can see himself in John, because this doctor has real financial promise. Paul does not, as Flan discovers, and thus he is no candidate for Flan's son (however Flan feels about homosexuality, which we don't know). At the start of *Guess Who*, the father's prospective son-in-law, named Simon Green, whose name just happens to be the beautiful color of money, is known to the father only by his job—a high-powered one—and his credit report ("a thing of beauty," the father says, "I almost cried"). Hence the daughter says to Simon: "I feel like he's more in love with you than I am."

The plot largely turns on Simon's hiding, from his fiancée and her father, that he has quit his job. When the father finds this out, he feels fully justified in blocking the marriage; and Simon's lack of money, and further dishonesty over his lack of it, serve as alibis for the black father to shun the white son. Only by the end does the father discover (the mother and daughter seem beside the point again) that Simon quit his job because his boss was racist and said racist things about his fiancée. The father, sitting side by side on a bench with his former bedmate whom he has cuddled when he's been asleep, tells the white boy: "What you did with your boss was honorable, impressive, and stupid: you can't quit your job every time someone rolls their eyes at the two of you—you'll never make any money." Here's a fascinating Oedipalization, the truest sense of American paternity. Simon needs to recognize his father is the dollar. Quite simply, and fully tautologically, Simon must stay Green—or become Green, once again, as he has been. Just as tautologically, fulfilling the pleonastic logic of *Guess Who's Coming to Dinner*, the father that Simon has been sleeping with needs to renew his vows to his wife (which he does at a party, in front of all their friends), since "after twenty-five years, all I've asked you is to let me be me," the father says redundantly, even though "I think I forgot what love is until . . . Simon showed up." This intrusion, too, has renewed and birthed a father.

The upshot of all of this? The father's embrace of a future in suspension:

"My future son-in-law: he's broke, unemployed, and white, but he loves [my daughter]. . . . welcome to the family." The father then dances a tango with his wife, which he has already danced with his "son" when both were drinking and Green said to him, in instruction: "There's got to be space between us — it's not like when we're sleeping together."

Money Is the Child's Queer Ride
Sexing and Racing around the Future

If a child of color, who is poor and queer, can be a mirror to whites with money, making them turn upon and look upon themselves, as is the case in *Six Degrees of Separation*, can a grown homosexual child mirror American money to itself? Andy Warhol actually did.[1]

He was the child from a Pittsburgh ghetto who drove commerce smack into art. He was the child who rode the wave of commerce, since he was a child so clearly queered by money. Rewarded by his mother for each of his drawings with a bar of chocolate, or so he said, he rose from "the humblest of backgrounds to become the most famous and famously controversial artist" of his time.[2] "He took the idea of art in the age of mechanical reproduction," says one critic, "to its logical extreme, breaching the wall dividing fine art from commerce, grasping as no one, before or since, the function of fame in a mass society" — "at once fulfilling the promise of the American dream and . . . redefining it, reinventing it."[3]

He was the mother of all (his) reinventions. He was "the ethnic Pole . . . who was gay and really swishy," with a "mysterious Albino-like loss of pigmentation in his skin," yet with splotches (reddish-brown) all over his face, who "thought it would be . . . nice to become Lana Turner, and art let him do that."[4] In fact, Andy Warhol gathers nearly all queer chil-

CANDY DOESN'T HAVE TO HAVE A POINT—THAT'S WHY IT'S CANDY.
—FROM *CHARLIE AND THE CHOCOLATE FACTORY*

dren in himself. He is the ghostly gay, queerly colored, Freudian-fixated-on-his-mother, deceptively "simple," and grown homosexual child of postwar American art and culture. In his persona, he also advertises growing sideways: "a girl from nowhere moving to somewhere," as one critic humorously puts it; or, as another critic formulates it earnestly: "I think he was an artist dealing with immediacy, intensity, vividness, the power of connection and the threat to all of that that comes with death."[5] This is not quite embrace of the death drive, as Lee Edelman asks us to conceive of it in *No Future: Queer Theory and the Death Drive*. But neither is it the blinkered embrace of "reproductive futurism" (Edelman's target). It is a plea for just more time. More fame. More: an extensive minimalism on his part.[6]

Maybe because of this plea for more, Warhol is, against all odds (and oddities, too), the original, creative copy of America—at least in many critics' estimations. Indeed, their estimates of him are grand: "He was the most American of artists and the most artistic of Americans—so American, in fact, we look at him and, knowing little of ourselves, learn little of Warhol because he *was* us—in all our innocence, ambition, and insecurity."[7] "In Warhol the simplicity of a typical American citizen and the simplicity of artistic genius are so intermingled that we cannot distinguish them." Yet another critic observes: "He's a touchstone . . . for the entire culture of the postwar period. . . . the most important artist of the second half of the twentieth century—maybe the most important artist of the . . . century." He continues: "If we needed to find a visual form to just distill what it was like to be alive for the last fifty years, the image would come somewhere from the corpus of Andy Warhol." A different critic summarizes: "How profoundly different the world before Andy and after Andy looked."

Aside from whether these claims are too large, too over-the-top about this queer child, they implicitly return us to the child queered by money most of all. One art critic, musing about the effects of Warhol's ghetto background in a Slavic enclave, says in passing: "I think the thing about Andy is that Andy had *no idea* of bourgeois life; he never saw it, he never lived it."

This decided distance from the object of his echoes, one might conclude, helped him reproduce it with the clarity that queered it.

Money Threads: A Recap

Warhol is my segue—and only a segue—into my conclusion for obvious reasons. He, like Capote, to whom he wrote fan letters that went unanswered, was a poster child for the queer child, a strangeness spreading out from a ghostly gayness that touched on money (for Warhol, most especially). But money problems—Capote's parents' relations to debt, with their love of luxury—are the clear setup, and background flavor, of many of Capote's childhood memoirs about the oddities of his Southern boyhood. One could surely say that his ghostly gayness seeps out in signifiers that have their roots in a tangled causality that is money—certainly in part. That is to say, financial relations clearly shape the form his strangeness as a sissy boy ends up taking.

In fact, Capote's boyhood had Jamesian elements, with a Southern twist. The parents' legal battles over a child that neither really wanted, and both neglected, left the child to avuncular figures—shades of James's bachelor figures—in the form of elderly spinster cousins and their old unmarried brother.[8] One of these cousins, in particular, a sixty-something woman, "as much of a child as I was," became his lateralized cousin-companion and synecdochal family, along with their beloved dog-child, Queenie ("we have a little rat terrier, a funny little thing," "but we both love her").[9] As Capote notes: "Perhaps it was strange for a young boy to have as his best friend an aging spinster," but "except for the hours I spent at school, the three of us" (boy, spinster, and dog) "were almost always together"—pushing their "buggy," "a dilapidated baby carriage . . . bought for me when I was born," which they filled with flowers, fishing poles, firewood, and their sleeping dog.[10] At least this is the picture we find in the memoirs—in no way contradicted by Gerald Clarke's biography.

Formal invention, as we have seen throughout my book, is again a strategy for circumventing strictures on representing children in a darkened light. To take just one example, a Capote story, A Christmas Memory, has a revealing narrative structure. Since it is told by a narrator who is not a child but whose voice subtly blends with the child's, and since it is told in the present tense but as a recollection—no small trick—it is possible for readers (especially for those who know Capote) to read these memoirs as now enacting, in their present past, portraits of Capote's protogay childhood. One should note, however—and this goes back to the complicated class and regional layers of Capote's parents' struggles with money (and their love of high life)—that these memoirs have a wonderfully estranging effect in relation to Capote's persona, even as a gay man. For a simple reason. Aspects of his childhood— "I was a real country boy"; "I believed in Jesus"; "my first oyster . . . was like a bad dream sliding down my throat"—do not always jibe with the urban sophisticated author whom we presume to be writing.[11] (This child's queerness queers adult gayness, which is birthing this "gay" child.)

Money is the child's queer ride in many ways. Not that the matter of children's sexuality is going to go away anytime soon. Even as children start to be "gay"—or "queer," or "nongay," or "gayish," or something we don't yet imagine—which they haven't yet been in History, they will be conceptually engrossing to follow, unless they disappear or fade in this century, which seems unlikely. Just as absorbing will be their money dreams, how they ride on the backs of coins into or around the futures they foresee, if they see in these terms. In a moment, Georges Bataille's *Visions of Excess*, with its stresses on destruction and luxurious expenditure, will prove useful for thinking about children and money. But first we need to gather where we've been on this front.

In fact, I laid down as a speculation in the introduction that money queers children as much as sex does. It can make them vulnerable and dangerous by turns, never mind make their motives—for motions, actions, or plottings—cloudy and complex. We have seen as much in the texts I address, in their umbrageous portraits of children. We have noticed, overall, that delaying children's moneyed relations to systematic labor, in the legal workforce, a pause enforced by law, has made them unique legal creatures. Legally, children cannot expend their energy in ways we call "work" *and* be systematically paid for these expenditures, even though they can perform certain labors—run a cash register, stuff envelopes, mow a lawn, shoot hoops—that are the basis of some adult work. In fact, we let them "play at" these labors in ways we don't let them play at sex, even if work-for-pay, like sex, is something delayed for them.[12] This delay gives them not a shelter from money's effects—they are affected, at every turn, by their financial circumstances—but a shelter, though often incomplete, from knowledge of money—often including the detailed workings of family finance.[13] (As *The Pupil*'s Morgan puts it: "I don't know what [my parents] live on, or how they live, or why they live! What have they got and how did they get it? Are they rich, are they poor, or have they a *modeste aisance*? Why are they always chiveying about?")[14] For this reason, labor relations take on imaginative, fantastical forms, including what one's parents do for money. Or, for parents, what their children will do for money in the future. Sex and money thus come together as sites of state and parental concern, however asymmetrical "having" these "things"—sex and money—proves to be for children. But sex and money also come together in a child's negotiations with the forging, discovering, unfolding, and bearing of her persona to herself—never mind to others.

These negotiations are not simple, even if children's grasp of money some-times is, as they play with fake money, funny money, game money (just as they might play doctor with each other). And pain that comes from money, from the myriad ways of having or not having it, may be decisive for how a child takes pleasure in ways that look sexual (and perhaps are). In James's *The Pupil*, labor relations and the closet of finance make a perfect storm for a child's specific suffering from his parents' ways with money. Ironically, as we extensively saw, parental abuse, in the context of money (what they feed him, how they clothe him), fosters an opening for man/boy love. Not only do the parents ever more surely slide this offspring toward the tutor, hoping he will take care of the boy ("off their hands"); boy and tutor oblige this wish by getting off on talking *about* this abuse, which forms their brotherly, eroti-cized bond.

In the fictions of girls-with-dogs by Woolf, Barnes, and Hall, which also indicate ghostly gay children, money, at first glance, seems more muted as a key feature of their dynamics. Dogs and money do not immediately im-plicate each other as a pairing of "objects" children make. But as we look closely, children's own moneyed positions—whether fully, quasi-, or feloni-ously aristocratic in these novels—shape their need for metaphoric transport through their dogs. Elizabeth Dalloway, poised to plunge into proper mar-riage (into "shoes and gloves" and the hosting of parties for wealthy elites), as is expected of a girl of her standing, uses her dog to signal her pause in advancing toward this future, which has been her mother's. But to this same mother's dismay, Elizabeth is also delaying this future by her relations with her tutor, tutor and dog both pointing to pause. Clarissa Dalloway could accept this stall—she herself had one with Sally Seton—if her daughter's tutor were not poor and shabby: "So insensitive was she, dressed in a green mackintosh coat. Year in year out she wore that coat; she perspired; she was never in the room five minutes without making you feel her superiority, your inferiority; how poor she was; how rich you were; how she lived in a slum without a cushion or a bed or a rug or whatever it might be, all her soul rusted with that grievance sticking in it, her dismissal from school during the War—poor embittered unfortunate creature! For it was not her one hated but the idea of her, which undoubtedly had gathered in to itself a great deal that was not Miss Kilman; had become one of those spectres with which one battles in the night; one of those spectres who stand astride us and suck up half our life-blood."[15]

This epic catalogue of the older woman who steals your daughter, making for your dramatic rejection of your daughter's reproduction of your queerness, has no analogue in *The Well of Loneliness*. There the mother outright rejects, cannot caress, the "queer fish" she birthed. She sees her daughter's—Stephen's—inability to wear aristocracy (land and money) in the form of a lady's posture, carriage, and clothing as her child's sad ill-suitedness for her love. But this failure-at-aristocratic-lady is not freestanding. It is part and parcel of what is sending Stephen, at age seven, in sexual ways, straight toward her housemaid (who mirrors her debasement) and aristocratic horses (who mirror her dignity)—each before she finds compensation in her dog as the sign of the only relation she can claim, given the impossible future she inherits as a child of her time. Robin Vote, perhaps, with her suffragette name, is yet another sign—this time in *Nightwood*—of an heir not apparent. In fact, her marriage to the farcical Baron, the closeted Jew, is not just a sign of her incurability on the score of sex (marriage doesn't cure her); her ill-fated marriage to a made-up aristocrat signals her turning her back on her class, a bold indication (and perhaps a happy one) that she, at the last, will "bow down," doglike, before her lover as a way to reach her.

There is one more dog-and-money show. Much more directly, *Lolita* signals all over the place that money matters to the child who would escape—escape from her mother, who has highly unpleasant plans for her, and from the pedophile who so bores and sometimes hurts her. Charlotte tells Humbert: "Little Lo, I'm afraid, does not enter the picture at all. . . . Little Lo goes straight from camp to a good boarding school with strict discipline and some sound religious training. . . . I have it all mapped out"; and, at the close, left only with the maps of the places he took her, Humbert sees: "In her washed-out gray eyes, strangely spectacled, our poor romance was for a moment reflected, pondered upon, and dismissed like a dull party, like a rainy picnic to which only the dullest bores had come . . . like a bit of dry mud caking her childhood."[16] These are the "parents" who hold her purse strings. In fact, Lolita's "purse"' is one of Humbert's euphemisms for her virginity, which she has spent in consensual manner (with girls and boy) before he can take it: "I had stolen the honey of a spasm [in the lap scene] without impairing the morals of a minor. Absolutely no harm done. The conjurer had poured milk, molasses, foaming champagne into a young lady's new white purse; and lo, the purse was intact. . . . I intended, with the most fervent force and foresight, to protect the purity of that twelve-year-old child" (62). As I have conveyed, Lolita, in ways that must surprise readers, and for all her pre-Humbertian sexual consent, has far less agency in the face of ads, and gives far less consent to their effects. Advertisements — and the objects they lure consumers toward (Quilty, as it happens, is one such object) — are far more powerful in seducing Dolly than Humbert ever imagines he could be. And, of course, it's money that makes Lolita stay with Humbert Humbert ("she had absolutely nowhere to go") — until dogs and cars (and Lolita's restless legs) move against the pedophile's controlling money plots.

As for the queer child's own hand at plotting, in the texts we've looked at that render famous murders, money is imaginatively bound up with motions that are their own reward. Perry Smith in *In Cold Blood* and Pauline Rieper in *Heavenly Creatures* both feel as children above the circumstances and the kind of culture that their parents can afford — to put it mildly, in Perry's case.[17] And, for both, money or a wealthy environment would seem to offer less the prospect of beautiful things than a life of the mind they both link to bodily expenditures and bodily adventures, whether in the form of diving for treasure or running in a garden toward a princess on a bridge. That these motions are tethered to seeming same-sex relations (boys' adventures for Perry with Dick or making love like the saints for Pauline with a willing Juliet) demonstrates how money is a central part of childhood queering that involves (but does not reduce to) sex.

This holds true for the child queered by color, who in some cases is not even sexual. *Blood Diamond's* soldier, an African child, who murders without motive though not without feeling (he has for reference the feelings of the boys who kill beside him), is not shown having sexual relations—

which might have proven more controversial than his murderous actions and drives. This boy, however, is queered by money by being made a laborer who kills for sustenance — at least to begin with — and who is the object of the final diamond swap (he is made equivalent to a pink stone) bringing the diamond markets to their knees, resulting in the Kimberley Process. That's quite a boy — quite unlike the child we think we are protecting from any experiences such as these ones. And the *Guess* sequence — *Guess Who's Coming to Dinner*, *Six Degrees of Separation*, and *Guess Who* — sharply turns on money meditations that take us from a black apprentice, to a black hustler, to a jobless white who is Green.

Bataille for Kids?

Turning toward an ending that opens onto problems, ones I leave to linger, I find I need Bataille. To confess the obvious: at first blush, the theories of Bataille do not seem fit for children. His visions of excess are gnarled contemplations and gnostic provocations on the topics of violence and debasement. With their cryptic titles — "Mouth," "The Solar Anus," "The Big Toe," "Rotten Sun"; with their crazed kind of SAT analogies — "an abandoned shoe, a rotten tooth, a snub nose, the cook spitting in the soup of his masters are to love what a battle flag is to nationality"; with their yoking of physical explosions and political rebellions, comparing a volcano, which he deems an anus, to the "scandalous eruption" of workers fighting against their masters; with Bataille's fixation on an ape's bottom: "There is no child who has not . . . admired . . . these filthy protuberances, dazzlingly colored excremental skulls, sometimes dappled, going from shocking pink to extraordinarily horrible . . . violet"; with this kind of ferment, these essays seem removed from a child's imagination.[18]

Or not at all. Somehow these ideas, these juvenile but intellectual copula, are not out of reach — not fully so — from how a child might use its fascination with dirty, naughty subjects to ask important questions (if just in its mind) about realms of value and exclusion. For Freud, we recall, the child must put away its natural attraction to anality, voyeurism, and sadistic cruelty in order to become a civilized adult. Must it also put away, relinquish, the violence of Greek and Roman myths? One specific myth is central to Bataille, and it is a myth one often learns in childhood, largely in

Anglo-American schooling. Many children know the myth of Icarus and his father, Daedalus: in order to enable their escape from capture on the island of Crete, Daedalus designed for them feathery wings, held together by wax. And though he warned his child not to fly too close to the sun, lest the sun melt the wax, Icarus, filled with the thrill of flying, flew too close and fell from the sky. Presumably, we are told this myth about a youth, especially in our youth, so as to cultivate a sense of moderation. (Listen to your parents: don't fly high.) Predictably, Bataille, in his *Visions of Excess*, sees a different point. In Bataille's way of thinking, our ideals are "rotten sun." They contain the doubleness of an elevation we desperately seek (in Icarean flights) and the guarantee of a violent fall (courtesy of the ideal itself). As Bataille words it: "The myth of Icarus is particularly expressive from this point of view: it clearly splits the sun," our most poetic and elevated concept, into "two—the one that was shining at the moment of Icarus's elevation, and the one that melted the wax, causing failure and a screaming fall when Icarus got too close" (58). For this reason, Bataille's own protodeconstructions of the ideality/reality binary always show reality, by definition, as a set of failed ideals. Nothing is more real than ideals that fail us and also fell us. And human life, as Bataille conceives it, is about watching our flights fall to earth, dropping down in real time. Nothing, moreover, is more violent than ideals—ideals that we laud to children all the time, even making children *our* ideal, which can be violent in itself (as the film *Hard Candy* shows).

Given his propensity to praise destructive flight, we are not surprised that, famously, Bataille, in "The Notion of Expenditure," speaks to what he calls "the insufficiency of the principle of classical utility." By "utility" Bataille means the goal, which he doesn't like at all, of taking one's "pleasure" in "moderate form," while one aims at the "acquisition," "conservation," and "reproduction" of goods and life. And though this moderation forms the basis of the "struggle against [human] pain" (116), Bataille proceeds to say that "personal experience" proves the falseness of this view. "Human society," he goes on to claim, has "an *interest* in considerable losses, in catastrophes that, *while conforming to well-defined needs*, provoke tumultuous depressions, cries of dread, and, in the final analysis, a certain orgiastic state" (117). Perhaps thinking once again about Icarus, Bataille produces a father/son example: "The father may provide the son with lodging, clothes, food, and, when absolutely necessary, a little harmless recreation"; "but the son does not even have the right to speak about what really gives him a fever"; "humanity recognizes the right to acquire, to conserve, and to consume rationally, but it excludes in principle *nonproductive expenditure*" (117). What, exactly, is this nonproductivity that Bataille embraces? Any outlay (Bataille in no way minds the word *wasting*) of money or energy or life itself—outlays that (happily) do not serve, that indeed defy, the ends of production; these would be wastings such as "luxury," "mourning," "competitive games," "artistic productions," and "perverse sexual activity (i.e. deflected from genital finality)." For Bataille, the ultimate question thus becomes: who has this power to lose and destroy? With undeniable Marxist strains running through his thoughts (though they are sometimes simplistic and confused), Bataille scorns forms of "conspicuous consumption." As his translator, Allan Stoekl, tells us: "'Conspicuous consumption' for Bataille is not a pernicious remnant of feudalism that must be replaced by total utility; instead, it is the perversion of man's 'need to destroy.' The noble, and even more hypocritically the bourgeois, use this 'destruction' not to destroy completely, but simply to reaffirm their place in the hierarchy" (xvi). What Bataille affirms is the wish to create so as to destroy—and to lose anyone who would lose loss. But the measure of destroying is elusive in his *Visions*, for all his talk of one's total destructions.

Can there be, then, Bataille for kids? Can they dream destruction or bodily expenditure? Do they lose loss? Or is the picture more mixed than Bataille's excessive visions would allow? Do some children, because they are not laborers, particularly dream of destroying *for a living* or *getting paid* to waste time well? This may seem an eccentric set of questions with which to move toward closure. Yet I find they open onto several crucial registers of the sideways futures we may still need to grasp. Two distinct films present two different slants on futures tipping sideways into themes from Bataille.

Losing Face to Shoes: Seductions in Hoop Dreams

A shoe is a strange thing to see your image in, a foreign mirror for a child's face. But it is stranger to lose face *to* shoes, when you discover you cannot really "be" who your shoes say you are. Of course, these thoughts are strange only if you don't play sports, or watch Nike ads, or believe you must spend a mint on your sneakers—that is, if you happen not to be a kid with the violent dream, the dangerous, limpid, luxurious dream, of rising to the level of the NBA. *Hoop Dreams* (dir. Steve James, 1994) follows two black boys who hold these dreams.

Here is a compendium of failed ideals. *Hoop Dreams* is full of Icarean flights, which tie together the poignant changes in a boy's face, due to his dreaming and the failure of his dreams, and his wish to be a shoe (like "Air Jordans" or some other brand). (The tag line of Michael Jordan's shoes has been "The History of Flight": "an ongoing legacy to the potential that lies within all of us to fly.") What links these aspects—causing the boy's loss of face to his shoes—is something also striking: the black boy's posture of having to seduce, maybe wanting to seduce his coaches' attention—and also ours—in a *kind* of culturally encouraged pedophilia based on this child giving us pleasure.[19]

Using documentary's collage of techniques—interviews, photography, close-ups, and action—*Hoop Dreams* makes stunning use of its cuts, its skillful edits that are hiding many hours of the boys' lives from us. It takes hours of documentary footage (almost three) for us to grasp that the optimistic faces, detailed with subtleties and modulations, which at many points have held us arrested, are slipping from our sight. Carefully, the camera captures both boys' little-boy hopefulness at the start (figure 39). Then, in a fully devastating portraiture, over the course of the three-hour film that spans five years (following events in the players' lives and their games on court), we see these hopeful looks disappear. They are replaced not only by the boys' worn-out demeanors, but by the more determined motions of their bodies, caught in the brilliantly edited action segments of the film. Ironically, the more the boys are filmed in these motions, *increasing* their beauty, the more the brightness of their faces slips away, as if it is banished to the realms of hands and feet, which might still, against all odds, bring them fame. Here are effects running counter to the theory of visual pleasure famously propounded by Laura Mulvey. As I discussed in the contexts of *Lolita* (both the Lyne and Kubrick films) and Peter Jackson's *Heavenly Creatures*, Mulvey assigns visual pleasure to the stilled figures of beautiful women—not to the fluid, athletic motions of (black) boys, such as we discover here. Nor does Mulvey theorize how a form of beauty could slide from one zone of the body to another, leaving one part bereft of the attractiveness that another part of the body now enjoys.[20]

39. Arthur busts a smile. From the film *Hoop Dreams* (1994).

Because these are changes occurring in the cuts over many years' time, we cannot determine when, precisely, these lit faces fell from view, offering a history of their fade. We may only sense that the cuts themselves, at various junctures, lure us out of the film altogether. They make us imagine the off-camera scenes, or those cut for time, that contribute to the losing of a lit-up look: a slow accumulation that a camera cannot catch, despite its technical, mechanical prowess. This is a dynamic — being launched as a viewer outside a frame — that the frame of the basketball court, with its courtings, helps the film explore (by thematizing frames). And of course complicating all these consequences are the basketball motions themselves: the bodily rhythms, drives, styles, and finesse that are pleasures to begin with, attracting the child by being energy expenditures s/he tremendously enjoys. *Hoop Dreams*, in this way, speaks to Bataille — speaks back to him. For one of our insights as viewers may concern the difficulty of our neatly separating "nonproductivity" (which many viewers may shorthand as "child's play") from "utility," when it comes to these boys' dreams. "Competitive games" are not unproductive in their most developed forms, since they are framed by a massive, moneymaking system of utility. So when children play them, with "eyes on the prize," can they feel the "orgiastic" wastings Bataille would lovingly assign them?[21] Or is the frame of the NBA almost always already framing and *causing*, lending flavor to, these childish pleasures? Have these boys already lost loss (the loss Bataille embraces)? If they have, do they care? Do we care more than they do? Does *Hoop Dreams* make the audience long for the days in which these children could enjoy the wasted time they spent in motion? Do we idealize, by the film's end, a "lost innocence" of nonproductivity we assign to children's games — as if Bataille and innocence (of all the screwy things) could somehow come together — even as we wish these boys had prepared themselves for the brutality of sinking to utility? This odd mixture of nostalgia and judgment is certainly a possible reaction to the film. So is the sense that a pure embrace of wasting isn't likely on anyone's part, since we do create, even if to destroy. Luxury may be the only necessity, according to Wilde's *Dorian Gray*, but necessity gives tremendous force to luxury, just as the act of projecting ourselves into future states, according to our dreams that are bound to fail, is one of our chief *present* expenditures, which forms our pleasure.[22]

Another reaction to these questions is anger, or just dislike, despite *Hoop Dreams'* enormous acclaim. For instance, the film critics Paul Arthur and Jane Cutler argue that the film "adds absolutely nothing to the current arsenal of documentary codes and techniques."[23] Specifically, the film's "nuanced elaboration of family dynamics is overwhelmed by the familiar momentum of parallel-edited [basketball] contests," "a numbing courtside litany of performance highlights" (22–23). In its depictions of "the plight of the underclass," they proclaim, the film "lack[s] a fully articulated analysis of social context" and "ignores information that could be truly useful to a younger audience" (24). The writer bell hooks agrees: "There is nothing spectacular or technically outstanding about the film"; rather, it offers "a victim perspective" on African Americans, along with images of black men and women that "simply confirm negative stereotypes."[24]

Critics, however, who praise *Hoop Dreams* do not mind being overwhelmed by details. As one critic puts it: "The movie fills up with multitudes of detail"; "to the average viewer, these particulars may seem repetitive, even downright exhausting, but only a fool would give them up."[25] For appreciative critics, the "extraordinarily detailed" nature of *Hoop Dreams* may be a

boon precisely because its overall themes seem familiar: "Elevating basketball players to mythic status has been a favorite American pastime. So has
debunking the possibility of an Algeresque climb from the ghetto to the playground to the coliseums of the NBA."[26] The dream-as-full-as-an-empty-hoop
is cited by any number of reviewers as the film's clear message: "It's about
. . . what passes for the American dream," "the worst dream a boy can have,"
says Richard Corliss of *Time* magazine.[27] bell hooks only ups the ante on why
these themes might seem familiar: "The film's most powerful moments are
those that subversively document the way in which these young, black male
bodies are callously objectified and dehumanized by the white-male domi-
nated world of sports administration in America . . . [characterized by] an
'auction block' mentality that has to call to the mind of any aware viewer the
history of slavery and the plantation economy."[28]

Yet, for all this déjà vu, much finer shades to these themes emerge. Here
are instructive, seductive versions of capitalist ideals and stunning letdowns:
boys as hopeful "workers" in the basketball system of the 1990s, preparing
for work they feel as play; fathers and brothers as the already let-down sup-
pliers of these dreams, backed by television's steady offerings; mothers and
girls who prop, mediate, scrutinize, and temper basketball dreams that both
are and never could be their own dreams in the early nineties; and, of course,
coaches, who are white-collared and largely white, looking to serve "professional meat" to basketball buyers.[29]

A look, in particular, at syntagmatic chains—*Hoop Dreams'* edited order
of images—shows how their brilliance is less "spectacular" than exquisitely
deft in form. The film's beginning sequence, in a first chain, puts together
faces, frames, and motions, and then money, shoes, and seductions (between
boys and scouts, boys and coaches, boys and idols). After a few establishing
shots that put viewers in the projects of Chicago—rumbling trains on the
creaking "L," making their way among soulless towers—we are in front of
the TV with William (one of the two boys) watching him watch men run
around a court. From the start, his face, expansive with expression—wide
sudden smiles, explosive laughter—is connected to this frame: the TV framing the court that frames the motions that, in a moment, we see him try
to match. When the camera captures him in slow motion, as it next does,
as he launches skyward in Jordanesque flight, already having a feel for the
hook he has seen a hundred times, the camera's seduction of us may begin,

helping us grasp how these motions could become such a scene of devotion for those who perform them. Before we can pass into praising the purity of motion, however, there are Arthur's words—Arthur is the other boy—describing what he'll buy when he hits the NBA: a house for his "momma" and "a Cadillac Oldsmobile" for his father "so he can cruise into games." His mother, in her kitchen, reports about the shoes: "He dreams about it"; "He look at those basketball commercials where they be advertising these Nike shoes and he tells his brother, 'Joe, Joe, that's me.'" Next, a scout is admiring Arthur (the latter shirtless, looking lithe), then taking Arthur, just out of grammar school, off to "perform" for Coach Pingatore at St. Joseph's School: "Your role today, Arthur, is to impress the coaches; try not to be too fancy." Arthur can still smile at this juncture when talking of his fears, but the mention of "Isiah" (Isiah Thomas, his greatest idol, an NBA star who went to St. Joe's) is enough to make him blushingly giddy and demure. Then Isiah appears on court, further seducing all boys present, especially Arthur, who, in a gesture common to boys, shyly, more than coyly, pulls his shirt up toward his face, as if he could cover his youthful embarrassment, while in the process baring his stomach. The moment is deflated only by the coach, speaking off camera, saying of Arthur: "I can see the playground in him: I can see the talent, but I don't see the confidence." He does see this assurance in William: "He flows with a smoothness and confidence and strength you don't see in every kid." A beautiful shot of William follows—a liquid rise to a slammed reverse—so as to grant the attraction just stated. And this motion of elegant power is next framed as a future by his brother who, already a basketball failure by his own reckoning, is living through William by his side (making the brother the means of his growth): "All those basketball dreams I had, they gone; all I see, all my dreams, is in him now; I want him to make it so bad, I don't know what to do." William's mother follows, revealing *her* dream, one that attaches to basketball plans yet forks off in a new direction: a high school diploma, never mind a degree, is "very important to me," she says, as if it will be hers. Here's a different frame for the bodily motions Bataille finds unproductive. Nonproductivity can buy diplomas. And here is a window into what the film is missing in a much larger sense: girls of color. Where are they hidden, held submerged inside these dreams, and what lens is fixed on them in their acts of dreaming? We are left to find them, if we even look for them, in their mothers' bodies (the mothers who are read through

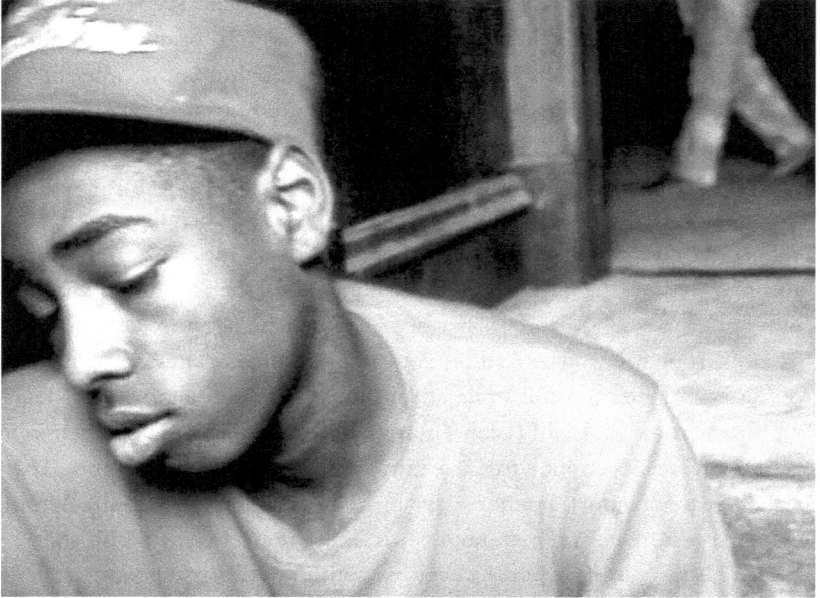

40. The dropping of a face. From the film *Hoop Dreams* (1994).

the dreams of their boys). That is, we might wonder: who were the girls who became these mothers? What was the texture of their specific hopes, which now directly or diffusely are tethered to a ball and court? Just how wry is their perspective on this game? Does it seduce *them*?

Past these first seductions, the film presents the forces that will make faces sink. Arthur is the first to have a change in his demeanor. It comes from his fall out of favor with his coach, as if Pingatore has lost his attraction to this boy, in a basketball sense. Against the backdrop of what is strikingly new to Arthur by his own report—"flowers," "clean hallways," houses in suburbs, "being around a lot of white people," along with a three-hour round trip to school—Coach Pingatore accuses him of "reverting back to his environment, where he came from" (as the coach uses the language of reversion and arrested development). Indeed, back he goes, when Arthur and his family can't make tuition, and Coach Pingatore does nothing to help them, despite his earlier passionate recruitment. Arthur, with a new look on his face (checked out, bitter, and jilted all at once) (figure 40), looks away

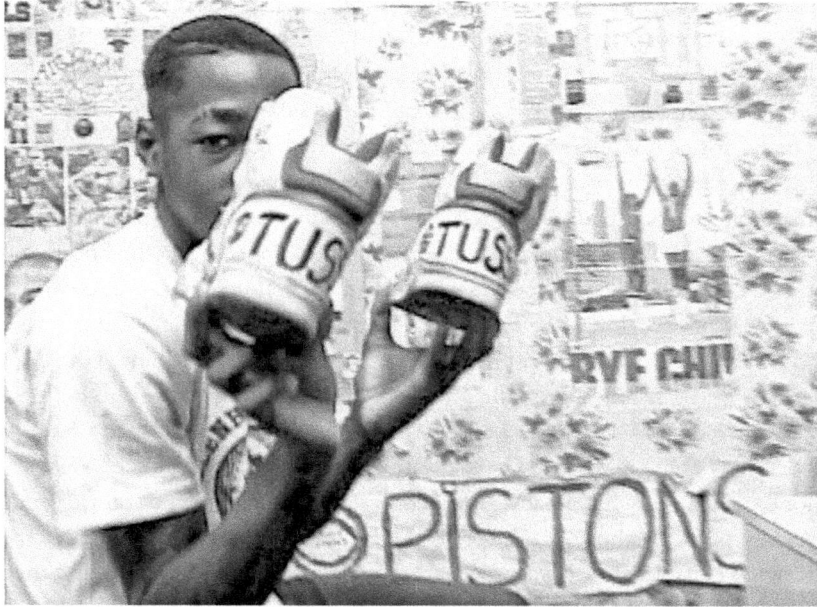

41. Arthur posing as a pair of sneakers. From the film *Hoop Dreams* (1994).

from the camera, shaking his head from side to side, then down toward the floor, as he comments to us: "Well, you know, he thought I wasn't going to grow; he kept on saying like 'when you going to grow?' or something like that"; "so why would he just waste some money on me staying there?" Arthur's mother tells us: "If I had to know he was going to go through this type of pain and myself the anguish of it—and then to put him out in the middle of the school year. . . ." (A voice-over says that she has lost her job and that Arthur's father, "after twenty years of marriage . . . is leaving the family.") Still, Arthur shows us his sneakers at one point, which he's adorned with Isiah's nickname in large letters, as if this nickname is his own (and the name of the shoe) (figure 41). William, by contrast, has stayed at St. Joe's, where the "whole school" sees him "as Isiah"—in a kind of group Lacanian Imaginary his school projects—which he doesn't seem to like. Watching high school films of Isiah with Coach Pingatore, who seems unable to let go of Thomas (as his greatest pupil), William is accosted by his coach's expectations: "Can you handle it? . . . you have two years to get us down there [to the state finals] and it's all going to be on your head." Not long after, William has an injury that ends his season. Now his face literally drops—head down low, as we saw with Arthur, and face getting cloudy—when looking at his X-rays and holding a model of the cartilage he's damaged. (These are other objects to see oneself in.) His change of fate that is changing his face affects his brother Curtis too; as William expresses it: "It was like my injury was making him look bad—I always felt Curtis should not be living his dream through me." Indeed, Curtis, whose lean, once-ripped basketball body has turned to fat, makes sad confessions about his self-image (fat, once again, is a sign of growing sideways): "Sometimes I just sit around and my eyes just kind of get watery and I believe I ain't amounted to nothing, I ain't got nothing; I be sitting there telling myself 'You ain't going to get no better.'" Meanwhile, in this section, we learn information that dramatizes what has been happening in the cuts (between the parts of the story we see). William, for example, now has a baby. And Arthur's family has been cut off from aid. At one point, Arthur's mother tells the camera what lies hidden inside the movie's edits. In an angry, exasperated voice, she faces the camera and then announces (more to the filmmakers than to any viewer): "Now I'm on welfare that I wasn't on then. . . . We was cut off for three months; we was cut off from aid, complete with no income. So, therefore, do you know what happened? Our lights were cut off, our gas was cut off and we were sitting in the dark." Comments such as these (oddly allegorical: the cut lights, the sitting in the dark) remind us that films are adept at hiding time. Every film cut, at least in documentaries, is potentially a part of a life we fall out of: in this case, roughly three months of a family's hardship, during which we as viewers were away.

Twin seductions bring us back. They coil about each other and conduct us to the end. William, on the one hand, is being wooed by colleges. Arthur, on the other, is part of a miracle run to take his team downstate to the basketball finals, a push that leads viewers to care about the details and outcomes of his games. It's as if the filmmakers haven't yet trusted us with extended footage of basketball games, fearful that we might consume these images all too readily or too lustily. Or, quite simply, these motions haven't yet added up to anything. Whatever the case, by the time we're now brought into these excitements, we have acquired a knowing mode of watching; we know our euphoria is shockingly fleeting, even if it is infectious. Besides, as schools are pursuing William, which should be the climax to his jubilation, the arc of his rise has already been dropping. While Marquette University has made a strong play for him, St. Joe's still shows its own ineptitude. Watching William back on court, Pingatore, who clearly thinks he's not on camera, says, succinctly, "[William] *stinks*," with another coach adding that other players "are not in awe of him anymore." Later, at a banquet, William's face looks fallen—palpably dulled, emptied, or resigned: "It became more of a job," he says, "than a game to play; Coach Pingatore just had these dreams in his head; he just wanted me to go the same route as he took Isiah, and when I had some real problems . . . with Catherine's [the mother of his baby's] family and my family . . . the only thing Coach Pingatore could tell me was 'write 'em off'; 'write 'em off'? what kind of advice is that?" Meanwhile, against our expectations, Arthur—with his more chaotic school life and his father in and out of the family (with domestic violence and drug-related charges)—is finally playing on a promising team. Now the filmmakers, more intensely, use all kinds of basketball clips, which, with faster-paced montage, draw us into the Cinderella story of Arthur's rise, along with his team's, to a third-place finish in the state of Illinois. Unless we are immune to sports, we cannot help but notice the ebullience that we feel. We might even see that certain ways of wasting time are pleasure-filled mini-projections of futures in a frame: what will happen, who will win, what will we see? But in the end these projections "die" or drop from their heights, necessarily so, when the clock runs out—before it starts again.

Juxtaposed to these seductions, as achievements to the side of Arthur's bid for glory, are two other milestones: Arthur's eighteenth birthday and his mother's school success. As for the first, his mother simply states: "It's his eighteenth birthday; he lived; to get to see eighteen, that's good"—as if the sheer act of his racking up years, given the deaths of so many black teens, is unquestioned achievement. As for the second, we see Arthur's mother completing a nurse's-assistant program, with the highest grades in class, and receiving her certificate in an empty room where nearly no one watches. The film, once again, makes its point syntagmatically, as it next tells us: "The gym is packed for Marshall [High School]." Still, the destination of the film for Arthur seems more sideways and pending than "up." He goes to school at Mineral Area Junior College, living in a sad-looking "basketball house," where he replies to a final question, which is telling on the filmmakers' part:

"You don't think you'll have the kind of tough times your dad went through?" (Just his dad? Not his mother or his largely invisible sister?) Arthur answers honestly: "I can't say I will, I can't say I won't." The film then ends, with the boys hanging in and still hanging on (William has almost dropped out but hasn't), making Arthur's statement an apt summation of their suspension.

Neither boy becomes a shoe.

The Economy of Candy: Charlie and the Chocolate Factory

As if it is replying to the need to fill shoes and pass on dreams, even fulfill them for white children, *Charlie and the Chocolate Factory* (dir. Tim Burton, 2005) imagines one can manufacture dreams, especially if a factory is given to a child. This is an Andy Warhol primer. (Warhol, we recall, called his studio The Factory.) But it is also Bataille for kids: children's unedited pleasure in obvious extremes of consumption and destruction. This is the quintessential instance of create-in-order-to-destroy: the dream of manufacturing what you will profusely and on the spot consume, not as a necessity but strictly as a luxury. And these emphases logically join "the child" to "the queer," as we are bound to see, when Willy Wonka, as played by Johnny Depp, is something of a fag. Rated PG, in this case amusingly for "Quirky Situations, Action, and Mild Language," the movie makes the grown queer child (namely, Willy) sit down to dinner with the innocent child (eponymous Charlie) in a way that should make conservatives shudder, to come full circle to where my book began.[30]

How does this movie get to this end? By several slanting moves. First, it makes the mystery of manufacturing akin to the mystery of sex itself. Where does chocolate come from? the child appears to question, making candy more mysterious than babies—and more alluring than any other pleasure. Willy to the children: "Did you guys know that chocolate contains a property that triggers the release of endorphins that give one the feeling of being in love?" An Indian palace of wealth and romance, in the tale's narration, is made all of chocolate (a house you can eat) until it all melts, looking more like excrement—perhaps to children's perverse delight. Indeed, one perceives—hardly an epiphany—that children want to grasp the production of a coin they do understand: namely, candy. They want to grasp the economy of candy that early structures their intense pleasure: where they do have agency, choice, access, a measure for barter, and clear permission to over-indulge. (One thinks of Warhol, who was paid in chocolate for each of his drawings by his doting mother.) In fact, Willy Wonka, parodying "parents" (a word he can't say), ironically warns the hedonists before him, actually goading them: "Don't lose your heads; don't get overexcited; no other fac-tory mixes its chocolate by waterfalls; and you can take *that* to the bank. . . . Everything in this room is edible, including myself, but that's cannibalism."

The dullness of industry here is a scene of imaginative and fantastic exer-tion ("don't lose your heads" means *do* get excited to the extreme) for those children who would comprehend the factory. In fact, from the start, we get hints that "it" (the factory, along with its methods, its products, and its owner) will be more than the children have bargained for in their fervent wish to tour it. Moreover, the children will not be chosen by Willy but by chance — shades of the vagaries of capitalist markets? — though they clearly must purchase his chocolate and hope, inside it, to find a Golden Ticket. (Thus, the chocolate proves golden and priceless.) Since there are only five such tickets, the candy contest would seem to privilege fat kids, who con-sume a lot, and wealthy kids, who can buy a lot — evidently also children who are driven ("eyes on the prize, Violet, eyes on the prize," a mother tells her daughter) and ones who can calculate, with their superior technical skills, how candy circulates in a global context (as does Mike Teavee). These are the children who win tickets, along with our protagonist — "this is the story of an ordinary boy named Charlie Bucket" — who seems destined to win out of sheer, exemplary normality (recalling those exceedingly normal Clutters from *In Cold Blood*). Here, however, "ordinary" is poor (poor and white); though this is clearly a happy poor, with two loving parents and both sets of grandparents, who, for warmth, share one bed at the center of the house (in a parody of coziness?). And though "they barely had enough to eat," Charlie was the "luckiest boy in the entire world," though he "didn't know it yet." And what exactly is it — luck, coincidence, or visual sight gag? — that a pair of effeminate men, walking their dogs, pass by Charlie just before he finds the money with which to buy the candy that bears a Golden Ticket?

Willy himself has a Wildean look: top hat, velvety long purple coat, a subtle shade of lipstick, and pageboy haircut (figure 42).[31] And he talks to children in a way Wilde might: "You're short," he chides them. "We're chil-dren," one replies. "That's no excuse," he answers back, "I was never as short as you." When the children meet him, it's on the heels of his Disney-style display of dolls bursting into flames, leaving the child-figurines with melting plastic flesh and hanging eyes. "Wasn't that just magnificent?" Willy asks the group. "I was worried it was getting a little dodgy in the middle part, but that finale — wow." This is the film's introduction to destruction, an interest that Willy and the children share. So much do these children run the risk of risking all, in this allowable economy of candy, that each child becomes a self-consuming artifact. All but Charlie, our innocent child, become some version of what they pursue. (Is this why the film has no children of color? Given that all the children but Charlie demonstrate "bad" sides, was it somehow safer, in someone's view of safety, to use no children of color at all?) One girl, for instance, a child named Violet, becomes an expansive violet ball when she consumes Willy Wonka's new gum (meant to be a series of meals all at once). Her mother complains of her round, purple child: "I can't have a blueberry as a daughter" (a comical echo of *Hoop Dreams'* problem of boys who would like to be basketball shoes). Another child, Augustus Gloop, becomes a kind of chocolate bar when, after gazing at himself in a river running with chocolate (as if he were a child-Narcissus having a Lacanian mirror moment), he falls into the river and becomes chocolate-dipped (figure 43). His mother has to tell him: "Don't eat your fingers." And Willy's workers sing:

> This revolting boy of course,
> Was so unutterably vile,
> So greedy, foul, and infantile,
> He left a most disgusting taste
> Inside our mouths, and so in haste
> We chose a thing that, come what may,
> Would take the nasty taste away.
> "Come on!" we cried, "The time is ripe
> To send him shooting up the pipe!"

The workers themselves — the Oompa-Loompas — have become workers by seeking their *pleasure*. And in Willy's fable of how he found them, then "imported" them from a "terrible country" "full of jungles," Willy gives these colonial connections a Marxist spin — or, more perversely, a twist from Bataille. It's as if he's offering non-alienation of a strange sort: eat at work what

42. Johnny Depp as Wonka/Wilde.
From the film *Charlie and the Chocolate Factory* (2005).

43. Chocolate-dipped Augustus Gloop: a self-consuming artifact.
From the film *Charlie and the Chocolate Factory* (2005).

44. The Oompa-Loompas about to dance on candy.
From the film *Charlie and the Chocolate Factory* (2005).

you make on the job: let what you make involve your play: eat playfulness.
In fact, in his story, the Oompa-Loompas were only too happy to change
locales, since "the food they longed for the most," and almost worshipped,
"was cocoa beans," which were in short supply where they lived. Willy
agreed to "pay" them their "wages in cocoa beans," if they wished, so they
flocked to his factory and became a part of this economy of candy. In Dahl's
book, they are African pygmies. Here, in the film, they are now clones of a
child-sized adult: shrunk down, digitized versions of the Indian actor Deep
Roy, many times multiplied on the screen (figure 44). Does this spread defy
their personhood, as would seem to be the obvious reading? or does it give
them, rather strangely, a kind of unusual intensification? Whatever racial
critique one makes of them—this is not hard—they are an odd, racialized
mirror of *Wonka's* growth. They are mischievous, wry, ironic, and not so
much arrested as suspended in noncouplehood, with their Steinian childish
pleasures of repetition to the fore; their routinized labor is artistic, often
breaking out into song and dance; though, as one might picture, their work
seems less executive than Willy's seems to be.

What about Willy's growth? It is shown in flashbacks, tripped by the children's question to him (soliciting how he lost his virginity in the realm of

chocolate): "Can you remember the first candy bar you ever ate?" Moreover, Willy's youth is manufactured by this film, since Dahl left Willy Wonka's childhood ghosted in his text. Here Willy first shows up *as* a ghost, dressed as a goblin for the night of Halloween. Underneath the sheet, he wears a torturous set of braces that look like a muzzle more than anything else. And his dentist father throws the "evil candy" into the fireplace where he burns it; so candy, of course, is the sign of the boy's forbidden pleasure(s), whatever they encompass, whatever else is ghosted in Willy's young life, making young Willy a stranger in the family, before he runs away. (He never "grows up" to have a wife and children.)

Sideways growth, nonetheless, is on display. It can be seen in the Wildean embrace of wasting time, which also sounds like unproductive expenditure. Building on the sense that "candy is a waste of time," as Willy's father told him, one child asks: "Why is everything here completely pointless?" Charlie answers: "Candy doesn't have to have a point—that's why it's candy." More important still is the literal motion of Willy Wonka's elevator: "[It's] not an ordinary up and down elevator," he tells the kids; "it can go sideways, slantways, [and] any way you can think of." Intriguingly, its upward and downward movements can seem pointless, whereas its sideways journeys conduct the children into each new room, where they see fanciful modes of manufacturing.[32] For example, they see a cow being whipped—hence, the making of whipped cream—in a light masochistic joke for children. Then, pink cottoncandy sheep come into view: "I'd rather not talk about this one," Willy slyly offers. He is also working on other new motions—such as how to send a chocolate bar by television.

But it is the last two moves in the film that hold queer Willy and innocent Charlie in a relation strung with money. Up to this point, the film has had more of a horizontal feel than a building sense of drama, as the children encounter one marvel, then another. But, at the end, with the other children having disappeared themselves, due to their brattishness or their greed, only Charlie and his elderly grandpa (Charlie's chaperone?) remain on Willy's tour. Willy takes them to an unsought climax. Shot to the heights of his "Up and Out" room, in the elevator with mysterious powers, Willy and his guests (the boy and his grandfather) look as though they're riding to self-destruction. (The movie clearly toys with this prospect.) They shoot through the smokestack of Willy Wonka's factory, in a novel version of Icarean flight, and free-fall to earth, where they land unharmed. Now Willy makes an offer to Charlie: if he leaves his family to come to live with Willy, he can own the factory — take it from Willy and run it himself. Willy wants an heir, which he pronounces "hair." As we can predict, Charlie says no to this queer choice. Instead, he ushers Willy to the family dinner table. (Guess who's coming to dinner?)

Here, as if they are nodding to the child inside Willy Wonka — this queer man who is a queer child, who will make an unrelated child his legal "hair" — the family invokes Willy-the-flamer as a "boy" by Charlie's side. Charlie, the innocent, now has something in his future to inspect: a factory of dreams, where dreams build sideways and fly toward destruction, as is shown to him by a queer.

Introduction

1 Here, as many readers will obviously recognize, I begin with the standard linguistic definition of "queer" that exists at this time: "*adj.* 1) deviating from the expected or normal; strange; 2) odd or unconventional in behavior; eccentric; 3) arousing suspicion; 4) *Slang.* Homosexual"; "*n.* A homosexual" (*The American Heritage Dictionary*, New College Edition).

2 Stadler, "Homo Sex Story," 168.

3 Sikov, "Chemistry," 230–31.

4 See Funny Gay Males (Jaffe Cohen, Danny McWilliams, and Bob Smith), *Growing Up Gay*, 127–28.

5 I am referring to scenes from *The Hanging Garden*, *The Children's Hour*, Vladimir Nabokov's *Lolita*, *Six Degrees of Separation*, and Djuna Barnes's *Nightwood*, respectively.

6 Throughout the book, I will use *History* to refer to what historians call "historiography": what appears in books *marked as* histories. Readers interested in history and spectrality from other, different angles, mostly focused on trauma, ethics, or the spectral force of what is already to some degree *in* History as a matter of historians' writings (for example, Marxism, slavery, or adult forms of homosexuality), should consult Derrida, *Specters of Marx*; Gordon, *Ghostly Matters*; and Freccero, *Queer/Early/Modern*. For my first thoughts on "the ghostly 'gay' child," see Stockton, "Growing Sideways, or Versions of the Queer Child." My work on ghostliness takes as its focus sideways relations and sideways growth, as becomes apparent throughout this introduction.

7 The phrase I cite is from Charlotte Brontë's novel *Villette*, 200; an apt phrase, I find, for the problem of children's visible obscurity.

8 As again will be familiar, many queer adults abjure the word *gay* since it smacks

of fixed identities, which the word *queer* is meant to renounce. In this book, I experiment with bringing back the word *gay*—in the context of children—as the new *queer*, which I explain later in this introduction.

9 The 1992 Republican National Convention is only the most famous instance of this coupling. The linkage of "homosexuality" and "family values" is so well established at this point in time that mention of the latter phrase, in most contexts, is tantamount to saying "values that specifically oppose gay lifestyles."

10 For an explanation of how the word *queer* performs both this touting and this sharing, see Stockton, *Beautiful Bottom, Beautiful Shame*, 27–33.

11 *Webster's New World Dictionary* defines the child as "1) an infant; baby 2) an unborn offspring; fetus 3) a boy or girl in the period before puberty 4) a son or daughter; offspring 5) a descendant 6) a person like a child in interests, judgment, etc., or one regarded as immature and childish." All of these meanings will appear in this book.

12 I first coined this phrase for my MLA paper "The Child, the Pedagogue, the Pedophile, and the Masochist," presented in December 1997, and have maintained it ever since. For this reason, forming almost a joke on belatedness, Heather Love's fascinating *Feeling Backward* has appeared too late for my consideration. Happily, it's not too late for my readers to be schooled by Love.

13 On the point of "no established forms to hold itself," see, as evidence, Eve Kosofsky Sedgwick's "How to Bring Your Kids Up Gay."

14 *The Oprah Winfrey Show*, November 17, 2005. The episode itself was inspired by Robert Trachtenberg's 2005 book, *When I Knew*, a rich gathering of anecdotes from gays and lesbians about when and how they "first knew." And, of course, *Doubt* (dir. John Patrick Shanley, 2008)—the new motion picture of the 2004 play—will strike viewers with its portrayal of a gay child in the present tense.

15 For my discussion of this diagnosis, via the work of Eve Kosofsky Sedgwick, see my section "Why Speak of Growing Sideways?" in this introduction.

16 "The century of the child"—actually the title of a book by Key—was a well-known treatise at the turn of the century. Nearly every major history of Anglo-American childhood mentions Key's book or her phrase, and the important recent volume edited by Koops and Zuckerman, *Beyond the Century of the Child: Cultural History and Developmental Psychology*, is obviously referencing Key in its title.

17 See, for example, Cunningham, *Children and Childhood in Western Society since 1500*; West, *Growing Up in Twentieth-Century America*; Sommerville, *The Rise and Fall of Childhood*; DeMause, ed., *The History of Childhood*; and Pinchbeck and Hewitt, *Children in English Society*, vol. 2, *From the Eighteenth Century to the Chil-*

dren Act of 1948. For further evidence of this absence, one can consult the excellent bibliographies offered by a group of childhood scholars (Nina Bandelj, Viviana Zelizer, and Ann Morning) at Princeton University (see www.princeton .edu/~children) under the title "Materials for the Study of Childhood." Organized according to twelve different categories (including "historical and cross-cultural perspectives" and "inequality"), not one entry gives any indication of childhood sexual orientation or homosexuality in reference to children. I should also say that, to my knowledge, as of the summer of 2007, there has been no history of gay and/or queer childhood (nothing of any scale announced as such) by any historian working in the history of sexuality. When I Googled "the history of gay childhood" on July 13, 2007, what immediately appeared were gay memoirs and books on "gay men and childhood sexual trauma." Memoir, of course, is related to History — it is personal history — but is not synonymous with it, in my view. I place it in the domain of self-confession, on the one hand, and literature, on the other — the two categories I invoked at the start of this introduction.

18 This is true, for instance, of Cunningham's 2005 edition of *Children and Childhood in Western Society since 1500.*

19 In other words, whether or not the concept of a "gay child" will be around, say, twenty years hence in the general culture of that time does not mean that it won't show up in histories of the twentieth century as a concept that was alive during this time.

20 All thanks here to my colleague Scott Black, who listened to me talk through versions of this claim and offered his invaluable wisdom.

21 Of course, retrospectively, there are reasons why it looks like someone flipped a switch in relation to children at the beginning of the twentieth century: the start of juvenile justice takes place in 1899 and the agitation for ending children's labor for wages begins, according to most scholars, in 1900; as for the "gay" child, the word *homosexual* enters English sometime in the early 1890s and the first inklings of any public notion (outside of novels, memoirs, or films) of gay children appear around 2005 (in my estimation). However, it is obvious that even these developments, especially the crucial roots to them, not to mention their flowerings, do not precisely obey the dates attributed to them or the parameters of what we call "the twentieth century."

22 Stockton, "Growing Sideways, or Versions of the Queer Child." This being said, though Michael Moon didn't claim to write a monograph on the queer child in the twentieth century — the child is "one pole" of his work, he says, and he was writing specifically on boys — I would say that Moon, both delightfully and brilliantly, did write something close to such a monograph in his book *A Small*

Boy and Others: Imitation and Initiation in American Culture. And though his book is focused on the 1960s, it richly ranges across a spread of times. Moreover, one can now put next to Moon's book Carol Mavor's just now appearing and elegant *Reading Boyishly.*

23 For a representative sample of texts along these lines, see Shyer and Shyer, *Not Like Other Boys;* Sanderson, *A Stranger in the Family;* Ryan and Futterman, *Lesbian and Gay Youth;* Mallon, *We Don't Exactly Get the Welcome Wagon;* D'Augelli and Patterson, *Lesbian, Gay, and Bisexual Identities and Youth: Psychological Perspectives;* Lipkin, *Beyond Diversity Day;* and Macgillivray, *Sexual Orientation and School Policy.*

24 All of these definitions are from the *Oxford English Dictionary.*

25 This scientific notion has been given a popular dimension through the IMAX documentary *Wired to Win: Surviving the Tour de France* (2006).

26 On the violence embedded in ideals in general, see Bataille, "Rotten Sun" and "The Language of Flowers" in *Visions of Excess.* And for a book that powerfully, creatively takes off from and extends Kincaid's notion of "erotic innocence," see Kevin Ohi's *Innocence and Rapture.*

27 Kincaid, "Producing Erotic Children," 10. Hereafter cited in the text.

28 Lee Edelman, in his use of Lacan's term "Imaginary," is referring to the domain of images by means of which the ego creates a set of falsely coherent and stabilizing representations of itself and its relations. Lacan's translator, Alan Sheridan, famously defines the Imaginary in *Écrits* as "the world, the register, the dimension of images, conscious or unconscious, perceived or imagined" (ix).

29 Edelman, *No Future,* 2. Hereafter cited in the text.

30 Creatively drawing on the kind of resistance to notions of "the social" that Leo Bersani has put forward, Edelman actually attacks our culture's standard notions of the social order and sociality — not just the social order that props up the child. See also Bersani, *Homos* and "Is the Rectum a Grave?"

31 Sedgwick, "How to Bring Your Kids Up Gay," 161.

32 Derrida, "Freud and the Scene of Writing," 81. The phrase "deferred action" is James Strachey's translation of *Nachträglichkeit;* "deferred effect" and "deferred comprehension" also appear in his translations of Freud's discussion of this concept; see *The Standard Edition of the Complete Psychological Works of Sigmund Freud,* 1: 356–59; 3: 166–67; and 17: 44–45 n. 1. See also Mather and Marsden, "Trauma and Temporality."

33 See Freud's long footnote to the "Wolf Man" case in *Standard Edition,* 17: 45, n. 1. See also McGrath, "The Transmission of Trauma," and Fonagy et al., "Measuring the Ghost in the Nursery."

34 In other words, the child may consciously to itself apply the words *gay* or *homo-*

sexual or *queer*, even though there is no context—not even among friends or family—in which these words may be uttered out loud in relation to itself. It is also possible, instead—or in addition—that this child will use a metaphor both to grasp and suspend itself.

35 Derrida, *"Différance,"* 413.

36 Ibid.

37 Platt, *The Child Savers*, 187–88. See also Shelden, *Delinquency and Juvenile Justice in American Society*, 11–39.

38 Until 2007, all of network TV's flirtations with this category involved gay or experimenting teens and gender-identity issues for children—never (to my knowledge) an explicitly same-sex-oriented child. (Even the boy on *Ugly Betty*, which started airing in 2006, has been played as gender-crossed, even gay-seeming, but not yet as full-on attracted to a boy.) If one counts subscription channels not governed by network regulations, then the show *Weeds* (which began its run in 2005 on the Showtime channel) does show a preteen girl's attractions to other girls. And on *Private Practice*, in an episode that aired on ABC on October 17, 2007, a preteen boy (who looks about twelve and is not gender bent) *is* shown having an attraction for a friend. Tellingly, he is beaten up by this boy (hence "endowed" with abuse for viewers' sympathies) and is suicidal afterward. The latter may be the first network instance of a "gay" child.

39 Sanderson, *A Stranger in the Family*, 8. Hereafter cited in the text.

40 Shyer and Shyer, *Not Like Other Boys*, viii. Hereafter cited in the text.

41 Savin-Williams, *". . . And Then I Became Gay."* Hereafter cited in the text.

42 This is not the end of his story, however. As I discuss further on in this chapter, Savin-Williams's newest take—a fascinating one—on his earlier work is no less rich to consider or discuss. See his pathbreaking book *The New Gay Teenager* and my engagement of it below.

43 Cole Moreton, "Christian Centre 'Turns Gays Straight,'" *The Independent*, November 20, 1994, 6.

44 Henry Makow, "We're Being Brainwashed to Be Gay," *Toogood Reports*, December 12, 2001, 3. The next reference occurs on the same page.

45 Charles Darwin, *The Descent of Man*, 421. The next reference occurs on the same page.

46 Nordau, *Degeneration*, 8th ed., 554–55.

47 Cesare Lombroso, *Crime: Its Causes and Remedies*, 418.

48 "A Letter from Freud," *American Journal of Psychiatry* 107 (April 1951): 786.

49 Freud, *Three Essays on the Theory of Sexuality*. The next reference occurs on the same page.

50 Quoted in Lewes, *The Psychoanalytic Theory of Male Homosexuality*, 149.

51 To be precise, both the term and the concept of "inversion" lasted into the twentieth century. Radclyffe Hall and Djuna Barnes, for instance, both refer to it in their fiction. Sigmund Freud, *Three Essays on the Theory of Sexuality* in *The Freud Reader*, ed. Peter Gay, 241. Hereafter cited in the text.

52 Boswell, *Christianity, Social Tolerance, and Homosexuality*, 43.

53 Stein, "Miss Furr and Miss Skeene," 255. Hereafter cited in the text.

54 For what I take to be the premiere book on the child in psychoanalysis in general, see Virginia L. Blum's fiercely intelligent *Hide and Seek*. See also Peter Coviello's "The Sexual Child; or, This American Life," which offers brilliant connections to American nineteenth-century contexts and our nation's use of the child.

55 Freud, "Femininity," 133–34.

56 Ibid., 130.

57 See Vito Russo's discussion in *The Celluloid Closet*, 121.

58 "The Little Black Boy," in *The Norton Anthology of Poetry*, 547.

59 The date of this volume is 1793. In 1794, Blake bound the two different *Songs* together in the volume *Songs of Innocence and Experience: Shewing the Two Contrary States of the Human Soul*.

60 See, for example, Harold Bloom's introduction to *William Blake's "Songs of Innocence and of Experience"*; Erdman, "Blake's Vision of Slavery"; Glazer, "Blake's Little Black Boys"; Gleckner, "The Strange Odyssey of Blake's 'The Voice of the Ancient Bard'"; Hirsch, *Innocence and Experience*; and Williams, *Ideology and Utopia in the Poetry of William Blake*.

61 For two completely different thinkers (from two different periods) who puzzle out delay, see the homosexual writer Edward Carpenter, in his essay "Affection in Education," from 1899; and Neil Postman, *The Disappearance of Childhood*, writing toward the end of the twentieth century.

62 See, for example, essays from Koops and Zuckerman, eds., *Beyond the Century of the Child*. See also the film *The Bad Seed* and its recent echoes in the film *Joshua*, both of which seem to index these issues.

63 See Neil Postman, for example, who puts this concern in the title to his book, *The Disappearance of Childhood*.

64 See Dinshaw, *Getting Medieval*, and Nealon, *Foundlings*. For their conversation back and forth with each other, see Freeman, ed., "Theorizing Queer Temporalities: A Roundtable Discussion."

65 Chris Nealon, I believe, is saying something similar in *Foundlings* about the force

of fictions for certain forms of emergent gay communities before the time of Stonewall; of course, at the time Nealon is writing, these communities are by and large apparent in History, whereas the gay child is not yet (or only just about to be) a publicly available category at the time I'm writing.

66 Edelman, quoted in Freeman, ed., "Theorizing Queer Temporalities," 181, 180.

67 Edelman and others for all good reason might not like the word *criteria* here. For myself, I accept it, not as prescriptive of how these nonlinearities must show themselves but as descriptive of patterns in fictions of how they do (at least so far in the fictions I'm discussing).

68 Ariès, *Centuries of Childhood*. Hereafter cited in the text.

69 For amplification of these claims, see Postman, *The Disappearance of Childhood*.

70 Even so, this is a figure recognized by two researchers from New Zealand, Julie Glamuzina and Alison J. Laurie, who wrote a study, *Parker and Hulme: A Lesbian View*, originally published by New Women's Press, 1991, of the circumstances surrounding the murder depicted in the film *Heavenly Creatures*. Nonetheless, one gets a sense that many readers, especially in the United States, have access to this study (written and published before the film) because of the film. Indeed, the introduction to their reprinted book is written by the American film critic B. Ruby Rich and the book is categorized (on its back cover) as "Film/Lesbian Studies."

71 Platt, *The Child Savers*, 3. Hereafter cited in the text.

72 Stearns, "Historical Perspectives on Twentieth-Century American Childhood," in Koops and Zuckerman, eds., *Beyond the Century of the Child*, 96. Hereafter cited in the text.

73 Zelizer, *Pricing the Priceless Child*, 3. Hereafter cited in the text.

74 Letts and Sears, eds., *Queering Elementary Education*, 42, 41, 42, 92. Hereafter cited in the text.

75 Savin-Williams, *The New Gay Teenager*, xi, 1. Hereafter cited in the text.

1. The Smart Child Is the Masochistic Child

This chapter has its origins in a 1997 talk I gave at the Modern Language Association in Toronto, Canada. Then titled "The Child, the Pedagogue, the Pedophile, and the Masochist," it contained the heart of the reading I present here. It then formed the nucleus of a playful essay, "Eve's Queer Child," I wrote for the volume *Regarding Sedgwick: Essays on Queer Culture and Critical Theory*, edited by Stephen M. Barber and David L. Clark (2002). It also formed parts of invited lectures at Harvard University, Cornell University, the University of Maryland, and New York University. I warmly thank the faculty and students at these places, who made my thinking on these matters so much sharper.

1 *The American Heritage Dictionary*, New College Edition, s.v. "ejaculation."

2 Witness the debates now taking place, at both state and national levels, about whether parents can be made to vaccinate their prepubescent daughters against the human papilloma virus that can lead to cervical cancer. Many parents would rather run the risk that their daughter could get cancer than possibly "encourage" her sexual activity by providing her with this vaccine.

3 For the purpose of this chapter, I will use the phrase "man/boy love," which to many ears denotes pedophilia, to connote a range of ways in which men and boys might say they love each other, including wanting to live together, as the man and boy want to do in James's story (the boy, at times, more than the man).

4 For my detailed engagement with Zelizer's *Pricing the Priceless Child*, which chronicles the disappearance of children's waged labor, at least in so-called developed countries, see my introduction.

5 Obviously, something like online sex (or, of course, phone sex) is a way that talking *can* be sex, or directly tied to it.

6 As the Mark Foley "Pagegate" scandal—centered on Congressman Foley's "sexually explicit" text messages to former pages—raged across the country during the fall congressional elections of 2006, we were immersed in these issues anew.

7 My characterizing of NAMBLA here—and throughout—is based in part on Jesse Green's article "The Men from the Boys." In what follows, I draw inferences, especially as I analyze, that Green doesn't make.

8 Actually, in most large cities NAMBLA marches at Gay Pride. However, Green's article "The Men from the Boys" begins with the dilemma of NAMBLA for would-be "respectable" gay groups: "The tale begins in July 1993, when after years of failure, the International Lesbian and Gay Association (ILGA). . . . representing more than 300 organizations worldwide, finally got the UN Economic and Social Council (ECOSOC) to grant it third-tier consultative status. . . . But Jesse Helms got wind of the fact that one of ILGA's signatories (and earliest members) was . . . NAMBLA" (76). Helms's bill "threatening to cut UN funding unless it expelled all pedophile groups passed the U.S. Senate 99–0" (76).

9 For my specific discussions of these models, see my introduction.

10 On contracts as a lateralizing relation, especially in a contract's requirement of

"mutual agreement," one could consult any legal textbook. But more importantly, readers may wonder what other critics have named or made of what I am calling "man/boy love" and "brotherly masochism" in this novella. F. O. Matthiessen, the famous and famously closeted homosexual author of *Henry James: The Major Phase*, states in this book, from 1944, that in *The Pupil* "there is no basis in homosexual attraction" and then implies that the story becomes consequently vague since there is no "accounting for why the tutor's attachment to his charge is so strong as to make him destroy his prospects on the boy's account" (93). Clifton Fadiman, in 1945, in *The Short Stories of Henry James* finds in the story a "perfectly unconscious homosexual love—of a type that could never ripen into overt action" (272), whereas Edward Wagenknect, in 1984, in *The Tales of Henry James* seems relieved to report that though "in days gone by, some readers were given to sniffing out homosexuality in the relations between Pemberton and his charge," "this nonsense seems now to have been abandoned." Despite this confidence, in 1991 Michael Moon gives *The Pupil* a whole new twist in perversity by reading "the boy Morgan's dead body" (at the story's end) as "occup[ying] precisely the place of the dirty suede gloves" the pupil's mother wears at the start, where "suede gloves" (with the help of the dictionary) translates as "undressed kid"; Pemberton is holding a metaphorically undressed boy at the climax of *The Pupil*. See Moon's "A Small Boy and Others." Not long after, in 1992, Fred Kaplan, in *Henry James: The Imagination of Genius: A Biography*, not only sees Pemberton "fall[ing] in love" with Morgan but also finds Pemberton lacking the will to be seen as homosexual at the story's end, thus indicating his "homosexual panic" that *results* in Morgan's death. Helen Hoy, by contrast, in 1993, in "Homotextual Duplicity in Henry James's 'The Pupil,'" considers Henry James to be the story's coward, since he kills off the boy, or so Hoy claims, to repress the homoerotic subtext threatening to break through the surface of the text. Linda Zwinger, two years later, says that *The Pupil* is *about* "disavowal," so that "James' tale insidiously suggests . . . that disavowal is all there is" (on many levels), making *The Pupil* "like most of the rest of James's fiction . . . an *investigation* of sexuality" ("Bodies That Don't Matter," 669, 674). At around the same time, Philip Horne, in "Henry James: The Master and the 'Queer Affair' of 'The Pupil,'" revisits all this history in order both to express his "skepticism" that homosexuality is "there" in the text and to suspend judgment about its full absence. As he states quite helpfully: "The real test, perhaps, would be a 'fuller' account of 'The Pupil' in which a homoerotic reading came into serious and interesting tension with the complex balance of other more explicit strains in the story, about duty and sacrifice, money and honour, education and experience" (88). Horne concludes: "So far it seems to me a convincing case has not been presented for such dynamics" (89–90). Of course, I think I present such a case.

11 This is how Eve Kosofsky Sedgwick has read Henry James—James as fascinated with his own shame. (See her remarks on James in "Shame, Theatricality, and Queer Performativity.") Sedgwick has written of her own fascinations along these lines in "A Poem Is Being Written." For my "fictional" (serious spoof) analysis of this revealing nexus, which is a precursor of this chapter, see my essay "Eve's Queer Child." For very different readings of literary masochism from my own, see Kucich, *Imperial Masochism*; Mansfield, *Masochism*; Siegel, *Male Masochism*; and Noble, *The Masochistic Pleasures of Sentimental Literature*.

12 Green, "The Men from the Boys," 80.

13 For a book-length study of the Mary Ellen Wilson story, which resulted in the first organization to prevent childhood cruelty—the New York Society for the Prevention of Cruelty to Children—see Shelman and Lazoritz, *The Mary Ellen Wilson Child Abuse Case and the Beginning of Children's Rights in the Nineteenth Century*.

14 By contrast, could the child consent to punching an adult in the stomach, if the adult asked the child to give him pain?

15 James, *The Pupil*, 2, 9, 4, 6, 10. This is the version James reprinted in book form in 1892. Hereafter cited in the text.

16 See note 4 above. Also, for an account of the rise of the juvenile justice system as a system of child protection that emerges in 1899, see my introduction.

17 Rind, Bauserman, and Tromovitch, "A Meta-Analysis of Assumed Properties of Child Sexual Abuse Using College Samples," 22. Hereafter cited in the text.

18 Garrison and Kobor, "Weathering a Political Storm,"165. Hereafter cited in the text.

19 Thirteen members of Congress voted "present," instead of voting "yes." As the authors tell us: "Although all of the 13 House members who voted 'present' were reelected in 2000, a significant number of them . . . suffered conservative grassroots and media attacks" (173).

20 See Silverstein and Auerbach, "Deconstructing the Essential Father."

21 Carpenter, *Selected Writings*, vol. 1, *Sex*.

22 Noël Greig, Introduction, in Carpenter, *Selected Writings*, 22.

23 Carpenter, "Affection in Education," 221–22.

24 Ibid., 222.

25 Ibid.

26 Ibid., 223–25.

27 Ibid., 226–27.

28 Ibid., 225, 228.

29 These biographical facts about Leopold von Sacher-Masoch can be found in Deleuze, "Coldness and Cruelty," 9–14. Hereafter cited in the text.

30 There are hints that the Greek is bisexual, raising the question of whether part of this excessive cruelty that is too much for Severin lies in the homosexualizing feel to this beating. Of the Greek, we are told: "Like a woman, he knows he is beautiful and behaves accordingly. Always elegant, he changes his costume four or even five times a day like a courtesan. He has been seen in Paris dressed as a woman and men showered him with love letters" (*Venus in Furs*, 250).

31 Sacher-Masoch, *Venus in Furs*, 189. Further references appear in the text.

32 Sacher-Masoch, "A Childhood Memory and Reflections on the Novel," in *Masochism*. Hereafter cited in the text.

33 Krafft-Ebing, *Pyschopathia Sexualis*, 150. Hereafter cited in the text.

34 As an aside, if one would like to know if there were female masochists, Krafft-Ebing tells us that only two cases of masochistic women "have been scientifically established" (178)—although, oddly, he presents three. Presumably, the difficulty of discerning them is due to the fact that "ideas of subjection are, in women, normally connected with the idea of sexual relations" (177). Even so, he presents these details from one patient, details which again stress the role of ideas. She recalls, "In former years I seriously contemplated going into a lunatic asylum whenever these ideas worried me. I fell upon this idea while reading how the director of an insane asylum pulled a lady by the hair from her bed and beat her with a cane and a riding-whip. I longed to be treated in a similar manner at such an institute. . . . I liked . . . best to think of brutal, uneducated female warders beating me mercilessly" (179). This patient contemplates scenes from Defoe's *Robinson Crusoe*, while the patient from the second case thinks about Rousseau's *Confessions*. A third (apparent) case involves a woman who seeks out "gynecological examinations" for her torture: "She [told the doctor] she would make resistance, but he must take no notice of that, on the contrary ask her to be calm and proceed with the examination. . . . She would resist, and thus work herself up into a high state of sexual excitement" (180).

35 I say lateral because I am not claiming that any of these texts had an influence on James. There is no evidence James read these texts or that he saw himself transforming them. They are lateral to *The Pupil* only in the sense that I'm making them so; the same is true of Deleuze to follow. What gives James his ideas of masochism? In part, what offered the author of *Venus*, in some respects, his own: his reading of fictions. Obviously, Sacher-Masoch's reading of the *Legends of the*

Saints, for example, indicates how crucial were "'cruel' . . . fiction[s]" — across a range of times — to his feelings, thoughts, and writings.

36 There are no references to penetrative sex in *Venus in Furs* — only mentions of passionate kissing and caressing (and, of course, nights spent together by the lovers) in addition to bruisings. A passage like the following shows this insistent focus on surface: "In a frenzy of passion I flung my arms around my lovely cruel mistress and covered her face, her mouth, her breasts with burning kisses, which she returned with equal fervor, her eyes closed as in a dream" (207). This kind of depiction of passion is why Deleuze draws attention to the novel's surprising absence of obscenity.

37 Of course, there are aspects of family finance that Morgan doesn't know, but he knows he doesn't know them. Responding to the closet of his family's moneyed circumstances, Morgan exclaims: "I don't know what they live on, or how they live, or *why* they live! What have they got and how did they get it? Are they rich, are they poor, or have they a *modeste aisance*? Why are they always chiveying about?" (27)

38 Making for a striking contrast with the pupil (and the tutor), the pupil's older brother is depicted as strongly resembling the father (again, in mocking tones). Here is how father and older son are rendered: "Mr. Moreen had a white moustache, a confiding manner and, in his buttonhole, the ribbon of a foreign order — bestowed, as Pemberton eventually learned, for services. For what services he never clearly ascertained: this was a point — one of a large number — that Mr. Moreen's manner never confided. What it emphatically did confide was that he was a man of the world. Ulick, the firstborn, was in visible training for the same profession — under the disadvantage as yet, however, of a buttonhole only feebly floral and a moustache with no pretensions to type" (5). He, too, is tagged "a man of the world" (37).

39 Any reader of Wilde will remember Henry's refinement and perception; these are the qualities that strike Dorian as so palpable after meeting Henry. The sense of Lord Henry as a gymnast of the mind emerges, too — perhaps in response to a character's claim that "to test Reality we must see it on the tight-rope; when the Verities become acrobats we can judge them" (*The Picture of Dorian Gray*, 64). Two pages later we read: "[Henry] played with the idea, and grew wilful; tossed it into the air and transformed it; let it escape and recaptured it; made it iridescent with fancy, and winged it with paradox. . . . It was an extraordinary improvisation. . . . He was brilliant, fantastic, irresponsible" (66). Unexpected hints of Henry's stoicism also surface in the text, especially in relation to his

aging: "I am wrinkled, and worn, and yellow. . . . I have sorrows, Dorian, of my own, that even you know nothing of. The tragedy of old age is not that one is old, but that one is young" (254–55).

40 This definition is from the *American Heritage Dictionary*, New College Edition.

41 Quoted in Green, "The Men from the Boys," 83.

2. An Interval of Animal

1 See www.lassie.net.

2 As cited on the webpage at www.rintintin.com. The next two quotations are from this same page.

3 For a more detailed discussion of delay in relation to the child, see the beginning of chapter 1.

4 Bersani, "Is the Rectum a Grave?," 203.

5 Not only does masochism offer a form for unexpected joy but the breaking of its frame is also, as we've seen, its own kind of form for holding emotions.

6 For example, in *The Norton Introduction to Poetry*, we are told that "often the vividness of the picture in our minds" from reading a poem "depends upon comparisons": "we are asked [through metaphors] to think of one thing as if it were something else" (134). "Things we can't see or which aren't familiar to us are pictured as things we can; for example, God is said to be like a father, Italy is said to be shaped like a boot."

7 In Matthew 9:36 we are told that "when [Jesus] saw the multitudes, he was moved with compassion on them, because they fainted, and were scattered abroad, as sheep having no shepherd." In John 10:27, Jesus himself says: "My sheep hear my voice, and I know them, and they follow me."

8 Barnes, *Nightwood*, 169–70. Hereafter cited in the text.

9 For my discussion of linguistic delay as it relates to the protohomosexual child, see the section "The Ghostly Gay Child" in the introduction. Readers may also wish to consult Dana Seitler's wonderful study, *Atavistic Tendencies*—a treatise that appeared while my book was being edited. Our two takes on Barnes's *Nightwood*, for all of their differences, speak to each other.

10 We meet this character Robin, in *Nightwood*, in a chapter titled "La Somnambule" (The Sleepwalker).

11 Freud, "Femininity," 130. "Femininity" appeared in 1933, three years prior to *Nightwood*'s publication in 1936.

12 For a reading of the banning of *Well* that argues that the issue of women's au-

tonomy was central to that act—not just the matter of homosexuality—see Doan, "The Mythic Moral Panic."

13 See Shelman and Lazoritz, *The Mary Ellen Wilson Child Abuse Case and the Beginning of Children's Rights in the Nineteenth Century.*

14 Deleuze and Guattari, *A Thousand Plateaus*, 237. Hereafter cited in the text.

15 I first discussed this pattern at the annual conference of the Society for the Study of Narrative Literature in 1998 at Ohio State University. See also my essay "Growing Sideways, or Versions of the Queer Child."

16 Woolf, *Mrs. Dalloway*, 16. Hereafter cited in the text.

17 See Cunningham, *The Hours.*

18 One sees that Woolf's trademark sentence—which makes central, frequent use of the semicolon and often suspends completion of a sentence base for many lines—is perfectly suited for this project in this novel.

19 Here Woolf gives a pleasurable spin to the clichéd metaphor of woman as flower.

20 In *The Hours*, Cunningham makes Clarissa the longtime lesbian companion of Sally Seton. The memorable passion Clarissa has for Sally in *Mrs. Dalloway* is transferred in *The Hours* to the Richard figure, who is not Mr. Dalloway (as he is in Woolf) but instead a gay man, dying of AIDS, whom Clarissa once kissed and can't forget. The Sally of *Mrs. Dalloway* is not even clearly herself a sapphist (perhaps not at all) in Woolf's depiction. She is a bohemian. She has "that quality," thinks Clarissa, which "she [Clarissa] always envied—a sort of abandonment, as if she could say anything, do anything; a quality much commoner in foreigners than in Englishwomen. Sally always said she had French blood in her veins, an ancestor had been with Marie Antoinette" (48). In fact, at the end, when Clarissa's party finally takes place, Sally is revealed to have married "quite unexpectedly, a bald man with a large buttonhole who owned, it was said, cotton mills at Manchester"—"and she had five boys!" (277). "The luster had gone out of her. Yet it was extraordinary to see her again, older, happier, less lovely" (260–61).

21 Intriguingly, Woolf also makes Miss Kilman a religious devotee—and thus as judgmental of the Dalloways as they are of her. ("She pitied and despised them . . . as she stood on the soft carpet, looking at the old engraving of a little girl with a muff," 188.) In *The Hours*, the Kilman figure (called Mary Krull), a "queer theorist" the daughter is "in thrall to," also deprecates Clarissa, making the latter think: "You respect Mary Krull . . . living as she does on the edge of poverty, going to jail for her various causes, lecturing passionately at NYU . . . but she is

finally too despotic in her intellectual and moral intensity. . . . You know she mocks you, privately, for your comforts and your quaint (she must consider them quaint) notions about lesbian identity" (23).

22 Mrs. Dalloway even imagines her daughter as somehow foreign (or alien): "She was dark; had Chinese eyes in a pale face; an Oriental mystery" (186); "she was a pioneer, a stray" (208); "in many ways, her mother felt, she was extremely immature, like a child still, attached to dolls, to old slippers; a perfect baby; and that was charming" (208–9).

23 Even Mrs. Dalloway metaphorizes her daughter in this way, thinking Elizabeth "like a hyacinth, sheathed in glossy green, with buds just tinted" (186).

24 Hall, *The Well of Loneliness*, 99. Hereafter cited in the text.

25 For a volume that helpfully gathers some of the most influential critical essays, past and present, written on *The Well of Loneliness*, see Doan and Prosser, eds., *Palatable Poison*.

26 For a discussion of the critical role of clothing in *The Well*, see "Cloth Wounds, or When Queers are Martyred to Clothes: Debasements of a Fabricated Skin," in my book *Beautiful Bottom, Beautiful Shame*, 48–50.

27 With Seitler's new book, *Atavistic Tendencies*, as a bold exception (see note 9 above), one could consult Baxter, "A Self-Consuming Light"; Pochoda, "Style's Hoax"; Plumb, Introduction; Herring, *Djuna*; Gerstenberger, "Modern (Post)-Modern."

28 Herring, *Djuna*, xv. Hereafter cited in the text.

29 For an interpretation of this relationship as both a case of incest and a safe harbor against patriarchy, see Mary Lynn Broe, "My Art Belongs to Daddy," 53.

30 Barnes at times even offers metaphors that seem to figure this aspect of her metaphors: "as if privacy . . . by the very sustaining power of its withdrawal kept the body eternally moving downward, but in one place, and perpetually before the eye" (51).

31 The best index to this issue is Jane Marcus's essay "Laughing at Leviticus."

32 For example, this child's father, Guido, "had walked, hot, incautious and damned, his eyelids quivering over the thick eyeballs, black with the pain of a participation that, four centuries later, made him a victim . . . the degradation by which his people [the Jews] had survived" (2); "it had made Guido, as it was to make his son, heavy with impermissible blood" (3).

33 Jane Marcus examines Doctor O'Connor as a parody of Freud in "Laughing at Leviticus."

34 Duncan, *Picasso and Lump*. Hereafter cited in the text.

3. What Drives the Sexual Child?

I first presented ideas from this chapter at Harvard University in 1998 and at the Modern Language Association in 2002 (in New York City) under the title "Motive's Mysterious Motions, or What Drives the Out of Place Child." I later had the pleasure of developing these readings for plenary lectures — "American Hotbed" and "Lolita's Queer Children: New Directions in American Studies" — at the American Literature Association's Fall Symposium in Cancun, Mexico and at Dartmouth's Institute for American Studies in 2004, the same year in which ideas from this chapter were published as part of my essay "Growing Sideways, or Versions of the Queer Child" in Bruhm and Hurley, eds., *Curiouser: On the Queerness of Children.*

1 One could be tempted to think of the more recent JonBenet Ramsey, who was murdered in 1997 at the age of six, as a depiction of a sexual child who was not fictional. On closer examination, however, one remembers that she was more of a sexual*ized* child, by virtue of her costumes and her abuse at death, not the figure of sexual agency as Lolita appears to be. For the ongoing use of the name "Lolita" for any sexual girl, one need only recall Amy Fisher, tagged by the press the "Long Island Lolita" in 1992, after her nationally publicized affair at age sixteen with Joey Buttafuoco (age thirty-two), whose wife she subsequently shot in the face.

2 For a sense of the novel's ongoing relevance, even in new contexts, and its role as icon of forbidden literature, see Azar Nafisi's *Reading "Lolita" in Tehran.* One can understand why this memoir wasn't called "Reading 'Pride and Prejudice' in Tehran" — which the author also read with women in her country — since it wouldn't signify in the same way.

3 As anyone knows who has seen the show, the moment the journalist Chris Hansen catches the predator (when the latter has taken the bait and shown up on set) is just the beginning. Provided the predator doesn't run off, which he usually doesn't, Hansen interrogates the man onscreen (while also scolding him) as to what he thinks he is doing and why. Presumably, this moment of seeing someone squirm, in the midst of his attempting outlandish explanations, is part of the reason the audience watches.

4 *Lolita,* of course, is replete with references to Edgar Allan Poe (more than twenty), especially in the section on Humbert's boyhood when he falls in love with Annabel Leigh — whose name and age are meant to invoke Poe's real-life love for his thirteen-year-old bride and cousin, Virginia Clemm, whom he immortalized in his poem "Annabel Lee."

5 In point of fact, Nabokov "detest[ed] Dr. Freud": "I think he's crude, I think he's medieval, and I don't want an elderly gentleman from Vienna with an umbrella inflicting his dreams upon me." "Let the credulous and the vulgar continue to believe that all mental woes can be cured by a daily application of old Greek myths to their private parts. I really don't care." (Quoted in *The Annotated Lolita*.) Of course, many critics have found that this sound denial of Freud is a case of disavowal, since the fictions, especially *Lolita*, seem to be in conversation with him. Perhaps Nabokov's more salient point is that Freudianism as a ready-made key for decoding every fiction is a diminishment of aesthetic pleasure and its power to surprise. For more discussion of these matters, see Shute, "Nabokov and Freud."

6 Nabokov, *Lolita*, 306. Hereafter cited in the text.

7 *The American Heritage Dictionary*, New College Edition, s.v. "motive" and "motion."

8 It is hard to prove the absolute absence of a point in a body of critical literature as large as the one that exists for *Lolita*, but my voluminous searches have not turned up a discussion of the dog as metaphor. Even Alfred Appel Jr., in his meticulous annotations to the novel, does not call our attention to the dog as a sign of Lolita's stealthy movements toward Quilty, the pedophile she actively desires. Dog talk is also strikingly missing from Carl R. Proffer's *Keys to Lolita*, even though Proffer has a chapter titled "In Quest of Quimby-Quix-Quilty" in which he unravels all clues to Quilty. Proffer does mention the dog in passing as what kills Charlotte (see page 6), but all talk of the dog stops here. At a chapter's end, Proffer confesses: "It is certain there are parts of Nabokov's pattern which I have not seen — or, rather, which I have not *recognized*. . . . But my point in this chapter . . . has been to give an idea of the kinds of detail a reader of Nabokov must remark and the kinds of logical connections he must make . . . Nabokov's works are fabricated piece by piece with the author aware of the exact position in the puzzle of each little piece" (77–78).

9 For an early defense of *Lolita* as a love story, see Trilling, "The Last Lover." Page Stegner's *Escape into Aesthetics* represents early critical tendencies to read *Lolita* in aestheticizing ways, an approach that reaches its apotheosis in Trevor Mc-Neely's uncompromising essay on Nabokov's "nihilistic" aesthetics, "'Lo' and Behold." Two critics often cited for turning attention to Nabokov as a humanist and moralist are David Rampton (*Vladimir Nabokov*) and Ellen Pifer (*Nabokov and the Novel*). James O'Rourke, in *Sex, Lies, and Autobiography*, indicates a wish to engage the novel's "ethical issues" through narratology. David Andrews, in *Aestheticism, Nabokov and Lolita*, tries to steer a course between these poles of

criticism by arguing that *Lolita* essentially "damns an aesthete even as it cele-brates aestheticism" (9). Add to this list various feminist engagements with *Lolita*, among them Linda Kauffman, "Framing *Lolita*"; Susan Bordo, "The Moral Content of Nabokov's *Lolita*"; and Virginia Blum's feminist Lacanian reading, "Nabokov's *Lolita*/Lacan's Mirror," in *Hide and Seek*.

10 For a reading that makes this case, see Bordo, "The Moral Content of Nabokov's *Lolita*."

11 This is a question that has troubled many critics. For example, Margaret Morganroth Gullette, in "The Exile of Adulthood," begins her essay by stating: "Pedophilia is a curious phenomenon of twentieth-century fiction. Why should novelists of the stature of Thomas Mann and Vladimir Nabokov write about it, and why do readers with presumably minimal interest in the actuality continue to praise and analyze *Death in Venice* and *Lolita*—without considering what role this subject matter plays in the narratives?" (215). Gullette's essay stands against the background of other critics' arguments that the specificity of pedophilia as *Lolita*'s "subject matter" must be engaged; the critics she particularly cites on this point are Trilling and Pifer. See also Bordo.

12 To review a point from my introduction: before 1967, the child was not a "per-son" in the sense established by the Fourteenth Amendment. Only after the Supreme Court case *In re Gault* was it decided that this amendment applied to children.

13 Kincaid, "Producing Erotic Children," 11. Hereafter cited in the text.

14 This debate takes unusual form in the film *Little Children* (dir. Todd Field, 2006), where the story's pedophile castrates himself at the end of the film, a climax meant, at least in part, to critique these proposals.

15 This particular theory is discussed in Jesse Green's article on pedophilia, "The Men from the Boys." From 1951 until his death in 2006, Money was a profes-sor of pediatrics and medical psychology at Johns Hopkins University. For an interview with Money, see PAIDIKA: *The Journal of Paedophilia* 2, no. 3 (Spring 1991): 5.

16 See note 7 above.

17 Baker, *In Perpetual Motion*. Hereafter cited in the text.

18 Darwin, *The Expression of the Emotions in Man and Animals*. Hereafter cited in the text.

19 Lyne, as it happens, had actually filmed a version of this scene but didn't use it. Whether he finally deemed it unsuccessful in aesthetic terms or worried that it might undermine his chances of getting *Lolita* released in America isn't clear.

20 This is the scene that even Nabokov can't afford to show—not if he wants to

publish *Lolita*. It can only be folded inside the time Humbert specifies, hidden in this interval but visible as hidden.

21 For different thoughts on Lolita's wifeliness, see Freeman, *The Wedding Complex*, 151–52, 154, 171–77.

22 One could even wonder if the old woman who seems to own the spaniel is Quilty in disguise. Humbert describes Lolita as "still squatting, listening in profile, lips parted, to what the dog's mistress, an ancient lady swathed in violent veils, was telling her from the depths of a cretonne easy chair" (118). Indeed, only seven lines after this description, the hotel clerk is telling Humbert: "'Our beds are really triple. . . . One crowded night we had three ladies and a child like yours sleep together. I believe one of the ladies was a disguised man.'" Is this a clue to read Clare Quilty as the veiled lady? Adrian Lyne perhaps thinks so, since he makes Quilty (without disguise) the one who has the spaniel at the end of a leash at the hotel, as Lolita sinks down on her haunches.

23 Humbert confesses that he needed to offer Lolita only a sense of destination so as to prolong their aimless wanderings: "Every morning during our yearlong travels I had to devise some expectation, some special point in space and time for her to look forward to, for her to survive till bedtime. . . . The object in view might be anything. . . . By putting the geography of the United States in motion, I did my best for hours on end to give her the impression of 'going places,' of rolling on to some definite destination" (151–52).

24 Mulvey, "Visual Pleasure and Narrative Cinema." Hereafter cited in the text.

25 In recent years, largely after 2000, Hollywood films have allowed their women actors some motion. Angelina Jolie is an action figure in *Lara Croft: Tomb Raider* (2001) and the later *Mr. & Mrs. Smith* (2005)—with the one requirement that her active motions make her even hotter, provide even greater visual pleasure, for the viewing audience. (The covers of both DVDs unambiguously make this point.) Halle Berry in the James Bond film *Die Another Day* (2002) would be another relevant example. When Bond meets her in this film, Berry's character, Jinx Johnson, is, according to one official website, "coming out of the sea in a Honey Ryder (Ursula Andress in *Dr. No*) homage," nodding to women in earlier Bond films.

26 Metz, "The Imaginary Signifier." Hereafter cited in the text.

27 For readings of these films that cover different ground and offer perspectives different from my own, see Corliss, *Lolita*; Hatch, "Fille Fatale"; and Andrews, *Aestheticism, Nabokov and Lolita*, especially his chapter "A Litter of *Lolita*'s: Three Adaptations of an Uncooperative Novel."

28 As for Kubrick's hotel scene, the long, drawn-out tomfoolery surrounding Hum-

bert and the rollaway bed—he and the bellman struggle over it like they're in a Three Stooges routine—marks the film's need to displace the energies of what it cannot show onto something to be seen (the bed itself, in this case). Even more bizarrely, Kubrick has Lolita wake up Humbert with her joking line, "Wake up, Humbert! The hotel's on fire," presumably as at least some reference to the heat we will not see or even hear about (since we see Lolita whisper in his ear, but are never told her content).

29 Lyne supplies these lines for Quilty when the latter addresses Lolita, who is squatting, caressing his dog: "It's a nice dog, huh? That's my dog—he likes you. He doesn't like everybody. He can smell when people are sweet. He likes sweet people—nice young people, like you."

30 Nor do they guarantee that Lyne gets the tone of the novel right. In fact, the effect of not situating visual pleasure in the body of a woman (or even a girl) is the seeping of visual pleasure into every other corner of the film. Lyne's film—its images and soundtrack—is achingly beautiful and therefore seems unable to encompass the kind of campiness and black humor that permeate the novel.

31 Adrian Lyne, as readers may recall, became an antifeminist poster boy after his direction of 9 1/2 Weeks (1986), Fatal Attraction (1987), and Indecent Proposal (1993); see, for example, Susan Faludi's well-known critique of Fatal Attraction in her book Backlash.

4. Feeling Like Killing?

Certain critical ideas from this chapter first emerged in a talk I gave, "The Queer Child and the Fantasy of Law," at Harvard University in 1998, and in a later presentation, "Who Feels Like Killing? Narrative Trials for the Queer Child," at the Modern Language Association in 2004 (in Philadelphia). I thank my audiences in both cases, especially David Kennedy and William Cohen, who raised fascinating, helpful questions. I am also tremendously grateful to the editors of the special issue "Queer Temporalities," GLQ: A Journal of Lesbian and Gay Studies 13, nos. 2–3, 2007—namely, Elizabeth Freeman, Ann Cvetkovich, and Annamarie Jagose—and their anonymous readers for remarkably insightful suggestions for improvement.

1 Capote, In Cold Blood, 245. Hereafter cited in the text.
2 The American Heritage Dictionary, New College Edition, s.v. "motive."
3 For suggestive work that examines spoiling in the realm of identity, see Goffman, Stigma, and Love, following Goffman, in "'Spoiled Identity.'"

4 This is why children are a form of legal strangeness, as I explained in my introduction. As I also stated there, Anthony M. Platt and others have pointed out
that, even in the nineteenth century, before the rise of the juvenile courts (in
1899), rules of criminal responsibility for children made them considerably different from adults: children under seven were deemed by the law "incapable"
of committing crimes; and children between seven and fourteen were said to be
"destitute of criminal design," though the prosecution could rebut this presumption, albeit with a heavy burden of proof. See Platt, *The Child Savers*, 187–88. See
also Shelden, *Delinquency and Juvenile Justice in American Society*, 11–39. For more
details on the emergence of juvenile justice, see the section "Horizontal History,
or Sitting beside the History of the Child" in my introduction.

5 Derrida, "Freud and the Scene of Writing," 81.

6 Ibid. See also *The Standard Edition of the Complete Psychological Works of Sigmund
Freud*, 1:356–59, 3:166–67, 17:44–45 n. 1; and Mather and Marsden, "Trauma and
Temporality."

7 See Freud's long footnote to the "Wolf Man" case, in *Standard Edition*, 17:45 n. 1.
See also McGrath, "The Transmission of Trauma," and Fonagy et al., "Measuring the Ghost in the Nursery."

8 For a more detailed discussion of these matters, particularly the question of the
child's consciousness, see my introduction, especially the section "Why Speak
of Growing Sideways?"

9 Freud, *The Interpretation of Dreams*, 258. Hereafter cited in the text.

10 Freud, *Three Essays on the Theory of Sexuality*, in *The Freud Reader*, 255.

11 Lehman and Phelps, eds., *West's Encyclopedia of American Law*, 2nd ed., 130. Hereafter cited in the text.

12 Williams, *The Mental Element in Crime*, 9. Williams, a fellow of Jesus College,
Cambridge, delivered the remarks that constitute his book as the Lionel Cohen
Lectures at the Hebrew University of Jerusalem in 1957–58, a period between the
murders depicted by Jackson and Capote. Hereafter cited in the text.

13 Specifically, Williams writes: "There is a very great measure of concurrence in
the definitions of intention . . . advanced by such writers as Salmond in New
Zealand (if he may be claimed in this respect as an academic), Turner in England, and Wechsler in the United States; and this agreement is notably reflected
in the series of definitions set out in the American Law Institute's Model Penal
Code" (9).

14 Duff, *Intention, Agency, and Criminal Liability*, 31. Hereafter cited in the text.

15 As Derrida explains in a now-familiar passage: "It is because of *différance* that the

movement of signification is possible only if each so-called 'present' element . . . is related to something other than itself, thereby keeping within itself the mark of the past element, and already letting itself be vitiated by the mark of its relation to the future element" ("*Différance,*" 405).

16 Butler, "Imitation and Gender Insubordination," 24.

17 Plimpton, *Truman Capote,* 33. Hereafter cited as *TC* in the text. The film *Infamous* (dir. Douglas McGrath), largely based on Plimpton's book and starring Toby Jones as Capote, was released in October 2006, after this chapter was in press for *GLQ.* In interesting ways, which I take as confirmation of my interpretations, this film explores the Truman-Perry coupling as eroticized and marked by sympathetic bonding, especially on Capote's part.

18 Capote's search for fame through his book is the focus of the film *Capote,* based on Gerald Clarke's eponymous biography, with Philip Seymour Hoffman in the title role. (This film, too, along with *Infamous,* which followed it by about a year, appeared after this essay was written.) Though this film, unlike *Infamous* (see note 17 above), only hints at Perry's homosexuality, it does suggest Capote's attraction to Perry through identification.

19 See Platt, *The Child Savers,* on this central point.

20 So we learn in Glamuzina and Laurie, *Parker and Hulme,* 82–99. Hereafter cited in the text.

21 See Bataille, *Visions of Excess,* 116–29. For a fine essay, with a different thesis, that complements my reading of *Heavenly Creatures* — that appeared after and independently of my 2004 MLA talk ("Who Feels Like Killing? Narrative Trials for the Queer Child") — see Jay, "'Let's Moider Mother.'"

22 In fact, it doesn't seem outlandish to imagine Frodo and Sam, in Jackson's *Lord of the Rings* films, as two hobbits extremely cozy with each other, who move together as a pair in the world, as if this is what the saga of the ring was really all about. Their farewell scene, in which Sam and Frodo are parted from each other, is destined to seem gay to many viewers (children among them).

23 See Metz, "The Imaginary Signifier," and Mulvey, "Visual Pleasure and Narrative Cinema." Mulvey is hereafter cited in the text.

24 In chapter 3, I examine the girl as spoiled visual pleasure in the two different films of *Lolita,* directed by Stanley Kubrick (1962) and Adrian Lyne (1996), respectively.

25 See Lacan, "The Mirror Stage as Formative of the Function of the I," in *Écrits,* 1–7.

5. Oedipus Raced

I am extremely grateful to audiences at the University of Pittsburgh and Michigan State, where I gave talks based on parts of this chapter. In-depth conversations with Ellen McCallum, Todd Reeser, Tom McWhorter, Kathryn Flannery, and Randall Halle were especially beneficial.

1 As viewers of this film will recall, there are at least two dinner-table scenes that depict this sense of a family's hosting. At the first — Pauline at Juliet's house, set to opera — Pauline seems seduced by the family's wealth as she is entertained at a candlelit table beautifully set. We see her dab her mouth with her napkin in admiring imitation of Juliet's mother. In a different scene, Juliet comes to eat at Pauline's — a lunchtime affair, at which both girls behave rather badly with their unique blend of childish humor and condescension.

2 This intermediary was Floyd Wells. And, indeed, it was he who "solved" these murders by coming forward to prison authorities to tell of his connection — and what he said — to Dick and Perry, the Clutters' killers.

3 Obviously, there are numerous ways to approach the notion of the child queered by color. Though I purposely specifically address black children here — my past and current domain of expertise — I believe this category, "children queered by color," does apply broadly to other so-called racial designations. In a future project, I plan on interrogating this book's arguments and taxonomies in the domain of international fictions, including depictions of children in Brazil, Uganda, India, Japan, and Southeast Asia. For other, earlier work of mine that addresses girls of color, see my two essays "Bottom Values: Anal Economics in the History of Black Neighborhoods" and "Prophylactics and Brains: Slavery in the Cybernetic Age of AIDS" in my book *Beautiful Bottom, Beautiful Shame: Where "Black" Meets "Queer."* We might also ask: how should we read the strange, estranging, and specific circumstances of the Jewish child in Holocaust fiction or documentaries? On this point, see the recent documentary *The Hidden Child* (2006). And for my connections between Cynthia Ozick's *The Shawl* and Toni Morrison's *Beloved,* see Stockton, "Prophylactics and Brains."

4 Obviously, it remains striking and absurd that individual African countries continue to be reified under the singular term of "Africa" (a move I will mark by putting this term under erasure).

5 This is clearly unusual footage, showing children wielding machine guns, rifles, and knives, inflicting bloody and lethal violence. Two of the very few texts to

show children in this light are *City of God* and *City of Men*, both of which focus on children and teens in the barrios of Rio de Janeiro.

6 The recent bestseller, *A Long Way Gone: Memoirs of a Boy Soldier*, by Ishmael Beah, details how this forcing unfolded. This book was an Alternate Selection of Book-of-the-Month Club, History Book Club, Military Book Club, and Quality Paper-back Book Club. It was also promoted and sold at Starbucks coffee shops.

7 One of the characters in the film is called Captain Rambo, indicating the film's own nod to the irony of this humble father's resemblance (in his guise as rescuer) to the iconic movie character.

8 The fact that the smuggler articulates a version of this structure shows the extent to which the film's screenwriter and director self-consciously employ it, though the smuggler puts it differently than I do.

9 One could be reminded here of Patrick Brantlinger's comment that as more light was shone on "Africa" by "Western" writers and explorers, the darker it (metaphorically) got. See *Rule of Darkness*.

10 For a fascinating rendering of this history, originally published in 1868, see Sibthorpe, *The History of Sierra Leone*. The name of the capital, Freetown, refers to Sierra Leone's status as a British colony and destination for freed slaves at the end of the eighteenth century. Sadly, postindependence for this country in 1961 saw a series of failed governments famous for their corrupt profits from the diamond trade.

11 Lest we think that the rap music here is a heavy-handed Hollywood touch, Ishmael Beah's memoir, *A Long Way Gone*, explains the great appeal of this music for young African males and its presence in their culture.

12 Here the black captain, with obvious irony, continues his speech: "The Freetown government and their white masters have raped your land to feed their greed; I have freed you—no more master and slave here." Of course, he utters these lines as he stands above the father (who is kneeling in the water) with his big machete hanging from his belt.

13 For Louis Althusser's explanation of how interpellation works, see his essay "Ideology and Ideological State Apparatuses."

14 At first glance, the DVD cover looks like it bears the usual action-picture image—two men (the smuggler and the father, DiCaprio and Hounsou) with shirts open and determined faces looking out at danger. But a subtle difference may or may not catch the viewer's notice: Hounsou has no weapon. He is Rambo without any guns to brandish or use; he is a man who looks and moves like an action stud but is "only" a father.

15 The journalist will be there for part of this action, including the moment at

which a well-meaning African teacher, who rescues boy soldiers, is gunned down by one of them, as he falsely believes his good intentions will spare his life. Actually, the filmmakers spare his life; we are predictably told that he will recover from his wounds.

16 This child, metaphorically, is a diamond-in-the-rough, as this stone also is. Both, in the future, must be polished.

17 The filmmakers arrange it so that just as the father is handing over the diamond, his family runs to him from a private plane that has delivered them. The film thus crafts a one-to-one correspondence.

18 As we learn at www.kimberleyprocess.com, "The Kimberley Process Certification Scheme is an innovative, voluntary system that imposes extensive requirements on Participants to certify that shipments of rough diamonds are free from conflict diamonds. The Kimberley Process is composed of 45 Participants, including the European Community. Kimberley Process Participants account for approximately 99.8% of the global production of rough diamonds."

19 Indeed, on August 13, 2007, CNN ran a story, "Diamond Obsession," explaining that the poverty-stricken population of Sierra Leone continues to scour the exhausted mines in hopes of finding its ticket out of poverty.

20 See, for example, the book I discuss in my introduction: Sanderson, *A Stranger in the Family*.

21 Of course, it is possible that viewers in 1967 made these connections even then.

22 Spillers, "Mama's Baby, Papa's Maybe." Hereafter cited in the text.

23 See Meillassoux, "Female Slavery."

24 See Freud, "Femininity," 118–19.

25 See my discussion of William Blake's poem in the introduction.

26 For this notion of (mis)recognition, see Jacques Lacan's by now exceedingly well-known essay "The Mirror Stage as Formative of the Function of the I," in *Écrits*, 1–7.

27 Colomina, "The Split Wall." Hereafter cited in the text.

28 Quite simply, the house can have views on itself because it has windows onto itself. The windows are frames for views of the house, back into the house, and onto its terrace or even side wings. For a discussion of the woman's body as the man's phallus in its extended sense, providing the place to which he penetrates, see Butler, *Gender Trouble*, where she explains: " 'Being' the Phallus and 'having' the Phallus denote divergent sexual positions. . . . For women to 'be' the Phallus means, then, to reflect the power of the Phallus . . . to 'embody' the Phallus, *to supply the site to which it penetrates*" (44; my emphasis).

29 Those familiar with this film will recall that the character Hilary, who works at Christina Drayton's art gallery, does respond to the interracial lovers in more overt racist ways. In a key scene, Christina fires her for this reason; the film even seems to link Hilary's bad taste in art to her tastelessness in being racist.

30 *The American Heritage Dictionary*, New College Edition.

31 For an index to these fears, see Patterson, *"Brown v. Board of Education": A Civil Rights Milestone and its Troubled Legacy*, which informs us: "For many whites, the very idea of desegregated schools prompted the ugliest imaginable images of racial mixing. No one expressed this feeling more clearly than Herbert Ravenel Sass, a South Carolinian, in the *Atlantic Monthly* in 1956: 'To suppose that . . . we can promote all other degrees of race mixing but stop short of interracial mating is . . . like going over Niagara Falls in a barrel in the expectation of stopping three fourths of the way down. The South is now the great bulwark against intermarriage. A very few years of thoroughly integrated schools would produce larger numbers of young Southerners free from all 'prejudice' against mixed matings'" (6). Notice that "mating," in a context such as this one, does the double-duty work of signifying both "intermarriage" and "interracial" reproduction. For my discussion of whether there could be same-sex miscegenation, see my chapter "Erotic Corpse: Homosexual Miscegenation and the Decomposition of Attraction" in *Beautiful Bottom, Beautiful Shame*.

32 In humorous ways, the film implies that a whole new world is emerging through the youth of the 1960s. In a particularly amusing scene, a delivery boy gets down and funky with a young black woman who works at the Draytons'; they literally dance their way to his delivery truck.

33 For an interpretation of Lacan's mirror stage that makes much of the metaphor "thrown," see Borch-Jacobsen, *Lacan*, 43–71.

34 Compare with the stage set designed for the play: "a bright red carpeted disc, two red sofas, and, hanging over the stage, a framed double-sided Kandinsky. . . . [The set designer] encased the back wall, made of black scrim, in a gilt picture frame and then divided that into two levels. The openings on either level were framed in gold. When actors appeared in the upper level doors, the set would give the feeling that they floated in the dark" (John Guare, "Production Note," *Six Degrees of Separation* [New York: Vintage, 1994]).

35 Not having seen the play, I don't know what effect good acting would have had upon lines such as these.

36 There are many dissolves involving Paul in the film's shot selections. When he first enters the Kittredge apartment, the celluloid image of a Cézanne that Flan

is showing the rich South African dissolves over Paul as he makes his entry. At the film's end, after Paul has disappeared, Ouisa hallucinates in a shop window an image of Paul that quickly dissolves.

37 The DVD cover shows characters mugging in exaggerated fashion befitting a farce.

38 Ouisa obviously does get over it. This is what causes her split from Flan by the film's end.

39 He touches him, however, with medical gloves—a key AIDS signifier from that time, in the early 1990s. Do the gloves, then, stress sexuality? Or do they signal threat? Or both? It's hard to say.

Conclusion

1 The character of Paul, in *Six Degrees of Separation*, is a child in the dual, important senses that he is posing as the son of Sidney Poitier and would like to be the child of Flan and Ouisa Kittredge.

2 *American Masters: Andy Warhol: A Documentary Film* (2006). See also Moon, *A Small Boy and Others*, 95–116.

3 *Andy Warhol: A Documentary Film.*

4 Wayne Koestenbaum in *Andy Warhol: A Documentary Film.*

5 Koestenbaum and Stephen Koch in *Andy Warhol: A Documentary Film.*

6 Of course, it might be that a *fear* of death can produce a kind of Wildean *carpe diem* that, in its own right, is quite opposed to reproductive futurism.

7 *Andy Warhol: A Documentary Film.* Subsequent quotations in this section are from the film unless otherwise noted.

8 See Clarke, *Capote*; and Capote, *"A Christmas Memory," "One Christmas,"* and *"The Thanksgiving Visitor."*

9 Capote, *One Christmas*, 47, 40.

10 Capote, *The Thanksgiving Visitor*, 60–61; *A Christmas Memory*, 5.

11 Capote, *One Christmas*, 39.

12 Even if we don't let children materially play at all labors—don't let them literally play at putting out fires, for instance—we do let them imaginatively go through these motions with their friends, in ways we don't let them play at sex acts, for example, with each other.

13 The curious relation between harm and shelter, in relation to money and sex, can be queered, retrospectively, by "children's" own accounts. I recall a student telling my class that the sex he had with his uncle, when he was only ten, was not

a traumatic event for him; but being moved by his parents to Montana, where he was made to play Little League baseball, was deeply damaging to his sense of self. (The parents had moved due to economic circumstance.)

14 James, *The Pupil*, 27.

15 Woolf, *Mrs. Dalloway*, 16–17.

16 Nabokov, *Lolita*, 83, 272.

17 A major part of Perry's childhood story is his alcoholic mother and abusive father; detailed renderings of his childhood memories are woven into *In Cold Blood* at various points by Capote.

18 Bataille, *Visions of Excess*, 6, 8, 75. Hereafter cited in the text.

19 At the very least, these are matters of libidinal force — deep cathexes — between boy and coach, coach and boy, and even back and forth between the boy and spectators.

20 For my earlier discussions of Mulvey's theories on these points, see chapters 3 and 4.

21 Needless to say, this is not a question raised by the famous documentary film on civil rights, *Eyes on the Prize* (1987).

22 Wilde's specific phrase is "unnecessary things are our only necessities" (*The Picture of Dorian Gray*, 122).

23 Cutler and Cutler, "On the Rebound," 24. Hereafter cited in the text.

24 hooks, "Dreams of Conquest," 22.

25 Klawans, "Hoop Dreams,"592.

26 Raymond, "Outside Shots," 46.

27 Corliss, "False Hoops," 76.

28 hooks, "Dreams of Conquest," 22.

29 One scene even shows Spike Lee addressing a group of NBA hopefuls, saying to them: "You have to realize that nobody cares about you: you're black, you're a young male. . . . The only reason you're here [is] . . . this whole thing is revolving around money."

30 For two different critical perspectives on the success of Depp's performance as Willy Wonka, and its effects on the movie's success, see Ebert, "Charlie and the Chocolate Factory," and Clarke, "An Improper Charlie." Ebert begins his piece by saying: "Now this is strange. 'Charlie and the Chocolate Factory' succeeds in spite of Johnny Depp's performance. . . . Depp . . . has never been afraid to take a chance, but this time takes a wrong one. His Willy Wonka is an enigma. . . . When [moviegoers] see Willy opening the door of the factory . . . they will be relieved that the kids brought along adult guardians. . . . In a creepy way we're not sure of his motives." Ebert finds a strong pedophilic undercurrent to Depp's

Willy Wonka, believing that Depp's performance inescapably calls up Michael Jackson. Clarke, by contrast, deems Depp's Wonka "playfully weird," just shy of pedophilia: "Here Johnny Depp performs the same trick he pulled off with *Finding Neverland*—like his J. M. Barrie, his Willy Wonka is a man you could trust with your sons, despite Burton's exaggeration of his dandyish qualities" and "Prince Valiant hair." Still, Clarke writes, "He is also a man-child—repulsed by the sexual blandishments of one of the mothers and more comfortable, one suspects, with little boys than little girls." For discussions of Roald Dahl's fiction that explore directions different from my own, see Nicholson, "Dahl, the Marvelous Boy"; Warren, "Roald Dahl"; West, *Roald Dahl*; Gould, "Magical, Funny, and Deliciously Disgusting"; and Talbot, "The Candy Man." Given the title and admirable detail of the latter piece, it's surprising that Talbot has so little to say about candy itself, never mind its economy in childhood and in Dahl's imagination.

31 Or, according to numerous critics, he looks like Michael Jackson. Roger Ebert, for instance, insists that "Johnny Depp may deny that he had Michael Jackson in mind when he created the look and feel of Willy Wonka, but moviegoers trust their eyes. . . . Depp's Wonka—his dandy's clothes, his unnaturally pale face, his makeup and lipstick, his hat, his manner—reminds me inescapably of Jackson. . . . Bad luck that the movie comes out just as the Jackson trial has finally struggled to a conclusion."

32 To be precise, the elevator takes one up or down to a space that allows for sideways travel (in the elevator) into interesting rooms. It is the exuberant, scary movement upward, through the "Up and Out Room" (see my subsequent discussion in the text), that may seem both excessive and pointless from conventional standpoints.

Althusser, Louis. "Ideology and Ideological State Apparatuses." *Lenin and Philosophy*, 127–87. Translated by Ben Brewster. New York: Monthly Review Press, 1971.

Andrews, David. *Aestheticism, Nabokov and Lolita*. Lewiston, N.Y.: Edwin Mellen Press, 1999.

Appel, Alfred Jr., ed. *The Annotated Lolita*. New York: Vintage, 1991.

Ariès, Philippe. *Centuries of Childhood*. Translated by Robert Baldick. New York: Vintage, 1962.

Baker, Bernadette M. *In Perpetual Motion: Theories of Power, Educational History, and the Child*. New York: Peter Lang, 2001.

Barber, Stephen, and David L. Clark, eds. *Regarding Sedgwick: Essays on Queer Culture and Critical Theory*. New York: Routledge, 2002.

Barnes, Djuna. *Nightwood*. New York: New Directions, 1961.

Bataille, Georges. *Visions of Excess: Selected Writings, 1927–1939*. Translated and edited by Allan Stoekl. Minneapolis: University of Minnesota Press, 1985.

Baxter, Charles. "A Self-Consuming Light: *Nightwood* and the Crisis of Modernism." *Journal of Modern Literature* (1974): 1175–87.

Beah, Ishmael. *A Long Way Gone: Memoirs of a Boy Soldier*. New York: Sarah Crichton Books, 2007.

Bersani, Leo. *Homos*. Cambridge, Mass.: Harvard University Press, 1995.

———. "Is the Rectum a Grave?" *AIDS: Cultural Analysis, Cultural Activism*, edited by Douglas Crimp, 197–222. Cambridge, Mass.: MIT Press, 1988.

Blake, William. "The Little Black Boy." *The Norton Anthology of Poetry*, rev. ed., edited by Alexander W. Allison, et al., 547. New York: W.W. Norton, 1975.

Bloom, Harold. Introduction to *William Blake's "Songs of Innocence and of Experience,"* edited by Harold Bloom, 1–28. New York: Chelsea House, 1987.

Blum, Virginia L. *Hide and Seek: The Child between Psychoanalysis and Fiction*. Urbana-Champaign: University of Illinois Press, 1995.

Borch-Jacobsen, Mikkel. *Lacan: The Absolute Master.* Translated by Douglas Brick. Stanford, Calif.: Stanford University Press, 1991.

Bordo, Susan. "The Moral Content of Nabokov's *Lolita.*" *Aesthetic Subjects,* edited by Pamela R. Matthews and David McWhirter, 125–52. Minneapolis: University of Minnesota Press, 2003.

Boswell, John. *Christianity, Social Tolerance, and Homosexuality.* Chicago: University of Chicago Press, 1980.

Brantlinger, Patrick. *Rule of Darkness: British Literature and Imperialism, 1830–1914.* Ithaca, N.Y.: Cornell University Press, 1990.

Broe, Mary Lynn. "My Art Belongs to Daddy: Incest as Exile: The Textual Economics of Hayford Hall." *Women Writers in Exile,* edited by Mary Lynn Broe and Angela Ingram, 41–86. Chapel Hill: University of North Carolina Press, 1989.

Brontë, Charlotte. *Villette.* New York: Penguin, 1979.

Bruhm, Steven, and Natasha Hurley, eds. *Curiouser: On the Queerness of Children.* Minneapolis: University of Minnesota Press, 2004.

Butler, Judith. *Gender Trouble: Feminism and the Subversion of Identity.* New York: Routledge, 1989.

————. "Imitation and Gender Insubordination." *Inside/Out: Lesbian Theories, Gay Theories,* edited by Diana Fuss, 13–31. New York: Routledge, 1991.

Capote, Truman. *"A Christmas Memory," "One Christmas," and "The Thanksgiving Visitor."* New York: Modern Library, 1996.

————. *In Cold Blood.* New York: Vintage, 1994.

Carpenter, Edward. "Affection in Education." *Selected Writings,* vol.1, *Sex,* 221–33.

————. *Selected Writings.* Vol.1, *Sex.* London: GMP, 1984.

Clarke, Gerald. *Capote.* New York: Carroll and Graf, 2001.

Clarke, Roger. "An Improper Charlie." *Sight & Sound* 15, no. 8 (August 2005): 22–25.

Colomina, Beatriz. "The Split Wall: Domestic Voyeurism." *Sexuality and Space,* edited by Beatriz Colomina, 73–130. Princeton, N.J.: Princeton Architectural Press, 1992.

Corliss, Richard. "False Hoops." *Time,* October 24, 1994, 76.

————. *Lolita.* London: British Film Institute, 1994.

Coviello, Peter. "The Sexual Child; or, This American Life." *Raritan* 27, no. 4 (2008): 134–57.

Cunningham, Hugh. *Children and Childhood in Western Society since 1500.* 2nd ed. London: Pearson Longman, 2005.

Cunningham, Michael. *The Hours.* New York: Picador, 1998.

Cutler, Arthur, and Jane Cutler. "On the Rebound: *Hoop Dreams* and its Discontents." *Cineaste* 21 no. 3 (1995): 24.

Darwin, Charles. *The Descent of Man.* New York: Modern Library, 1936.

———. *The Expression of the Emotions in Man and Animals.* New York: D. Appleton, 1896.

D'Augelli, Anthony R., and Charlotte J. Patterson, eds. *Lesbian, Gay, and Bisexual Identities and Youth: Psychological Perspectives.* Oxford: Oxford University Press, 2001.

Deleuze, Gilles. "Coldness and Cruelty." *Masochism,* 9–138. New York: Zone, 1991.

Deleuze, Gilles, and Félix Guattari. *A Thousand Plateaus: Capitalism and Schizophrenia.* Translated by Brian Massumi. Minneapolis: University of Minnesota Press, 1987.

DeMause, Lloyd, ed. *The History of Childhood.* New York: Psychohistory Press, 1974.

Derrida, Jacques. "*Différance.*" *Deconstruction in Context: Literature and Philosophy,* edited by Mark C. Taylor, 396–420. Chicago: University of Chicago Press, 1986.

———. "Freud and the Scene of Writing." Translated by Jeffrey Mehlman. *Yale French Studies,* no. 48 (1972): 74–117.

———. *Specters of Marx: The State of the Debt, the Work of Mourning, and the New International.* Translated by Peggy Kamuf. New York: Routledge, 1994.

Dinshaw, Carolyn. *Getting Medieval: Sexualities and Communities, Pre- and Postmodern.* Durham, N.C.: Duke University Press, 1999.

Doan, Laura L. "The Mythic Moral Panic: Radclyffe Hall and the New Genealogy." *Fashioning Sapphism: The Origins of a Modern English Lesbian Culture,* 1–30. New York: Columbia University Press, 2001.

Doan, Laura, and Jay Prosser, eds. *Palatable Poison: Critical Perspectives on "The Well of Loneliness."* New York: Columbia University Press, 2001.

Duff, R. A. *Intention, Agency, and Criminal Liability: Philosophy of Action and the Criminal Law.* Oxford: Blackwell, 1990.

Duncan, David Douglas. *Picasso and Lump: A Dachshund's Odyssey.* New York: Bullfinch, 2006.

Ebert, Roger. "Charlie and the Chocolate Factory." *Chicago Sun-Times,* July 15, 2005, http://www.suntimes.com.

Edelman, Lee. *No Future: Queer Theory and the Death Drive.* Durham, N.C.: Duke University Press, 2004.

Erdman, David V. "Blake's Vision of Slavery." *Blake: A Collection of Critical Essays,* edited by Northrop Frye, 88–103. Englewood Cliffs, N.J.: Prentice Hall, 1966.

Fadiman, Clifton, ed. *The Short Stories of Henry James.* New York: Random House, 1945.

Faludi, Susan. *Backlash: The Undeclared War against American Women*. New York: Crown Books, 1991.

Fonagy, Peter, et al. "Measuring the Ghost in the Nursery." *Journal of the American Psychoanalytical Association* 41 (1993): 957–89.

Freccero, Carla. *Queer/Early/Modern*. Durham, N.C.: Duke University Press, 2006.

Freeman, Elizabeth. *The Wedding Complex: Forms of Belonging in Modern American Culture*. Durham, N.C.: Duke University Press, 2002.

———, ed. "Theorizing Queer Temporalities: A Roundtable Discussion." GLQ: *A Journal of Lesbian and Gay Studies* 13, nos. 2–3 (2007): 177–95.

Freud, Sigmund. "Femininity." Translated and edited by James Strachey. *New Introductory Lectures on Psychoanalysis*. Lecture 33, 112–35. New York: Norton, 1965.

———. *The Interpretation of Dreams*. Translated by James Strachey. New York: Avon Books, 1965.

———. *The Standard Edition of the Complete Psychological Works of Sigmund Freud*. Translated and edited by James Strachey. London: Hogarth Press, 1955.

———. *Three Essays on the Theory of Sexuality*. *The Freud Reader*, edited by Peter Gay, 239–93. New York: W.W. Norton, 1989.

———. *Three Essays on the Theory of Sexuality*. *The Standard Edition of the Complete Psychological Works of Sigmund Freud*, vol. 7, 135–245.

Funny Gay Males (Jaffe Cohen, Danny McWilliams, and Bob Smith). *Growing Up Gay: From Left Out to Coming Out*. New York: Hyperion, 1995.

Garrison, Ellen Greenberg, and Patricia Clem Kobor. "Weathering a Political Storm: A Contextual Perspective on a Psychological Research Controversy." *American Psychologist* 57, no. 3 (March 2002): 165.

Gay, Peter, ed. *The Freud Reader*. New York: W.W. Norton, 1989.

Gerstenberger, Donna. "Modern (Post)Modern: Djuna Barnes among the Others." *Review of Contemporary Fiction* 13, no. 3 (1993): 33–40.

Glamuzina, Julie, and Alison J. Laurie. *Parker and Hulme: A Lesbian View*. Ithaca, N.Y.: Firebrand, 1995.

Glazer, Myra. "Blake's Little Black Boys: On the Dynamics of Blake's Composite Art." Bloom, ed., *William Blake's "Songs of Innocence and of Experience,"* 85–100.

Gleckner, Robert F. "The Strange Odyssey of Blake's 'The Voice of the Ancient Bard.'" Bloom, ed., *William Blake's "Songs of Innocence and of Experience,"* 101–121.

Goffman, Erving. *Stigma: Notes on the Management of Spoiled Identity*. Englewood Cliffs, N.J.: Prentice Hall, 1963.

Gordon, Avery F. *Ghostly Matters: Haunting and the Sociological Imagination*. Minneapolis: University of Minnesota Press, 1997.

Gould, Alice. "Magical, Funny, and Deliciously Disgusting." *New Welsh Review* 16 (Spring 1992): 55–56.

Green, Jesse. "The Men from the Boys." *Out*, September 1994, 75–83, 128–36.

Greig, Noël. Introduction to Carpenter, *Selected Writings*, vol. 1, *Sex*, 9–77.

Gullette, Margaret Morganroth. "The Exile of Adulthood: Pedophilia in the Midlife Novel." *Novel* (Spring 1994): 215–32.

Hall, Radclyffe. *The Well of Loneliness*. New York: Anchor Books, 1990.

Hatch, Kirsten. "Fille Fatale: Regulating Images of Adolescent Girls, 1962–1996." *Sugar, Spice, and Everything Nice*, edited by Frances Gateward and Murray Pomerance, 163–82. Detroit: Wayne State University Press, 2002.

Herring, Phillip. *Djuna: The Life and Work of Djuna Barnes*. New York: Penguin, 1995.

Hirsch, E. D. Jr. *Innocence and Experience: An Introduction to Blake*. New Haven, Conn.: Yale University Press, 1964.

hooks, bell. "Dreams of Conquest." *Sight & Sound* 5 (April 1995): 22–23.

Horne, Philip. "Henry James: The Master and the 'Queer Affair' of 'The Pupil.'" *Critical Quarterly* 37, no. 3 (1995): 75–92.

Hoy, Helen. "Homotextual Duplicity in Henry James's 'The Pupil.'" *Henry James Review* 14, no. 1 (Winter 1994): 34–42.

James, Henry. *The Pupil. The Faber Book of Gay Short Fiction*, edited by Edmund White, 1–47. Boston: Faber, 1992.

Jay, Betty. "'Let's Moider Mother': *Heavenly Creatures* and the Politics of Delusion." *Genders* 42 (2005): 222.

Kaplan, Fred. *Henry James: The Imagination of Genius: A Biography*. London: John Curtis, 1992.

Kauffman, Linda. "Framing *Lolita*: Is There a Woman in the Text?" *Special Delivery: Epistolary Modes in Modern Fiction*. Chicago: University of Chicago Press, 1992, 53–79.

Kincaid, James R. *Erotic Innocence: The Culture of Child Molesting*. Durham, N.C.: Duke University Press, 1998.

————. "Producing Erotic Children." Bruhm and Hurley, eds., *Curiouser*, 3–16.

Klawans, S. "Hoop Dreams." *Nation*, November 14, 1994, 592.

Koops, Willem, and Michael Zuckerman, eds. *Beyond the Century of the Child: Cultural History and Developmental Psychology*. Philadelphia: University of Pennsylvania Press, 2003.

Krafft-Ebing, Richard von. *Pyschopathia Sexualis: A Medico-Forensic Study*. New York: Putnam, 1965.

Kucich, John. *Imperial Masochism: British Fiction, Fantasy, and Social Class.* Princeton, N.J.: Princeton University Press, 2007.

Lacan, Jacques. *Écrits: A Selection.* Translated by Alan Sheridan. New York: W.W. Norton, 1977.

Lehman, Jeffrey, and Shirelle Phelps, eds. *West's Encyclopedia of American Law.* 2nd ed. Detroit: Thomas Gale, 2005.

Letts, James J. IV, and James T. Sears, eds. *Queering Elementary Education: Advancing the Dialogue about Sexualities and Schooling.* Lanham, Md.: Rowman and Littlefield, 1999.

Lewes, Kenneth. *The Psychoanalytic Theory of Male Homosexuality.* New York: Simon and Schuster, 1988.

Lipkin, Arthur. *Beyond Diversity Day: A Q & A on Gay and Lesbian Issues in Schools.* New York: Rowman and Littlefield, 2004.

Lombroso, Cesare. *Crime: Its Causes and Remedies.* Translated by Henry P. Norton. Boston: Little, Brown, and Co., 1918.

Love, Heather. *Feeling Backward: Loss and the Politics of Queer History.* Cambridge, Mass.: Harvard University Press, 2007.

———. "'Spoiled Identity': Stephen Gordon's Loneliness and the Difficulties of Queer History." *GLQ: A Journal of Lesbian and Gay Studies* 7, no. 4 (2001): 487–519.

Macgillivray, Ian K. *Sexual Orientation and School Policy: A Practical Guide for Teachers, Administrators, and Community Activists.* New York: Rowman and Littlefield, 2004.

Mallon, Gerald P. *We Don't Exactly Get the Welcome Wagon: The Experiences of Gay and Lesbian Adolescents in Child Welfare Systems.* New York: Columbia University Press, 1998.

Mansfield, Nick. *Masochism: The Art of Power.* Westport, Conn.: Praeger, 1997.

Marcus, Jane. "Laughing at Leviticus: *Nightwood* as Woman's Circus Epic." *Silence and Power: A Reevaluation of Djuna Barnes*, edited by Mary Lynn Broe, 221–50. Carbondale: Southern Illinois University Press, 1991.

Masochism. Comprising Gilles Deleuze, "Coldness and Cruelty," and Leopold von Sacher-Masoch, *Venus in Furs.* New York: Zone, 1991.

Mather, Ronald, and Jill Marsden. "Trauma and Temporality: On the Origins of Post-Traumatic Stress." *Theory and Psychology* 14, no. 2 (2004): 205–19.

Matthiessen, F. O. *Henry James: The Major Phase.* New York: Oxford University Press, 1944.

Mavor, Carol. *Reading Boyishly: Roland Barthes, J. M. Barrie, Jacques Henri Lartigue, Marcel Proust, and D. W. Winnicott.* Durham, N.C.: Duke University Press, 2008.

McGrath, Tom. "The Transmission of Trauma." *Psychoanalytische Perspectieven*, nos. 41/42 (2000): 123–37.

McNeely, Trevor. "'Lo' and Behold: Solving the *Lolita* Riddle." *Studies in the Novel* 21, no. 2 (Summer 1989): 182–99.

Meillassoux, Claude. "Female Slavery." *Women and Slavery in Africa*, edited by Claire C. Robertson and Martin A. Klein, 49–67. Madison: University of Wisconsin Press, 1983.

Merla, Patrick, ed. *Boys Like Us: Gay Writers Tell Their Coming Out Stories*. New York: Avon, 1996.

Metz, Christian. "The Imaginary Signifier." Stam and Miller, eds., *Film and Theory: An Anthology*, 408–36.

Moon, Michael. *A Small Boy and Others: Imitation and Initiation in American Culture*. Durham, N.C.: Duke University Press, 1998.

————. "A Small Boy and Others: Sexual Disorientation in Henry James, Kenneth Anger, and David Lynch." *Comparative American Identities*, edited by Hortense J. Spillers, 151–56. New York: Routledge, 1991.

Mulvey, Laura. "Visual Pleasure and Narrative Cinema." Stam and Miller, eds., *Film and Theory: An Anthology*, 483–94.

Nabokov, Vladimir. *Lolita*. New York: Vintage, 1997.

Nafisi, Azar. *Reading "Lolita" in Tehran*. New York: Random House, 2003.

Nealon, Christopher. *Foundlings: Lesbian and Gay Historical Imagination before Stonewall*. Durham, N.C.: Duke University Press, 2001.

Nicholson, Catriona. "Dahl, the Marvelous Boy." *A Necessary Fantasy? The Heroic Figure in Children's Popular Culture*, edited by Dudley Jones and Tony Watkins, 309–26. New York: Garland, 2000.

Noble, Marianne. *The Masochistic Pleasures of Sentimental Literature*. Princeton, N.J.: Princeton University Press, 2000.

Nordau, Max. *Degeneration*. 8th ed. New York: Appleton, 1896.

The Norton Introduction to Poetry. 2nd ed., edited by J. Paul Hunter. New York: W.W. Norton, 1981.

Ohi, Kevin. *Innocence and Rapture: The Erotic Child in Pater, Wilde, James, and Nabokov*. New York: Palgrave Macmillan, 2005.

O'Rourke, James. *Sex, Lies, and Autobiography: The Ethics of Confession*. Charlottesville: University of Virginia Press, 2006.

Patterson, James T. *"Brown v. Board of Education": A Civil Rights Milestone and its Troubled Legacy*. New York: Oxford University Press, 2001.

Pifer, Ellen. *Nabokov and the Novel*. Cambridge, Mass.: Harvard University Press, 1980.

Pinchbeck, Ivy, and Margaret Hewitt. *Children in English Society*. Vol.2, *From the Eighteenth Century to the Children Act of 1948*. Toronto: University of Toronto Press, 1973.

Platt, Anthony M. *The Child Savers: The Invention of Delinquency*. Chicago: University of Chicago Press, 1969.

Plimpton, George. *Truman Capote*. New York: Doubleday, 1997.

Plumb, Cheryl. Introduction to Djuna Barnes, *Nightwood: The Original Version and Related Drafts*. Normal, Ill.: Dalkey Archive Press, 1995.

Pochoda, Elizabeth. "Style's Hoax: A Reading of Djuna Barnes' *Nightwood*." *Twentieth-Century Literature* (1976): 179–91.

Postman, Neil. *The Disappearance of Childhood*. New York: Vintage, 1982.

Proffer, Carl R. *Keys to Lolita*. Bloomington: Indiana University Press, 1968.

Rampton, David. *Vladimir Nabokov*. New York: St. Martin's, 1993.

Raymond, C. "Outside Shots." *Esquire*, November 1994, 46.

Rind, Bruce, Robert Bauserman, and Philip Tromovitch. "A Meta-Analysis of Assumed Properties of Child Sexual Abuse Using College Samples." *Psychological Bulletin* 124, no. 1 (1998): 22.

Russo, Vito. *The Celluloid Closet: Homosexuality in the Movies*. Rev. ed. New York: Harper and Row, 1987.

Ryan, Caitlin, and Donna Futterman. *Lesbian and Gay Youth: Care and Counseling*. New York: Columbia University Press, 1998.

Sacher-Masoch, Leopold von. *Venus in Furs*. Translated by Jean McNeil. *Masochism*, 143–272. New York: Zone, 1991.

Sanderson, Terry. *A Stranger in the Family: How to Cope If Your Child is Gay*. London: Other Way, 1996.

Savin-Williams, Ritch C. "*. . . And Then I Became Gay": Young Men's Stories*. New York: Routledge, 1998.

———. *The New Gay Teenager*. Cambridge, Mass.: Harvard University Press, 2006.

Sedgwick, Eve Kosofsky. "A Poem Is Being Written." *Tendencies*, 177–214. Durham, N. C.: Duke University Press, 1993.

———. "How to Bring Your Kids Up Gay: The War on Effeminate Boys." *Tendencies*, 154–64.

———. "Shame, Theatricality, and Queer Performativity: Henry James's *The Art of the Novel*." *Touching Feeling: Affect, Pedagogy, Performativity*. Durham, N.C.: Duke University Press, 2003.

Seitler, Dana. *Atavistic Tendencies: The Culture of Science in American Modernity*. Minneapolis: University of Minnesota Press, 2008.

Shelden, Randall G. *Delinquency and Juvenile Justice in American Society.* Long Grove, Ill.: Waveland Press, 2006.

Shelman, Eric, and Stephen Lazoritz. *The Mary Ellen Wilson Child Abuse Case and the Beginning of Children's Rights in the Nineteenth Century.* Jefferson, N.C.: McFarland, 2005.

Shute, Jennifer. "Nabokov and Freud: The Play of Power." *Modern Fiction Studies* 30, no. 4 (1984): 637–50.

Shyer, Marlene Fanta, and Christopher Shyer. *Not Like Other Boys: Growing Up Gay: A Mother and Son Look Back.* Boston: Houghton Mifflin, 1996.

Sibthorpe, Aaron Belisarius C. *The History of Sierra Leone.* New York: Routledge, 1970.

Siegel, Carol. *Male Masochism: Modern Revisions of the Story of Love.* Bloomington: Indiana University Press, 1995.

Sikov, Ed. "Chemistry." Merla, ed., *Boys Like Us,* 230–237.

Silverstein, L. B., and C. F. Auerbach. "Deconstructing the Essential Father." *American Psychologist* 54 (1999): 397–407.

Sommerville, C. John. *The Rise and Fall of Childhood.* Rev. ed. New York: Vintage, 1990.

Spillers, Hortense J. "Mama's Baby, Papa's Maybe: An American Grammar Book." *Diacritics* (Summer 1987): 65–81.

Stadler, Matthew. "Homo Sex Story." Merla, ed., *Boys Like Us,* 167–75.

Stam, Robert, and Toby Miller, eds. *Film and Theory: An Anthology.* Oxford: Blackwell, 2000.

Stearns, Peter. "Historical Perspectives on Twentieth-Century American Childhood." Koops and Zuckerman, eds., *Beyond the Century of the Child,* 96–111.

Stegner, Page. *Escape into Aesthetics: The Art of Vladimir Nabokov.* New York: Dial, 1966.

Stein, Gertrude. "Miss Furr and Miss Skeene." *A Stein Reader,* edited by Ulla E. Dydo, 254–59. Evanston, Ill.: Northwestern University Press, 1993.

Stockton, Kathryn Bond. *Beautiful Bottom, Beautiful Shame: Where "Black" Meets "Queer."* Durham, N.C.: Duke University Press, 2006.

———. "The Child, the Pedagogue, the Pedophile, and the Masochist." Talk given at the Modern Language Association in Toronto, Canada, 1997.

———. "Eve's Queer Child." Barber and Clark, eds., *Regarding Sedgwick,* 181–99.

———. "Feeling Like Killing? Queer Temporalities of Murderous Motives among Queer Children." GLQ: *A Journal of Lesbian and Gay Studies* 13, nos. 2–3 (2007): 301–25.

———. "Growing Sideways, or Versions of the Queer Child: The Ghost, the Homosexual, the Freudian, the Innocent, and the Interval of Animal." Bruhm and Hurley, eds., *Curiouser*, 277–315.

———. "Motive's Mysterious Motions, or What Drives the Out of Place Child." Talk given at the Modern Language Association in New York, 2002.

———. "Prophylactics and Brains: *Beloved* in the Cybernetic Age of AIDS." *Novel Gazing: Queer Readings in Fiction*, edited by Eve Kosofsky Sedgwick, 41–73. Durham, N.C.: Duke University Press, 1997.

———. "The Queer Child and the Fantasy of Law." Talk given at Harvard University, 1998.

———. "Who Feels Like Killing? Narrative Trials for the Queer Child." Talk given at the Modern Language Association in Philadelphia, 2004.

Talbot, Margaret. "The Candy Man: Why Children Love Roald Dahl's Stories and Many Adults Don't." *New Yorker*, July 11, 2005, 92–98.

Trachtenberg, Robert, ed. *When I Knew*. New York: Regan Books, 2005.

Trilling, Lionel. "The Last Lover." *Encounter* 11 (1958): 9–19.

Wagenknecht, Edward. *The Tales of Henry James*. New York: Ungar, 1984.

Warren, Alan. "Roald Dahl: Nasty, Nasty." *Discovering Modern Horror Fiction*, edited by Darrell Schweitzer, 120–28. Mercer Island, Wash.: Starmont, 1985.

West, Elliott. *Growing Up in Twentieth-Century America: A History and Reference Guide*. Westport, Conn.: Greenwood Press, 1996.

West, Mark. *Roald Dahl*. New York: Twayne, 1992.

Wilde, Oscar. *The Picture of Dorian Gray*. New York: Penguin, 1985.

Williams, Glanville L. *The Mental Element in Crime*. Jerusalem: Magnes, 1965.

Williams, Nicolas M. *Ideology and Utopia in the Poetry of William Blake*. Cambridge: Cambridge University Press, 1998.

Woolf, Virginia. *Mrs. Dalloway*. New York: Harvest, 1925.

Zelizer, Viviana. *Pricing the Priceless Child: The Changing Social Value of Children*. Princeton, N.J.: Princeton University Press, 1985.

Zwinger, Linda. "Bodies That Don't Matter: The Queering of Henry James." *Modern Fiction Studies* 41, nos. 3–4 (1995): 657–80.

Films

A.I. Artificial Intelligence. Directed by Steven Spielberg. Based on a short story by Brian Aldiss. Warner Bros., 2001.

American Masters: Andy Warhol: A Documentary Film. Directed by Ric Burns. PBS, 2006.

The Bad Seed. Directed by Mervyn LeRoy. Based on the novel by William Marsh. Warner Bros., 1956.

Bastard out of Carolina. Directed by Angelica Huston. Based on the novel by Dorothy Allison. Showtime, 1996.

Blood Diamond. Directed by Edward Zwick. Warner Bros., 2006.

Capote. Directed by Bennett Miller. Sony Pictures Classics, 2005.

Charlie and the Chocolate Factory. Directed by Tim Burton. Based on the book by Roald Dahl. Warner Bros., 2005.

The Children's Hour. Directed by William Wyler. MGM, 1961.

City of God (Cidade de Deus). Directed by Fernando Meirelles and Katia Lund. 02 Films, 2002.

City of Men. Directed by Fernando Meirelles. Fox Films, 2006.

Die Another Day. Directed by Lee Tamahori. MGM, 2002.

Doubt. Directed by John Patrick Shanley. Based on the play by John Patrick Shanley. Miramax, 2008.

Elephant. Directed by Gus Van Sant. HBO Films, 2003.

Eyes on the Prize. Directed by Henry Hampton. Blackside, Inc., 1987.

Guess Who. Directed by Kevin Rodney Sullivan. Sony Pictures, 2005.

Guess Who's Coming to Dinner. Directed by Stanley Kramer. Columbia Pictures, 1967.

The Hanging Garden. Directed by Thom Fitzgerald. Alliance Communications Corp., 1996.

Hard Candy. Directed by David Slade. Lions Gate, 2006.

Heavenly Creatures. Directed by Peter Jackson. Fontana Productions, 1994.

The Hidden Child. PBS, 2006.

Hoop Dreams. Directed by Steve James. KTCA Minneapolis, 1994.

Infamous. Directed by Douglas McGrath. Warner Independent Pictures, 2006.

Joshua. Directed by George Ratliff. ATO Pictures, 2007.

Lara Croft: Tomb Raider. Directed by Simon West. Paramount Pictures, 2001.

The Lord of the Rings Trilogy. Directed by Peter Jackson. New Line Cinema, 2001–2003.

Little Children. Directed by Todd Field. New Line Cinema, 2006.

Lolita. Directed by Adrian Lyne. Lions Gate, 1996.

Lolita. Directed by Stanley Kubrick. A.A. Productions, Ltd., 1962.

Mr. & Mrs. Smith. Directed by Doug Liman. Regency Enterprises, 2005.

Six Degrees of Separation. Directed by Fred Schepisi. MGM, 1993.

Wired to Win: Surviving the Tour de France. Directed by Bayley Silleck. IMAX, 2006.

Carpenter, Edward, 53, 68, 71–73, 88, 250 n. 61

Catcher in the Rye (Salinger), 209, 211, 216

Century of the child, 8, 246 n. 16

Charlie and the Chocolate Factory (film), 51, 56–57, 238–44

Child: adult as not, 5, 7, 31, 40, 90; agency of, 63–65, 121, 139–40, 146, 225, 239; candy and, 56–57, 219, 238–44; as dangerous, 37–38, 41, 62, 222; defined, 246 n. 11; as disappearing, 37–38; as fascinated with debasement, 226–28; fear of, 37–38, 41–42, 62, 126, 188; as future, 5, 13, 120; harm to, 61, 63, 69–71, 122–23, 139–40, 153, 202, 271 n. 13; as idea, 5, 12–13, 31, 40–41; as innocence, 5, 30, 40, 45, 126, 138–40, 188; Internet as presumed threat to, 37–38, 126–27; labor of and labor laws governing, 38, 46–48, 62–63, 66–68, 71–88, 186–88, 222–23, 228–44, 271 n. 12; media enthrallment of and effects on, 37–38, 120, 126–29, 167–69, 172–77, 228–38; as not yet straight, 7, 121, 123; paradoxes surrounding, 37–38, 42; problem of consent and, 33, 38, 65, 121; as sacralized and sentimentalized, 47–48; protections needed by, 6, 16, 31, 33, 40–41, 94, 205; as seductive, 64, 66–67, 81, 126, 140, 228–38; as sexual, 53, 90–113, 119–53, 155, 166–80, 222, 260 n. 1; talking with, 63, 66, 72, 83–88, 223; visual pleasure and, 121–22, 126, 128, 146–53, 173–77, 264 n. 30; as vulnerable, 37–38, 41, 45, 62, 222. *See also* Law; Money; Queer child

Child abuse: parental neglect or engagement as, 63–67, 74, 85, 94, 172, 221, 223; sexual, 12, 68–71, 120–23, 126, 129, 139–40

Childhood studies, 4, 6, 8, 16–17, 37–38, 40, 121, 246 n. 17

Child queered by color, 5, 8, 31–33, 131, 183–218, 225–26, 267 n. 3; absence of, 240; American dream as bad for, 230–31; as animal, 194; architecture and, 196–213; becoming a shoe, 228–38; birthing parents, 55–56, 184–85, 188, 191–93, 196–97, 205–6, 209–13, 217–18; disappearing or suspended future of, 57, 184–97, 199, 207, 213–14, 217, 228–38, 270 n. 36; horizontal kinship and, 183–84, 195; matriarchy thesis and, 193–96; (metaphor of) slavery and, 187–88, 194–95; miscegenation and, 195, 204–5, 270 n. 31; "mixed" marriage and, 184, 192–93, 199, 204, 218, 270 n. 31; as reproductive problem, 193, 199, 202, 204–5; theme of art and, 202, 204, 207, 209–10, 213. *See also* Racism

Child queered by innocence: economy of candy as appealing to, 238–44; grown homosexuals paired with, 57, 64, 93, 110–11, 220; law and, 30, 55, 158–59; masochism of, 64; normative strangeness as defining, 30–31; Romantic poets as creating, 30–33; violence of, 123–30, 184–86

Children's Hour, The (film), 28–30

Child soldiers, 55, 184–91, 268 n. 6, 269 n. 15

City of God (film), 268 n. 5

City of Men (film), 268 n. 5

Clarke, Gerald, 221, 266 n. 18

Colomina, Beatriz, 56, 197–99

Columbine High School shootings, 178

Congress, U.S., 68–71

Congressional Task Force on Fatherhood Promotion, 71

Conrad, Joseph, 170
Coviello, Peter, 250 n. 54
Cunningham, Michael, 95, 258 nn. 20–21

Dahl, Roald, 51, 56, 242–43, 272 n. 30
Darwin, Charles, 22–24, 42, 54, 135–37
Death drive, 12–13, 220, 271 n. 6
Delay: as animal pause, 5, 90–102, 113;
    child's own control of, 68, 90–91, 120;
    Derrida's definition of, 4, 15, 164, 265
    n. 15; developmental sense of, 4, 62;
    ghostly gay child as form of, 18, 62,
    91–113, 196–97; of labor, 62–63, 222;
    as legally enforced, 4, 53, 62; as man-
    aged by parents and society, 40, 90,
    123; motions inside, 90–91, 97, 102; of
    sex, 57, 63, 72, 131, 222; as sideways
    growth, 37, 72, 90–94, 101–2, 107–10,
    113, 159–60, 164; talking as, 63, 72, 74,
    83–88. See also Arrested development
DeLay, Tom, 69–70
Deleuze, Gilles, 4, 53, 77–78, 94, 105–6
Depp, Johnny, 51, 57, 238, 241, 244, 272
    n. 30
Derrida, Jacques, 14, 159–60, 245 n. 6;
    definition of delay by, 4, 15, 164, 265
    n. 15
Dinshaw, Carolyn, 38–39, 250 n. 64
Doubt (film), 246 n. 14
Duff, R. A., 163–64

Edelman, Lee, 11–12, 220, 248 n. 30, 251
    n. 67
Education studies, 10, 48–49, 133–35
Elephant (film), 177–80

Family Research Council, 70
Family values, 3, 246 n. 9
Film theory, 146–53, 173–77, 229–32
Foley scandal, 53, 61, 252 n. 6

Foucault, Michel, 42
Freccero, Carla, 245 n. 6
Freud, Sigmund, 4, 52, 56, 64, 226; on
    lesbians, 93; on masochism, 77–78; on
    motives, 159–60; Nabokov and, 261
    n. 5; on Nachträglichkeit, 14, 159–60,
    164, 197, 248 nn. 32–33; on Oedipus
    complex, 55, 77–78, 113, 184–186, 193,
    196; as parodied in Nightwood, 111,
    259 n. 33
Freudian child, 8, 23–30, 121–22, 126, 184,
    220; as invert, 24–25; lingering of, 25;
    as robot child, 33–36; as sexual and
    aggressive, 27–30, 64, 121, 126–30
Futurism, reproductive, 13, 220, 271 n. 6
Futurity: of child, 5, 13, 120; of child
    queered by color, 57, 184–99, 207,
    213–14, 217, 228–38, 270 n. 36; of queer
    child, 53, 55–57, 90, 97–99, 109, 155,
    224, 228

Garrison, Ellen Greenberg, 69–71
Gay: as new form of "queer," 4, 246 n. 6;
    term, 2–4, 15, 26–27, 222, 245 n. 8
Gay child: as absent from History, 8–10,
    222, 246 n. 17, 247 n. 19, 251 n. 65;
    asynchronicity and backward birth
    of, 6–7, 11, 15–16, 20, 55, 158, 163, 222;
    closeting of, 3, 49, 98–102, 108–12,
    211–13; coming out as, 7, 15, 210–13;
    darkness of, 3, 6; as death of straight
    person, 6–7, 16–17, 22; existence of, 2;
    as a fiction, 4, 9; ghostliness of, 2–4,
    17–22, 48, 51–56, 98, 102, 110–12, 119,
    158–59, 184, 192, 196–97, 211–13, 220–
    23, 256 n. 6, 270 n. 36; as lesbian, 5,
    43, 53–54, 89–113, 121, 140, 157, 170–77;
    metaphors used by, 15–16, 19–20, 22,
    93–113, 249 n. 34; pain of, 3, 53, 62,
    64, 67, 78–88; in present tense, 7, 246

Gay child (*continued*)

    n. 14; as protogay, 6, 13–14, 64, 157–58, 221; sentiment surrounding, 3; sexuality of, 3, 19–22, 26–27, 48–53, 62–113, 140, 164–77, 207–214; sorrow and, 91, 101–2, 112, 177; as stranger in the family, 17–18, 192, 243; suicide and, 21, 28–30, 213; on television, 17, 249 n. 38; transgendering and, 8, 98; typicality of, 17, 19; word *gay* and, 2–6, 14–16, 19, 37–38, 48–49, 52, 248 n. 34. *See also* Homosexuals; Queer child

Gay teens, 10, 19–22, 49–51

gender identity disorder in childhood, 8, 14

Glamuzina, Julie, 251 n. 70

Gordon, Avery, 245 n. 6

Growth: Aristotle on, 134; arrested development and, 8, 22–27, 108, 131–32; definition of *grow* and, 11; as gradual, 4, 40; as "growing up," 4, 6–7, 11–15, 18–20, 93, 243; as sideways, 4–6, 11–13, 20–29, 33–37, 52–57, 90–94, 101, 107, 113, 158, 220, 233, 236, 243–44, 273 n. 32

Guare, John, 192, 270 n. 34

Guattari, Félix, 94, 105–6

Guess Who (film), 214–18, 226

Guess Who's Coming to Dinner (film), 56, 183–84, 192–96, 199–207, 209, 213–17, 226

Hall, G. Stanley, 133

Hall, Radclyffe, 10, 53, 95, 120–21, 155, 250 n. 51; banning of *The Well of Loneliness*, 91, 93, 257 n. 12; ghostly gay child and, 17; *Nightwood* and, 106–7, 112; *The Well of Loneliness* and, 98–102, 137, 223–24

Hanging Garden, The (film), 19–22, 24, 33, 92

Hard Candy (film), 123–30, 142, 227

Heavenly Creatures (film), 45–46, 54–55, 156–57, 164, 170–77, 183, 225, 251 n. 70

Helms, Jesse, 252 n. 8

Herbart, Johann, 133

Herring, Phillip, 103–4

History: of childhood, 9–10, 40–48; gay child absent from, 8–10, 222, 246 n. 17, 247 n. 19, 251 n. 65; as historians' writings, 2, 245; historical prematurity and, 93, 101–2, 110, 112; queers' desire for, 38; queer theoretical debates over, 38–39; as sideways growth, 9; as synchrony, 9, 51

Homosexuals: as animals, 23; as in arrested development, 8, 22–24, 27, 33, 62; conservatives' view of, 3, 22, 24, 246 n. 9; figured as children, 8, 22, 56, 64, 93, 99, 164–70, 184, 219–20, 238–44; historical prematurity of, 93, 101–2, 110, 112; impossible love and, 93, 101, 106; inversion of, 24, 98, 102, 104, 109–111, 250 n. 51; Jews and, 107, 110; in Kubrick's *Lolita*, 149–50; lesbians lovers as mother and child, 93, 105, 110; presumed pathology and perversion of, 14, 23–24, 150; as threat to children, 3; word *homosexual* entering into English, 63

hooks, bell, 231–32

Hoop Dreams (film), 56–57, 228–38, 240

Human papilloma virus, 252 n. 2

In Cold Blood (Capote), 41, 54–55, 155–59, 163–70, 177, 225, 239

Infamous (film), 266 n. 17

Innocence: of child, 5, 30, 40, 45, 126, 138–40, 188; as eroticized, 12, 122–23, 126; as normative, 30; as strange, 5, 30; as threatening, 123–30; as violent,

Kathryn Bond Stockton is a professor of English and a director of gender studies at the University of Utah. She is the author of *God Between Their Lips: Desire Between Women in Irigaray, Brontë, and Eliot* and *Beautiful Bottom, Beautiful Shame: Where "Black" Meets "Queer."*

Library of Congress Cataloging-in-Publication Data
Stockton, Kathryn Bond, 1958–
The queer child, or growing sideways in the twentieth century /
Kathryn Bond Stockton.
p. cm. — (Series Q)
Includes bibliographical references and index.
ISBN 978-0-8223-4364-6 (cloth : alk. paper)
ISBN 978-0-8223-4386-8 (pbk. : alk. paper)
1. Gender identity — Children. 2. Children — Sexual behavior. 3. Children and homosexuality. 4. Homosexuality. 5. Queer theory. I. Title. II. Series: Series Q.
HQ784.S45S76 2009
306.76'6083 — dc22   2009008988